STUDIES IN RELIGION AND CULTURE
John D. Barbour and Gary L. Ebersole, Editors

AMERICAN KOAN

IMAGINING ZEN AND SELF IN
AUTOBIOGRAPHICAL LITERATURE

BEN VAN OVERMEIRE

UNIVERSITY OF VIRGINIA PRESS
Charlottesville and London

The University of Virginia Press is situated on the traditional lands of the Monacan Nation, and the Commonwealth of Virginia was and is home to many other Indigenous people. We pay our respect to all of them, past and present. We also honor the enslaved African and African American people who built the University of Virginia, and we recognize their descendants. We commit to fostering voices from these communities through our publications and to deepening our collective understanding of their histories and contributions.

University of Virginia Press
© 2024 by the Rector and Visitors of the University of Virginia
All rights reserved
Printed in the United States of America on acid-free paper

First published 2024

1 3 5 7 9 8 6 4 2

LIBRARY OF CONGRESS CATALOGING-IN-PUBLICATION DATA

Names: Van Overmeire, Ben, author.
Title: American koan : imagining Zen and self in autobiographical literature / Ben Van Overmeire.
Description: Charlottesville : University of Virginia Press, 2024. | Series: Studies in religion and culture | Includes bibliographical references and index.
Identifiers: LCCN 2024002722 (print) | LCCN 2024002723 (ebook) | ISBN 9780813952086 (hardcover) | ISBN 9780813952093 (paperback) | ISBN 9780813952109 (ebook)
Subjects: LCSH: Koan. | Zen Buddhism in literature. | Literature—Criticism and interpretation. | Autobiography.
Classification: LCC BQ9289.5 .V366 2024 (print) | LCC BQ9289.5 (ebook) | DDC 294.3/443—dc23/eng/20240328
LC record available at https://lccn.loc.gov/2024002722
LC ebook record available at https://lccn.loc.gov/2024002723

Cover art: Figure, redzone/shutterstock.com; background, Lana Veshta/shutterstock.com
Cover design: Susan Zucker

For Mio

CONTENTS

Preface | ix

Acknowledgments | xv

Note on Language Conventions | xix

Introduction	1
1. Enlightenment: D. T. Suzuki and Philip Kapleau	23
2. Failure: Janwillem van de Wetering, David Chadwick, Natalie Goldberg, Shozan Jack Haubner	44
3. The Two Truths: Myoan Grace Schireson, Claire Gesshin Greenwood, Zenju Earthlyn Manuel	79
4. Detachment in Van de Wetering's *Afterzen*	104
5. Interdependence in the Work of Ruth Ozeki	131
6. Conclusion	161

Notes | 179

Bibliography | 205

Index | 221

PREFACE

This book is about koan and the self. I assume you know what the self is. Most people seem to think they have one. Some people discussed in this book claim they don't. We'll get to that. But what on earth are koan? As always with this kind of thing, it helps to have some examples. Here is my favorite koan. It consists of two parts, and features Nansen (C. Nanquan), an esteemed Chinese Zen master, a bunch of nameless monks, and one cat:

> Nansen Oshō saw monks of the Eastern and Western halls quarreling over a cat. He held up the cat and said, "If you can give an answer, you will save the cat. If not, I will kill it." No one could answer, and Nansen cut the cat in two.[1]

I have a cat, and this first koan breaks my heart. What's going on here? Who does Nansen think he is, sacrificing an innocent animal for his stupid games? I imagine myself on the scene, a garrulous monk stupefied by my teacher's behavior. I'm sure I would have remained silent as well, marveling at this odd behavior, demanding a word for a cat. And, like the monks in the story, I do not think I would have spoken after the cat's screams of agony had subsided.

Felinicide is not the end of the story, though. Another esteemed master called Joshu (C. Zhaozhou) pays Nansen a visit:

That evening Jōshū returned, and Nansen told him of the incident. Jōshū took off his sandal, placed it on his head, and walked out. "If you had been there, you would have saved the cat," Nansen remarked.[2]

You might have thought this was the script for an absurd theater play. How is putting your shoes on your head connected to saving the cat's life? Yet, for Zen Buddhists, what Nansen and Joshu are doing is a demonstration of supreme wisdom, of the unsurpassed enlightenment that Buddhists have strived for since the Buddha sat down under a tree in India and saw reality revealed. That's a lot. For now, I want to note a couple of things about the two koan we've just read:

1. They thrive on irrationality and violence. This might conflict with what you thought Buddhism was. Buddhism here is not the *kumbaya* religion of everyone getting along. Buddhism in these texts is not "make love not war"; it is "make love *and* war."
2. They are about interactions between authority figures (masters like Nansen and Joshu) and their students (the monks of the Eastern and Western halls).
3. They are about answering a question that has no clear answer.
4. They contain a sudden twist that is seen to demonstrate insight. When Joshu places his sandals on his head, this means something to Nansen. He sees something we do not, but that something is something Joshu sees as well. The tradition holds that Joshu and Nansen are enlightened, and if you don't understand their weird actions, you're not.

As you can see, there's a lot going on in these short texts. They're messy. And it gets even messier when they enter descriptions of modern lives, autobiographical narratives. That is what I examine in this book. Autobiography is usually understood as a narrative that describes the author's life. In Zen autobiography, the author's life is marked by a deep commitment to Zen Buddhism. This commitment often results in an engagement with koan, which are interpreted and reinterpreted for their relevance to modern life. In the process, old Nansen and Joshu begin to mean something to these authors. They are not dead, but they speak through the story of the modern self. In the process, koan become a genre of American literature, and they turn modern Americans into Zen Buddhist masters.

I show how this happens in an introduction, five chapters, and a conclusion. The introduction lays out the argument of the book through a reading of *Nine-Headed Dragon River,* an autobiography by the prominent Zen Buddhist author Peter Matthiessen. In doing so, it also gives you a better idea of the types of texts this book focuses on. I also review the relevant secondary literature, define the scope and methodology of the book, and sketch my own position in relation to Zen.

The five chapters that form the heart of the book explore the relationship between koan and autobiography through five themes: enlightenment, failure, the two truths, detachment, and interdependence. Each of these themes indicates one way of narrating selfhood through koan. To examine each theme, I focus on the primary sources that allowed for the best discussion of that theme. But that obviously does not mean that we cannot find these themes anywhere else. For example, Ruth Ozeki, whom I use to talk about interdependence, also has things to say about enlightenment. Shozan Jack Haubner, whom I focus on in relation to failure, also discusses the two truths.

Chapter 1 is about enlightenment. It shows how koan have been used to imagine two key concepts in Zen modernism: Zen experience and Zen mastery. In his best-selling *An Introduction to Zen Buddhism,* the famous Zen apologist Daisetz Teitaro "D. T." Suzuki uses koan to present Zen Buddhist awakening or enlightenment as a fundamental and timeless experience. At the same time, Suzuki locates this universal experience in the Japanese Zen temple. Because Suzuki claims to have had such a universal experience, he presents himself as superior to his readers. To demonstrate Suzuki's influence, I turn to the autobiographical section of one of the most influential Zen manuals written by an American, Philip Kapleau's *The Three Pillars of Zen.* The diary of Kapleau contained in that section describes a continuous struggle to match the image of Zen portrayed by Suzuki with the reality encountered in a Japanese temple. Kapleau eventually claims to reconcile these two realities in attaining awakening. Yet a close reading of Kapleau's personal correspondence and a comparison with a later account of this experience show that this was likely conditioned by Kapleau's changing relationship with Suzuki and his teacher, Yasutani Hakuun.

Chapter 2 is about failure. It shows that narrating failure is a way to contest the narrative of Zen outlined in chapter 1, namely that enlightenment is all that matters. It proves this argument by looking at four Zen memoirs: Janwillem van de Wetering's *The Empty Mirror,* David Chadwick's *Thank You and OK!*, Natalie Goldberg's *The Great Failure*, and Shozan Jack Haubner's *Single White Monk*. The first two books portray the gap between the enlightened behavior of patriarchs of koan and temple life in Japan. In doing so, Van de Wetering and Chadwick criticize naive readings of koan that present the Zen temple as a utopian space. The latter two books are about Zen sex scandals. Goldberg and Haubner describe how whole communities could have remained blind to the wrongdoing of their teachers, and how the narrative of the selfless Zen teacher played a role in that. Despite this insight, they do not abandon koan. Instead, this genre is used to reframe failure as success: to fail is to gain insight into the nature of reality.

Chapter 3 is about the Buddhist doctrine of the two truths, and thus about Zen understandings of difference. It surveys the work of three contemporary women Buddhist authors: Grace Schireson, Claire Gesshin Greenwood, and Zenju Earthlyn Manuel. For Schireson and Greenwood, koan are a way to think about how to be a feminist in Japan: Should you follow the monastic pecking order, even if that order is deeply patriarchal? Or should you refuse it and stand up for yourself? Manuel is different from Greenwood and Schireson in that she seeks to abandon the koan framework altogether, creating a separate lineage and separate communities for people who are not straight, able, white male Buddhists. The symbol that unites the whole chapter is the ritual of bowing down: when and how do you bow, and what does this bow express?

After the first three chapters, which focus on comparing different authors, I switch gears to focus on two individual authors. Chapter 4 is about detachment. In it, I examine the two Zen memoirs Janwillem van de Wetering published after *The Empty Mirror*. Throughout his career, Van de Wetering continued to use his experiences with Zen as material for his books. *A Glimpse of Nothingness* tells the story of his enlightenment experience, but at the same time contains cues that these experiences are fictionalized. This attitude becomes more explicit in *Afterzen*, which advocates for the free invention and reinterpretation of koan. In doing so, Van de Wetering urges his readers to adopt an attitude of detachment, which for him implies not identifying with any social roles we fulfill, but also doing our best for the well-being of others. His work ultimately attempts to loosen our attachment to the distinction between fact and fiction.

Chapter 5 is about interdependence. It looks at the autobiographical work of Ruth Ozeki, namely the novel *A Tale for the Time Being* and the autobiographical essay *The Face*. In these books, Ozeki contests the idea that there is such a thing as an isolated "self" existing in the "now." Instead, she maps out the endless connections between self and other, between present, future, and past. To do this, she heavily draws on the writings of the Japanese Zen Buddhist thinker Eihei Dogen. In *A Tale*, characters interact across time and space, and books are cowritten by the author, the reader, and even fictional characters. In *The Face*, Ozeki looks into a mirror to explore how her own face in fact carries within it the whole world, thus finding an answer to the classic koan question, "What is your original face?"

The conclusion describes the larger contributions of this book. First, I show that we can capture the diversity of functions of koan in these life narratives by studying them as neck riddles. Doing so not only makes koan amenable to comparative analysis but also gives us an account of why people's engagement with these texts sometimes results in life-changing experiences. Then, I discuss an idea very prominent in American Zen writing, namely that writing and reading autobiography can itself be a form of Zen practice. Finally, putting both of these things together, I discuss in more detail the mutual transformation of koan and autobiography, how in these books koan become American and Americans become Buddhas.

The most obvious path through this book is to read the chapters in order. However, depending on the specific interests you bring to this material, here are some alternative routes:

1. If you're interested in seeing how deeply Zen autobiographies can contrast in their usage of koan and their representation of enlightenment, compare chapter 1 with chapter 5.
2. If you only care about the Dutch adventurer and rebel Janwillem van de Wetering, read the first part of chapter 2 and then continue reading about him in chapter 4.
3. If you're interested in women Zen practitioners' accounts, read the discussion of Goldberg in chapter 2, all of chapter 3, and then all of chapter 5.
4. If you're interested in the Zen sex scandals and abuses of authority, read the second half of chapter 2 (Goldberg and Haubner) and then the discussion of good and bad masters in chapter 4.
5. If you feel like laughing out loud, check out the discussion of Haubner in chapter 2, the discussion of Greenwood in chapter 3, the material on

Afterzen in chapter 4, and the discussion of Ozeki's *A Tale for the Time Being* in chapter 5.

6. Finally, if you're convinced that American Zen practice means avoiding language, chapter 2 (sections on Haubner and Goldberg) and chapter 5 are good places to start.

ACKNOWLEDGMENTS

A koan records a conversation that can have various results. Sometimes, both parties feel wise. Often, one party feels stupid. This book is in many ways a compilation of cases where I felt stupid. If there is wisdom in it, I have my interlocutors to thank for it.

This project started while I was in graduate school, and Richard S. Cohen, my doctoral advisor, nurtured it from its very beginning until its very end. In addition to Richard, my dissertation committee at the University of California, San Diego, provided many helpful suggestions along the way. Thank you, Page Dubois, Pasquale Verdicchio, David Jordan, Wai-lim Yip, Emily Roxworthy, and Suzanne Cahill.

The project continued during a postdoctoral fellowship, founded by the Research Foundation, Flanders, at the Ghent Centre for Buddhist Studies at Ghent University. There, I particularly want to thank my supervisor, Ann Heirman, and Christopher Anderl for help with knotty passages in Chan Chinese. In Ghent, I also got to meet Marjan Beijering, who has been generous with advice on understanding the life and work of Janwillem van de Wetering.

At Duke Kunshan University (DKU), where the project was finished, I received ample support from the Humanities Research Center (HRC) and the Center for the Study of Contemporary China (CSCC). A manuscript workshop funded by the HRC helped shape an earlier version of this manuscript, and I want to thank Ann Gleig, James Shields, Jeff Wilson, Natasha Heller, Brooke Schedneck, Carlos Rojas, and James Miller for providing plenty of suggestions for improvement. An individual chapter was taken apart during a CSCC workshop, where Sarah Schneewind and Keping Wu, among others, showed me how far that chapter still had to go.

Apart from formal workshops, I benefited from a great many conversations with my wise DKU colleagues. Specifically, I want to thank Selina Lai-Henderson, Zach Fredman, Yitzhak Lewis, Bryce Beemer, Tommaso Tesei, Kim Hunter Gordon, and Jeff Nicolaisen. DKU undergraduate students Yuan Li, Anne Liu, Sadey Dong, and Jiachen Wu helpfully provided feedback on some of the chapters. Outside of DKU, I want to thank Jeff Kripal, Shoji Yamada, Brian Victoria, Steven Heine, Stuart Lachs, Benoît Vermander, Kathryn Lofton, and Michael Pye.

Portions of this book include material previously published as "DT Suzuki's Literary Influence: Utopian Narrative in American and European Memoirs of Zen Life," in *Beyond Zen: D. T. Suzuki and the Modern Transformation of Buddhism*, 247–67 (Honolulu: Hawai'i University Press, 2022); "'Mountains, Rivers, and the Whole Earth': Koan Interpretations of Female Zen Practitioners," *Religions* 9, no. 4 (April 2018): 125; "Portraying Zen Buddhism in the Twentieth Century: Encounter Dialogues as Frame-Stories in Daisetz Suzuki's *Introduction to Zen Buddhism* and Janwillem van de Wetering's *The Empty Mirror*," *Japan Studies Review* 21 (2017): 3–24; "Zen and the Body: A Postmodern Ascetic? Bodily Awakening in the Zen Memoirs of Shozan Jack Haubner," *Religions* 12, no. 2 (February 15, 2021): 122; "Understanding Chan Kōan as a Literary Genre," *Hualin International Journal of Buddhist Studies* 6, no. 1 (2023): 111–45.

One of the joys of doing a project on contemporary Zen Buddhists is that you get to speak to some of them. I wish to thank Thera van de Wetering for speaking with me about her father. Shozan Jack Haubner, Norman Fischer, and Natalie Goldberg helpfully replied to my emails. Mat Zepelin at Shambhala helped in various ways as well.

When not talking to the people in this book, I got to read about them in the archives. I particularly wish to thank the excellent staff at Duke Library's Arthur Rubinstein Archive, where Philip Kapleau's correspondence is held, and at Boston University's Howard Gotlieb Archival Research Center which holds various items connected to Van de Wetering.

My editor at the University of Virginia Press, Eric Brandt, was enthusiastic about this project from the moment he heard about it six years ago. Since then, he has been supportive every step of the way. Thank you for your faith. John Barbour introduced Eric to me and has been the best conversation partner about these books that fascinate both of us.

Finally, I want to thank my family, both my extended family in Belgium (my father, sister, and brothers) and my own family: my wife, Mio, and children, Kai and Yue. Without you, nothing would be worth doing.

NOTE ON LANGUAGE CONVENTIONS

In this book, I use the term "American" to refer to the United States, more specifically to individuals who have spent significant time in this country. Doing so has become the convention of the field but is not without its problems, since it takes the United States as synonymous with the continent of America itself.

Similarly riddled with problems is using the Japanese pronunciation of the character "Zen" to refer to a school that originated in China. Due to the complex history of Asia during the twentieth century, Japanese Zen has had an outsize influence on determining what constitutes proper "Zen" practice, and this also shows in the Japanese pronunciation of the school's name having become commonplace in English. The same goes for the Japanese pronunciation of the characters that make up the word "koan" to indicate the Zen Buddhist genre at the center of this book. I nevertheless use "Zen" and "koan" (for singular and plural forms of the noun) because all of the authors I examine refer to it by this term, and because it is better known.

Chinese Zen masters of koan can be named in Chinese or Japanese. I usually use the Japanese names of these teachers, except where the authors I examine themselves use the Chinese. For the first mention of any Chinese Zen master, I give both Chinese and Japanese pronunciations. For Japanese transcriptions, I do not give diacritics (e.g., koan not kōan; Soto not Sōtō) since most of these terms are unambiguous when used in the American Zen context.

The authors of books are usually identified with their last names. Sometimes, I use the author's first name to refer to the protagonist of an autobiographical narrative. For example, I use "Van de Wetering" to refer to Janwillem van de Wetering the author and narrator, but "Janwillem" to refer to the main character of his books. This separation allows me to distinguish what the author does ("Van de Wetering inserts a Zen master's biography") from what the protagonist of the narrative is doing ("Janwillem was surprised when he met the Zen master").

When I refer to the Chinese originals of koan, I refer to the editions contained in the so-called Taisho canon, the scholarly standard in my field. I use the italicized *T* to indicate this. Full citation is as follows: Takakusu Junjirō and Watanabe Kaigyoku, eds. Taishō shinshū daizōkyō (Buddhist Canon Compiled under the Taishō Era [1912–1926]). 100 vols. Tokyo: Taishō issaikyō kankōkai, 1924–32.

INTRODUCTION

THREE JAPANESE ZEN MASTERS ON AN AMERICAN DRIVEWAY

When American convert Zen Buddhists use koan in telling the story of their life, these Zen riddles deeply shape what they say, how they say it, and sometimes why they say it. In the process, koan become American, and Americans become Buddhas. This is the core argument of my book. These autobiographers use koan to articulate what they write, to structure how they write, and sometimes even to explain why they write. Koan become a way to say what cannot be spoken, a way to speak as a Zen master, a way to include and exclude, a way to imagine a bright future, a way to translate experience into narrative, and a way to transform writing and reading into Zen practice. Koan are mirrors reflecting, distorting, and warping what Zen is and should be, who these authors think they are and should be, and who they imagine their teachers are and should be.

Stories have to begin somewhere, and one good somewhere is the beginning of another book, where three mysterious beings appear suddenly on a suburban driveway:

> On an August day of 1968, returning home to Sagaponack, Long Island, after a seven-month absence in Africa, I was astonished by the presence in my driveway of three inscrutable small men who turned out to be Japanese Zen masters. Hakuun Yasutani-roshi, eighty-four years old, was a light, gaunt figure with hollowed eyes and round, prominent ears; as I was to

learn, he had spent much of that morning upside down, standing on his head. Beside him, Nakagawa Soen-roshi, slit-eyed, elfin, and merry, entirely at ease and entirely aware at the same time, like a paused swallow, gave off emanations of lightly contained energy that made him seem much larger than he was. The roshis were attended by Tai-san (now Shimano Eido-roshi), a compact young monk with a confident, thick-featured face and samurai bearing. Though lacking the strange "transparent" presence of his teachers, Tai-san conveyed the same impression of contained power. The teachers were guests of my wife, Deborah Love, a new student of Zen, but I was ignorant of this as of much else on that long-ago summer day.... No doubt I revealed what I presume was my great-grandfather's wary attitude toward unanticipated Orientals in outlandish garb. For years thereafter Tai-san would relate how Soen and Yasutani, perceiving my unenlightened condition at a glance, had shaken their shining heads and sighed, "Poor Debbo-lah."[1]

This is the opening of the celebrated author Peter Matthiessen's *Nine-Headed Dragon River: Zen Journals, 1969–1982*, a book that, according to the back cover, "embodies the spirit of Zen in America." In Matthiessen's own telling, his encounter with the three masters was the beginning of his lifelong engagement with Zen. From his condition of "unenlightenment," he would emerge as a Zen teacher in his own right, weaving the silences of meditation through his rich prose. Read today, though, the stereotypes through which he understands the three masters are obvious: they are scripted through a literary discourse that has become known as "orientalist." Their "outlandish garb" designates them as representatives of an exotic and mysterious place very different from the America Matthiessen grew up in.

However important this moment might be for Matthiessen, in his book it is merely the reflection of another, earlier confrontation between a clueless blockhead and an accomplished master. So it goes with Zen stories: one tale requires the telling of another. In this case, the other story is that of the Zen patriarch Bodhidharma facing the Chinese emperor Wu. Zen patriarchs like Bodhidharma are legendary masters who possess insight equal to that of *the* Buddha Shakyamuni himself. They understand what Siddhartha Gautama understood so many years ago under the Bodhi tree. Having reportedly traveled from India to bring this insight to China, Bodhidharma is given an audience with Wu, in which he dismisses the emperor's Buddhist building projects as having no merit whatsoever, proceeds to call the "holy truth" of

Buddhism "vast emptiness," and takes his leave by stating that he does not know who he himself is. One could imagine more productive conversations to be had with a powerful autocrat. But then again Bodhidharma is not interested in ordinary conversations, nor is he, by any account, an ordinary man. One legend has him sitting in meditation facing a wall for nine years, until his legs fell off. In another story, he conquers sleep by cutting off his eyelids, which grew to be the first tea plants.

Matthiessen tells us Bodhidharma's uncompromising attitude paid off: "Bodhidharma's arrival was followed by four centuries of great Zen prosperity in China, and its establishment in Korea and Japan. But in recent ages, almost everywhere, the Buddha Way had withered in the grasp of its own priesthood, and Master Soyen believed that the time had come for the teachings to travel eastward to the new world."[2] Who is this Master Soyen? He was not among the three masters on Matthiessen's driveway. Shaku Soen, as his name is more commonly spelled, is instead the teacher of these three masters. During the Chicago World's Parliament of Religions of 1893, the most important event in the history of convert Buddhism in America, Soen represented Japanese Zen to the world. Many of his students, not only those on Matthiessen's driveway, would go on to profoundly affect Americans' understanding of Zen. Matthiessen's comparison of Soen and Bodhidharma is thus a recognition both of Soen's past efforts and of the future: just like Bodhidharma, Soen and his students will spread Zen to new regions and, in doing so, revitalize the teaching. The twentieth-century history of Buddhism's coming to America is thus understood through a much older story, a koan.

I will have much more to say on koan below, but for now it's good to know that koan are a genre of Zen literature used in some versions of the Zen monastic training curriculum.[3] Koan often feature a student and a master engaging in enigmatic exchanges aimed at producing enlightenment. Within narratives like Matthiessen's, koan mediate between self and "Zen," between past and present, tradition and modernity, Asia and America. This book attempts to understand this dynamic of making sense of one's present experiences through recourse to the canonical literature of the past. It shows that the interpretation of stories like Bodhidharma's encounter with Wu has been essential for the convert imagination of Zen in America.

I became interested in this project because all the books I read about Zen as an undergraduate had koan in them. Indeed, many introductions to Zen, scholarly or not, emphasize these short, cryptic texts, often representing them as the essence of Zen Buddhist doctrine and practice. I later discovered that, in fact, this representation was inaccurate and that, while koan are important, Zen monastic practice does not typically involve rejecting the merits of infrastructure ventures or engaging in innovative botany. Why, then, did so many people want to talk about koan? This is something that prominent scholars within Zen studies have often wondered about.[4] In the pages that follow, I attempt to provide an answer.

WHAT IS ZEN?

Before I go any further, let me briefly summarize what "Zen" is. Zen originated as a Chinese school of Buddhism that called itself "Chan." Buddhists, mainly belonging to the Mahayana school, started traveling to China during the first centuries of the Common Era, and gradually people in China started to adopt practices associated with this religion. Over the years, Buddhism in China took on unique features, a process that has been called "sinification."[5] One of these sinified schools was the Chan, or "meditation," school, and it should be no surprise that adherents of this school would focus on contemplative practice more than the study of Buddhist religious doctrine and literature (at least in theory). Emerging in China as early as the sixth century CE, Zen Buddhists gradually distinguished their school from other schools by stressing a "special transmission outside the scriptures." They claimed that they did not need to read texts to understand what enlightenment was. Not even the words of Shakyamuni Buddha himself encoded in the sutras transmitted from India were deemed necessary for spiritual attainment. Instead, Zen Buddhists claimed that their masters had received a special instruction from the Buddha, a teaching beyond words. This instruction was far superior to textual understandings of enlightenment and, they said, had been transmitted across the ages through an enduring lineage of masters. Bodhidharma, whom we met earlier, was one of these masters.

In a well-noted irony, though, Zen Buddhists produced the largest volume of Buddhist literature in China. One scholarly interpretation of this paradox has been to see the Zen school as a "community of memory" that "denotes socially interdependent groups that share certain practices and are bound together by their communal remembrance of the past, which provides them with a sense of collective identity and a common heritage."[6] In other words, a narrative of the past that is articulated in sacred literature reinforces a certain idea of group identity, however much that identity might change over time. But one can go even further and dismiss the idea that Chan was never much more than its literature. One such interpretation startlingly proposes that "Chan was a utopic form of Buddhism that never existed; or, more exactly, existed only as the steady literary—and later, ritual—ability to produce convincing images of just this simple and pure form of Buddhism that never, and could never, exist [sic]."[7] Others have pointed out that literature and religious experience are not mutually exclusive.[8] Zen mind-to-mind transmission has to happen through a mastery of language that then allows one to transcend language.

Whatever one makes of Zen's connection to its literature, the written word was crucial for the school's success in gaining political support. From the Song dynasty (960–1279) onward, Zen would become the most important Buddhist school in China. Due to China's massive cultural prestige in medieval Asia, the school's ideas found their way into other states, such as Vietnam, Korea, and, most importantly for this study, Japan. By that time, the school had split into two different factions, one named the Linji (Japanese: Rinzai) lineage after the famous Zen master Linji Yixuan, the other named Caodong (J. Soto) after Dongshan Liangjie and Caoshan Benji. Though this split, like the purported split between the Northern and Southern Schools much earlier, might have been largely a matter of doctrine rather than practice, it was taken very seriously in Japan, where Rinzai and Soto see themselves as distinct until this day.[9] The split partly concerned the usage of koan as tools for awakening. With the master Dahui Zonggao, the Linji lineage had adopted the usage of such texts in formal Zen study: because they described the actions of living Buddhas, gaining insight into a koan was considered as gaining insight into enlightened behavior and enlightenment itself. Students focused on an individual phrase of the koan, a method called *kanhua* meditation. The Caodong school refused such tools and maintained that enlightenment was achieved through "silent illumination," denying that enlightenment is something that one has to strive toward by using tools such as koan. In Japan, the famous Zen masters Eihei Dogen (Soto) and Hakuin Ekaku (Rinzai) solidified these doctrinal differences, with Hakuin revitalizing the koan curriculum and Dogen rejecting *huatou* study (but not koan study altogether, as can be seen from the ample quotation of koan in his work).

After the Second World War, it was Rinzai that first captured the imagination of spiritual seekers in America and Europe. Through the works of the Rinzai-trained Daisetz Suzuki (chapter 1), koan studies were represented as the very essence of Zen, and Japanese Rinzai as the purest version of Zen. Early Westerners who went to Japan to train like Gary Snyder, Joanne Kyger, Janwillem van de Wetering (chapter 2), or Irmgard Schloegl were trained in Daitokuji, a Rinzai temple. Others, however, like Philip Kapleau (chapter 1), Robert Aitken, and Matthiessen would practice under both Soto and Rinzai masters, questing for the enlightenment that Suzuki's books held out as the ultimate reward to all of life's problems. But it was with the coming to America of Shunryu Suzuki, a Zen master who had a charismatic personality to match that of the other Suzuki, that Soto would become a force in American convert Zen.

KOAN AND EXPERIENCE

Let's now look a bit more closely at koan, which describe people like Bodhidharma in conversation with people who are usually less advanced than they are. Because Zen Buddhists believe the patriarchs are living Buddhas, these texts therefore give us an idea of what enlightenment looks like. If you can't find a Zen master in a temple near you, you can still read these texts to get an idea of what they're like. And again: the irony is that these Zen supermen constantly speak against the idea that you can capture what they have to teach in words.

As mentioned earlier, scholars have shown how koan were part of the literary arsenal Zen Buddhists used to gain political support. The need to appeal to those in power meant, for example, that the editors of a text describing the life of the patriarch Linji Yixuan, a text containing many snippets that would become koan, would strategically move around sections of the text to please their readers, for instance changing an opening aimed at dissing the Zen competition to an opening that included local magistrates in Linji's audience.[10] We know that Bodhidharma didn't always speak the way he did to Emperor Wu: in fact, the speeches of the masters were gradually "Zennified," changed from fairly clear discourse to increasingly mysterious exchanges to create the distinctive language now associated with the entire school.[11] According to this scholarship, koan came about partly as a literary style aimed to please those in power.

A foundational text for my own understanding of koan as rhetorical tools is Bernard Faure's often-cited article where he argues we need to move away from studying Bodhidharma as a real person and instead to treat him as a "textual and religious paradigm."[12] Rather than using koan and other genres of Zen hagiography to reconstruct the biography of a real person, Faure argues, we ought to pay attention to how the idea of Bodhidharma works in different contexts. The question of what it means for a school of Buddhism to imagine their saint as a bearded madman is more useful than attempting to ascertain whether that madman indeed existed. John McRae would summarize this insight in the first of his "Rules of Chan studies": "It's not true, and therefore it's more important."[13]

As in literary studies more broadly, the—arguably postmodern—bracketing of truth claims has deepened our understanding of the role representation played in Zen discourse. For example, until fairly recently it was a widespread belief that the Tang dynasty was the peak of Zen Buddhism: all the best masters were teaching, and there was enlightenment to be had anywhere. The Song dynasty, which followed the Tang and saw an immense production of Zen literature, was believed to be its downfall: Zen became repetitive, elite, boring. However, scholars have shown that this narrative is more reflective of Zen polemics than of historical reality. They have proven how the imagination of a "Golden Age" of Zen was always a rhetorical creation of Zen Buddhists themselves, who were attempting to capture the interest of those in power.[14] They did so by telling koan, stories of funny and eloquent teachers who lived in beautiful bygone days of glory.

So there are, in fact, two histories of Zen, which Steven Heine has characterized as the Traditional Zen Narrative (TZN) and the Historical Cultural Criticism (HCC).[15] The TZN, which has its home among practitioners, involves believing that there was a person called Bodhidharma who met an emperor and then sprouted plants from his body. Zen originated in India with Shakyamuni, and his timeless wisdom has been transmitted in unaltered form throughout the ages. All this time, Zen Buddhists have strived unselfishly for the enlightenment of all sentient beings. They only wrote literature because they had to and were never concerned with pleasing those in power. The HCC, which has its home in the academy, has deconstructed nearly all of these truth claims: Zen did not originate in India but in China. Bodhidharma is a fictional invention, as are many of the school's patriarchs. Zen Buddhists were political powerhouses, frequenting the halls of power to position their school as the most influential in China.

A similar deconstruction of truth claims has involved the nature of religious experience. For some of the authors I discuss in this book, koan provide access to an experience of enlightenment. I was initially attracted to Zen because I wanted this enlightenment as well. Finally figuring out my life seemed like bliss when I was twenty. But then I read a series of articles that shook my vision of the tradition. Arguably, these articles enabled the HCC scholarship cited above as much as did Faure's notion of Bodhidharma as a textual paradigm. In these articles, Robert Sharf showed how the idea that Zen is all about getting an "experience" is not a "traditional" idea but in fact a product of the twentieth century.[16] Only marginal Zen teachers in Japan focused on getting enlightenment, and for most enlightenment was a performance, not something you felt internally.[17] Sharf defined experience, in a phrase that has stuck with me, as "a mere placeholder that entails a substantive if indeterminate terminus for the relentless deferral of meaning. And this is precisely what makes the term so amenable to Buddhist ideological appropriation."[18] Anyone can claim to have had an experience of enlightenment. How would you know? A kung fu master can defeat his opponents with nothing but his bare hands, but a Zen master claims to have mastered nothing. Ok, "Nothing." But what is the difference between knowing Nothing and knowing nothing? Sharf had a point.

Sharf's rather dim view of experience as "a mere placeholder" clashes with how many American Zen practitioners see religious experience, namely as the single most important event of their lives. Here is one example of such an experience, from Matthiessen's *Nine-Headed Dragon River*. Matthiessen engages in the *kanhua* (koan) meditation described earlier. His first awakening happens during his training with "Joshu's Mu," a koan where the famous master Joshu (whom we met in the preface) is asked whether or not a dog has Buddha-nature, to which he replies "Mu" ("No" but also "There is not" and—more philosophically—"Nothing!"). After Matthiessen ritually shouts this "Mu," the following happens:

> Then I let my breath go, gave my self up to immersion in all things, to a joyous *belonging* so overwhelming that tears of relief poured from my eyes. For the first time since unremembered childhood, I was not alone, there was no

separate "I." Wounds, anger, ragged edges, hollow places were all gone, all had been healed; my heart was the heart of all creation. *Nothing was needed*, nothing missing, all was already, always, and forever present and forever known. Even Deborah's dying, if that had to be, was perfectly in place. All that day I wept and laughed.[19]

Why is Matthiessen laughing and crying? What has been healed? What has he understood? Scholars in the field of religious studies have disagreed on this question for half a century now, and the end of this debate is nowhere in sight. Everyone would agree that this experience is not an ordinary experience, like the experience of going to Disneyland or the experience of driving a car. But scholars have argued back and forth about almost everything else. Is what Matthiessen experiences the result of social conditioning? Was his "I" really no longer "separate?"

Whatever religious experience is, it is powerful. From the 1950s onward, Americans flocked to Zen temples and centers looking for the revelations Matthiessen describes. Like him, many would make sense of Zen and themselves by investigating koan, both in their practice on the meditation pillow and in their writing. Koan allow these writers to access and express the type of experience Matthiessen describes. They assume, like Matthiessen does, that these transformative experiences reveal a deeper truth about reality. They also believe that such experiences have remained essentially the same over time. By solving the "Mu" koan, you understand the same things as Matthiessen, Bodhidharma, and the Buddha.

Sharf is not the only one who has resisted these claims, arguing instead that religious experiences are culturally and historically specific and do not exist outside of the medium—language—in which they are communicated.[20] This position, called "constructivism," has become a common position in the field of religious studies. Constructivists believe to varying degrees that (1) religious experience does not exist separately from discourse about religious experience; and (2) religious experience is modern, and no equivalent exists prior to the nineteenth century. For constructivists, religious experience is not something that exists by itself that is then described in language. For example, an elephant exists outside of me writing about it, but religious experience does not. Instead, religious experiences *are* language, just like the words "morality" or "nation." The TZN alternative to this HCC position is called perennialism. Perennialists believe that religious experience exists as something distinct from sociolinguistics. It is something that really happens to people, like having a heart attack (no matter how much you talk about a heart attack, it'll still hit you). As the name "perennialism" implies, this means that experience is seen as possessing an unchanging, eternal element: all beings across human history have had to endure heart attacks and have had religious experiences.

In this book, I undertake what Jeffrey Kripal has called a "reflexive rereading" of religious experience.[21] This implies the following two steps: First, take constructivist interpretations of religious experience seriously: yes, religious experiences are conditioned by cultural circumstances; yes, they are a Freudian expression of our sex drive; yes, they are caused by the brain behaving in an unusual way. Second, then wonder: But isn't that really *weird*? Even if religious experiences are cultural, why are we imagining such things? If they are an expression of our sex drive, what is our sex drive? If our brain is misbehaving, what does that tell us about what we see when our brain is not misbehaving? If koan are just literature, and yet it causes people to feel healed, what is literature?

In reflexively rereading religious experiences, I aim to take seriously both sides of the debate. I am convinced that culture, history, memory, psychology and many other factors affect reports of religious experiences. In the book, I show this by comparing descriptions, separated in time, of the exact same experience by one single person. The differences can be significant, and that should tell us something about how unstable religious experience is. I am also convinced that religious experiences are deeply meaningful for those who have them, and that these experiences come across as genuine and life-changing. Practitioners like Matthiessen see koan as both catalyzing and expressing that experience, and that tells me something about the power of literature.

AMERICAN BUDDHIST LITERATURE

You may have noticed that most scholarship on Zen focuses on the East Asia of the distant past. This book, however, is about Zen literature in the twentieth and twenty-first centuries, one of the most important periods (if not *the* most important) in the history of the school. Zen has spread around the world to such an extent that nearly every secular state has a Zen Center in every major city. It has deeply influenced the way Westerners have come to see meditation, namely not as a transcendental and supernatural practice but as a productivity method. Zen has created its own modernist aesthetics, the bare "less is more" approach that inspired the music of John Cage as it did the interior architecture of Silicon Valley.[22] And yet very few scholars have written on this crucial period of Zen's history.

This needs to change, because it reflects normative assumptions about what "authentic" Buddhism is. Natalie Quli argues that the focus on pre-twentieth-century Asian Buddhism reflects the orientalist idea that contemporary Asian and American Buddhists are "tainted by Western culture, philosophy, and religion." Therefore, they are not "really" Buddhist and thus not worthy of study.[23] This bothers Quli, as it bothers me, because I don't think it's our job as scholars to evaluate what real Buddhism is.[24] I don't believe Buddhists were corrupting their religion when they adjusted it to the realities of China or Japan. Likewise, the way contemporary Zen Buddhists use koan to articulate modern ideas such as feminism or failure is a literary adaptation like so many in Buddhism's long history.

Despite their marginal position in Buddhist studies, scholars of American Buddhism have accomplished much in the past few decades. One area of research has been how American Buddhism differs from premodern Buddhism in Asia. For example, the modern emphasis on meditation as the core of Buddhist practice would have been unfamiliar to most Buddhists in India, China, Japan, Vietnam, Korea, and other locations where Buddhism was practiced before the eighteenth century.[25] David McMahan has shown that this focus on meditation is intimately connected to the idea that individual practice and experience are very important.[26] It also fits the idea that Buddhism is a "science," where we ourselves can see what the Buddha saw by sitting down and meditating. This is the scientific principle of reproducibility applied to religion, only the test laboratory is our minds.

Premodern Buddhists would likely have had trouble understanding this specifically modern notion of meditation. They might also have had trouble with American Buddhists' emphasis on the freedom of the autonomous individual, on the equality between men and women, on the world as a hospitable and not hellish place, and on daily life as a miracle. This leads McMahan to characterize Buddhist modernity as a composite entity, a "hybrid" that is the result of the interaction of Western and Buddhist discourses.[27] Jeff Wilson has shown what this dialogue looks like in the case of mindfulness meditation, demonstrating that mindfulness is not only a transformation of Buddhism, but that through it Buddhism also transforms America.[28] In this book, I take this concept of mutual transformation and apply it to individual Americans, who also transform koan in citing them in their life stories, and in turn are transformed into living Buddhas.

McMahan wrote about Buddhist modernism but gestured, at the end of his book, toward the possibility that a postmodern Buddhism was emerging in the United States. The challenge of analyzing this new form of Buddhism was taken up by Ann Gleig, who sees twenty-first-century American Buddhism as a "reaction against core modernist characteristics."[29] The core features of this reaction are a critique of Buddhist metanarratives ("Buddhism is a science"), a focus on community building (and not on individual accomplishment), and a historical awareness that American Buddhism is just one historical iteration of Buddhism and by no means a "universal" truth.

Within literary studies, Zen Buddhist (post)modernism has been mainly approached through an examination of what I would call "highbrow" authors. These authors' literary production usually involves significant formal experimentation. This is to be expected, since Buddhist poetic genres such as the Japanese haiku verse form were a significant influence on authors such as Ezra Pound. Other authors typically treated in examinations of American Buddhist literature include Ernest Fenollosa, Allen Ginsberg, Jack Kerouac, Gary Snyder, Lew Welch, Philip Whalen, Maxine Hong Kingston, Alice Walker, Charles Johnson, and Lan Cao.

Scholars studying these authors have seen American Buddhist literature as something that is not just read but that also creates and critiques. Jonathan Stalling, for example, sees American Buddhist poets' interest in emptiness as a way of critiquing the American obsession with possession.[30] Similarly, Kyle Garton-Gundling reads American Buddhist literature as supplementing American individualism with the Buddhist deconstruction of the individual.[31] Buddhist literature, however, also makes possible "the formation of a Buddhist imagined community" in that it connects Buddhists across America.[32]

Productive as it has been, this focus on canonized authors has obscured texts and authors that are formally less interesting but can tell us at least as much (perhaps even more) about how Zen is represented and understood in

America. Quantitatively, one of the most important genres in American Buddhism is not poetry or fiction, but autobiography. When I'm at the AAR, the convention of the American Academy of Religion, I always visit the stands of the Buddhist publishers Shambhala and Wisdom and buy half of their catalogue. This is partly because one of my many neuroses is buying way too many books but also because so many of the books they sell are autobiographical in some fashion: what we find are memoirs of studying with famous Buddhist teachers, manuals of Zen practice that are grounded in personal experience, philosophical treatises sprinkled with anecdotes from lives lived in temples of Zen Centers.

In some ways, then, I wrote the book you now hold in your hands to make sense of my growing collection of Zen autobiographies. What I've found in reading these texts is that many of the findings discussed above hold for autobiography as well. Zen Buddhist autobiographers deeply criticize American ideologies, such as the idea of success. They also criticize harmful ideas within American Zen, such as racist or gendered interpretations of Buddhism. They are deeply concerned with the larger Buddhist community they are a part of, and they speak to that community in their work. But these autobiographies also possess some special features, in that koan are deployed to articulate these positions. Interpreting koan becomes a way of seeing what it means to be a Zen Buddhist in contemporary America.

Now, autobiography is usually thought of as a genre that describes a self: I write a book that describes what my life has been like. What we find when we look at that life, though, is not something stable but something "dynamic, changing, and plural."[33] When I look at notes I made twenty years ago, I might not recognize myself in them anymore. Based on this type of observation, scholars have questioned whether there is an entity (called the self) that preexists its representation in autobiography. Instead, Sidonie Smith and Julia Watson propose to examine autobiographical writing not as representational but as "a performative act" that produces its own subject, namely the self.[34] Such a seemingly radical idea is supported by recent research in psychology and neuroscience, a field where autobiographical narrative is considered "a constituent part of self."[35]

The Zen life narratives I discuss in this book are deeply concerned with the construction and the transformation of the self. They often do this by connecting their life narratives to koan, an interaction that I understand through the concept of relationality. Pioneered in feminist analyses, relationality is the idea that the self is constituted in constant interaction with others. This makes life writing really a collection of biographies as well.[36] In her study of the Tibetan saint Sera Khandro, Sarah Jacoby has taken this insight one step further and has proposed that relationality can also mean that the self is in dialogue with nonhuman beings (such as ghosts and spirits).[37] As I show, relationality can also be used to understand how identity is constructed in dialogue with the Zen masters of old.

Various identities are the result of this dialogical construction of the self. One of these identities is that of the Zen practitioner. Helen Baroni has looked at how this image is constructed by examining personal letters written to and by the American Zen master Robert Aitken.[38] In analyzing Aitken's correspondence, she argues that his "distant correspondents"—people whom he never met but who nevertheless want Zen instruction—"write to create for themselves an identity as a Zen practitioner that they can present to Aitken."[39] Brooke Schedneck has also studied how gender and orientalism figure into this identity. In her study of Theravada practitioners, she maps out how autobiographies often portray a clash between an imagined "ideal" Buddhism and the realities of monastic life in often strongly patriarchal environments.[40]

In the case of Zen autobiography, koan are often taken as representative of an "ideal" Buddhism that individual authors measure their own practice against. This is how they define themselves as practitioners or masters. Some feel as if they understand the gnomic sayings of Bodhidharma, whereas others are stuck wondering what the bearded saint meant. However, koan ultimately turn all these authors into living Buddhas no matter what their ideas about themselves are, because the literary move of representing your life narrative through koan turns that narrative into that of a Zen sage.

The most recent contribution to our understanding of Buddhist autobiography is John Barbour's *Journeys of Transformation*, the direct predecessor to the present study. As its title implies, Barbour looks at travel narratives, a category that includes some of the authors (Matthiessen, Van de Wetering, Greenwood, Chadwick) I discuss as well. For Barbour, such books often portray religious experiences he calls "unselfing," which he defines as "moments when a person's sense of self is radically altered."[41] But, crucially, it isn't just that autobiographies describe such experiences but that autobiographical writing itself can be "an inherently religious action."[42] In interpreting what happened during their journey, religious experience is constructed both for the authors themselves and for their readers.

In this book, I develop Barbour's notion that the very act of writing and reading a Buddhist autobiography can be of great religious significance. I find that Zen autobiography is not just the writing of a self but also the unwriting, the unmaking of one. This happens because these books incorporate koan. In these texts, koan are much more than decorative quotations to give some oriental flavor to the narrative. They become important structural components. It isn't just that these authors read and interpret koan (they do) but that koan structure the narratives of their lives. As mentioned, koan become placeholders for awakening experiences. But they also become a way of interrupting linear time frames. They become a framework to interpret daily life, where any encounter becomes one between master and student with the potential for awakening. Koan become a way of telling a life, a way of reading a life, and ultimately, a way of unraveling who we think we are. This implies that these autobiographies are not just describing Zen practice. Writing and reading them *is* Zen practice.

One way of understanding the range of functions koan have had in American convert Zen autobiography is to imagine them as mirrors. Mirrors—including broken, shattered, or empty mirrors—show up everywhere in these autobiographies, often as a symbol of enlightenment. Look in this mirror. What do you see? Do you see Bodhidharma smiling back at you? Or is the mirror a "fun house mirror," to use Jonathan Z. Smith's description of religion in general, that both reflects and distorts reality?[43] All the authors described in this book tell us how they see themselves reflected in/by/through koan. But what they see in that mirror varies greatly. These mirrors can reflect, but they can also bend, curve, and warp.

ORIENTALISM AND UTOPIANISM

Sometimes convert Zen Buddhists look into the mirrors that are koan and they see a better place that is nowhere, a utopia. When Thomas More wrote *Utopia*, a book that came to define a whole subgenre of literature, he wrote it as a mirror of his contemporary Britain, and the wordplay in the title (*eu-topia* as good place, *ou-topia* as no-place) reflects this. Ideal and imaginary, utopian texts can be used as a tool to enforce compliance but also as a means of resistance. If utopian visions such as that of the classless society have united the downtrodden and brought about revolutions, they have also been used to exclude and reject.[44] Often, these two operations of utopia are inseparable: imagining an ideal world usually implies rejecting some people from that world. In More's case, the political radicalism of his perfect world, which is egalitarian in its politics and has abolished the use of money, goes hand in hand with a firmly patriarchal family system and a colonialist expansionist program (Utopia conquers neighboring countries for their own good).[45] Utopian narrative in the twentieth century shares this basic structure: often, its rejections of capitalism are coupled with a rejection of minority groups.

Unfortunately, this also affects how some Zen Buddhists have used koan to imagine better worlds. As we have seen, when Matthiessen looks at Shaku Soen, he sees Bodhidharma. And through this seeing, America becomes the new destination of Zen, and Zen's emissaries the storied monks of old. This vision proposes a better world, one where human beings devote themselves to the elimination of suffering, sit down in silence to observe their mind, to eventually see Reality revealed.

Yet this perfect world is constructed on the basis of dehumanization. Matthiessen suggests that his teachers are manifestations of the eternal essence of Zen by stereotyping them. As we've seen in the opening of his book, Yasutani, Nakagawa, and Shimano are cast respectively as a yogi, a samurai, and "entirely aware and at ease at the same time." In short, they are what Jane Iwamura has characterized as "oriental monks." Characteristic of the oriental monk is "his spiritual commitment, his calm demeanor, his Asian face, his manner of dress, and—most obviously—his peculiar gendered character."[46] In characterizing his teachers, Matthiessen neglects specificity (who is Yasutani, and how has he been shaped by a rapidly modernizing Japan?) for the stereotyped universal. Later in the *Nine-Headed Dragon River*, Matthiessen is confounded by a white Zen master because he cannot fit this teacher into such ready-made categories.[47] In the case of Matthiessen, then, utopianism is deeply connected to orientalism. He articulates this vision through koan, which is the type of canonized literary text that orientalists tend to privilege above the accounts of living Buddhists.

This representation of the Zen master as an oriental monk, scripted by a reading of koan that took these stories as accurate representations of living masters, was and remains dangerous. Read with the benefit of historical hindsight, there are remarkable silences in *Nine-Headed Dragon River*. Overtly, the book highlights similarities between the Zen patriarchs of koan and Matthiessen's own present-day teachers. But there are several hints that these teachers are anything but perfect. As is well-known today, even before he became a master Shimano was pursuing sexual relationships with his female students, something he continued to do throughout his career.[48] Matthiessen, who studied extensively with Shimano, mentions these problems briefly but then will not discuss them directly.[49] His analysis of Shimano places part of the blame for the abuse on the students: "But for idealistic American Zen students, seeking respite from our own disorderly lives, this practice [Zen] had seemed a clear oasis where life could be kept pure, spare, and simple, as in the Buddhist image of the white lotus rising from the muddy water. Now the image had been muddied, messy 'real' life had come flooding in, and we wrestled with 'oughts' and 'shoulds' on our black cushions; we had forgotten that the lotus needs the nourishment of mud, that it cannot grow in clear 'pure' water."[50] Here, Matthiessen reveals the utopian ideals his generation held regarding Zen. Shimano was supposed to act like Bodhidharma and benefit all sentient beings, but he did not conform to this script. Ironically, narratives of Zen success like Matthiessen's contributed to this idealization of Zen by continuing to imagine present-day Zen teachers by referring to the Zen patriarchs of koan. This caused some students to not see what was happening right before them, and others to turn a blind eye to what they did see. This blindness and silence allowed for abuse to continue uncensored, leading to much suffering and, ultimately, the scandals that have haunted American Zen since the 1980s.

Yet at the same time, utopian orientalism can also be a form of resistance. This is what some of the more recent work on orientalism and Asian religions has highlighted. For Urs App, the European encounter with Asian religions was not just a matter of colonialism, power, and privilege—though naturally these played a prominent role—but also "the largest-scale religiocultural encounter in human history," an encounter that profoundly affected, indeed enabled, the European Enlightenment and the abandonment of the biblical worldview.[51] For American Buddhism, Adeana McNicholl has demonstrated how orientalist portrayals of Shakyamuni were a form of resistance for Black Buddhists, allowing them to envision Shakyamuni as a civil rights activist.[52] In the very different historical moments studied by App and McNicholl, then, orientalism is never one-sided: it can close down worlds as well as open them up. The same is true for the orientalism that emerges in American Zen autobiographies that use koan.

The purpose of Zen practice, many an introductory manual will tell you, is to stop imagining things and to see the world as it is, right here, right now. Contrary to practices that focus on visuals such as Tantric Buddhism, we are told, in Zen visions and fantasies are distractions from the path. From this perspective, students like Matthiessen who were witnesses to sexual abuse simply weren't Zen enough, because they allowed their fantasies about their teacher blind them to the truth of who he actually was. But such a perspective would ignore how essential and pervasive, for good and bad, the imagination has been for convert Zen in America.[53] Without the imagination, there is simply no way that the authors I discuss here could see themselves as belonging to a tradition that is part of the cultural heritage of East Asia. In imagining themselves, their teachers, and their tradition as Zen (whatever that meant to them), Matthiessen and every other writer I discuss in this book were trying to make this alien tradition more comprehensible and more approachable. They did so by employing the—sometimes harmful—narratives that they were familiar with. In this respect, at least, they were not very different from Chinese, Japanese, Korean, Thai, Vietnamese, Khotanese, and so many other people across the ages who sought to understand what Buddhism was and how they, too, could be Buddhists.

SCOPE AND METHODOLOGY

A word, now, about the scope of this project. As source materials, I have chosen to examine autobiographical texts written by individuals like Matthiessen: American convert Zen practitioners who have studied with masters situated within Japanese lineages. Such individuals have published the largest volume of Zen autobiography in America, something that demonstrates both the immense influence Japanese Zen has had on American literary production and the dominance of convert Buddhist authors as spokespersons for American Zen. Within this group, I examine those who use koan in their work. These authors include Philip Kapleau, Janwillem van de Wetering, David Chadwick, Natalie Goldberg, Shozan Jack Haubner, Grace Schireson, Claire Gesshin Greenwood, Zenju Earthlyn Manuel, and Ruth Ozeki, among others.

With the exception of chapter 1, I limit myself to examining work published after the 1950s, a period that has become well known in the field as "the Zen boom," an era when Zen Buddhism moved far outside Chinese and Japanese American religious communities and started appearing widely in public intellectual discourse and writing.[54]

What are the characteristics of this group of Zen authors? In her largely anthropological study of recent developments in American Buddhism, Gleig used the term "meditation-based convert lineages" to characterize Buddhist groups that are largely composed of white, upper-class individuals like Matthiessen.[55] Such groups are lay-oriented: members rarely relinquish their families, as Asian monks and nuns were required to do. Instead, they participate in society while still keeping up a life of practice. That practice mainly consists of meditation, which in these communities overshadows most other ritual activities that lay Buddhists usually do in Asia (such as worshiping Buddha statues, repeating the name of heavenly Buddhas, and so on). Their understanding of Buddhism is shaped by a great variety of influences, most important among which are science and psychology. At the same time, progressive ideas such as democracy, feminism, and social justice also affect how they interpret Buddhism. Despite these progressive values, such groups also need to be understood as enjoying and exercising white privilege in determining what legitimate and "American" forms of Buddhism are and what the focus of practice should be. Ozeki, who is a Japanese American Zen Buddhist, and Manuel, who is queer and Black, are situated within such convert lineages. As we will see, Manuel in particular documents the subtle ways these communities can exclude those who are different.

As a scholar of comparative religious literature, I put aside what these individuals informally say about their practice or what it is they do on the meditation pillow. These topics are fascinating, but they are more within the purview of anthropological and sociological studies of Zen, of which many excellent examples exist already. Rather, I am fascinated by what happens when convert Zen Buddhists commit their lives to paper.

I interpret the category "autobiography" quite loosely. The literary scholars Julia Watson and Sidonie Smith argue that "autobiography" refers to a "particular practice of life narrative that emerged in the Enlightenment and has become canonical in the West."[56] For them, autobiography is only one type of life narrative, and a very Eurocentric one at that. This is a basic assumption of many early critics of the genre.[57] In contrast to autobiography,

Smith and Watson suggest the clunky term "life narrative," which for them means "a set of evershifting self-referential practices that engage the past in order to reflect on identity in the present."[58] While I appreciate Smith and Watson's attempt to decolonize the term, I don't think we should abandon the term "autobiography" altogether because it has such broad currency. Instead, I rely upon Smith and Watson's notion of "self-referential practices" to define a broad range of "autobiographical" texts: from personal correspondence to memoirs, and even postmodern novels that use the author's name in the narrative, there are indeed many ways to tell a life story.

Now that you have a better idea of what I mean by autobiography, I can turn to what I take to be koan. My approach to koan is, like my understanding of autobiography, quite flexible. A lot of ink has been spilled in disambiguating the terms "koan" from its cognates, which include "encounter dialogue" and "standard."[59] But these distinctions are not very important for my interlocutors, the authors of Zen autobiographies, who use the term "koan" for any type of enigmatic interaction between Zen masters and students. Moreover, unlike scholars of Chinese and Japanese Buddhism, I do not think that koan are only found in classic collections. Like jazz standards, new koan are being written today, and these koan, as we will see, continuously play with the genre conventions of the classics: What if the master's enigmatic silence is really a demonstration of his ignorance? What if the Zen master's strange behavior is due to a disability? What if the koan is any situation where two people come face-to-face? In the conclusion, I will return to this discussion to redefine koan (at least as they appear in the materials examined in this book) as story or "neck" riddles. For reasons of stylistic elegance, I also occasionally refer to them as riddles in the chapters preceding that conclusion.

I also need to talk about the tone of this book. As the chapters proceed, I will address you more and more often in the second person, adopting the conversational tone I use when teaching my classes. I do this primarily because I want my students to be able to read and understand this book without problems. I also hope that this stylistic choice will make the book accessible to nonacademics. But I also step to the fore to allow myself and the reader to examine who it is that I am. One lesson I have learned from this project is not to take myself too seriously. Hiding behind a scholarly "objective" voice would be to ignore that lesson. In this respect, I find inspiring Kripal's note on this in his recently published scholarly autobiography. Kripal tells his reader from the outset:

> It is my own growing conviction that my social sense of self—this dingbat other people keep calling "Jeff" or, astonishingly, "Prof. Kripal"—is in actual and literal fact a fiction, in short, a "myth" as most people understand that word. "Jeff Kripal" is a little unstable story that I tell myself over and over again (apparently, I need reassuring) from a few bits of memory, which I have selected out of millions of potential bits, that are then strung loosely together to make up a story line or plot that is "me." You are such a myth, too, of course. We all are. As are all our cultures and religions. It's all fiction.[60]

I have become convinced, though, that in the process of repeating this myth over and over again, it starts falling apart. We start getting bored with the ego and its insistence on self-affirmation, the stories it tells about itself. What comes after, I'm not 100 percent sure. I'm hoping you'll help me find out.

PERSONAL POSITION

Finally, something about why I wrote this book. I did so because I was on a quest for insight and liberation, much like the Zen practitioners discussed in this book. I first encountered Zen not on my driveway, like Matthiessen, but through its literature. Nowhere else had I read of beings who seemed so free as the Zen masters in koan. I wanted it, bad. I started meditating and had mind-blowing experiences that changed my life.

As a graduate student, I read Van de Wetering, in whose existential quest for meaning and perambulatory life from the Low Countries to Japan to America I saw a reflection of my own. Like Van de Wetering, I was disappointed to discover that living Zen masters weren't the supermen I had imagined them to be. At the same time, meditation retreats in China and the United States had established within me the certainty that Zen remained worthwhile. How could I solve this problem?

In narratives of Zen failure, I found that it was possible for Zen masters and their students to just be human beings, good and bad at the same time. This critique of the mainstream tradition I found valuable, and I began to read more voices who wrote outside of, and sometimes against, the mainstream, in turn exposing its underlying biases and thereby innovating a new type of American Zen. Though including all the voices that have guided me on my way would have made up a much longer book, many of them are here. In talking about Zen and themselves, all these authors have told me things about the riddle that is me. I can only hope that this study, which holds together their good and bad, conveys some of my deep love for the wordless teaching poured into language.

The first chapter takes us to Japan. The Second World War has just ended, and two Americans are about to meet a Zen sage.

ONE
ENLIGHTENMENT

—

D. T. Suzuki and Philip Kapleau

An iconic moment in American Zen's history was when two men climbed up the steep steps from the station at Kita-Kamakura to a temple called Engakuji.[1] The year is 1947, and the two men are American journalists, reporting on the war trials. They've come to meet someone who is already famous as the author of many English-language works explaining Zen. To Daisetz Teitaro "D. T." Suzuki (1870–1966), Zen was not a religion, or even a philosophy. What Zen gets at is the root of all human experience. If all religions point to something, and if that something is an experience, Zen's fingertip pointed the best.

"Zen" here means Japanese Zen. Suzuki had dismissed Chinese Zen as corrupted since the Song dynasty, a popular idea in the Japan of his day, and Indian Buddhism as too metaphysical. No, there was only one type of Zen that was worth discovering, a Zen that had rooted itself in the island-nation Japan and had become part of the very fiber of its society. In the sword flash of the samurai, in the silence of the tea ceremony, one could draw close to the Zen experience of enlightenment. What that experience was like, exactly, Suzuki would not say, though he alluded to it in that vague but powerful language all his own. Like all good Zen things, enlightenment stood outside of the realm of language. One could only talk around it but not describe it directly. And if one absolutely had to use language, koan would do the job.

Having never met Suzuki, Richard De Martino, one of the two men climbing the steps, found himself imagining what kind of person he would be: "Somehow I pictured a tall man with a long, flowing white beard and a remote, unworldly appearance who was, in some undefined manner, extremely 'Oriental.'"[2] His expectations matched those of his companion, Philip Kapleau, who forty years later recalled thinking he was about to encounter a "sage with long white hair and beard, flowing robes, and crooked walking stick."[3] Both were to be disappointed. At their destination, Kapleau finds a "short, clean-shaven, almost bald Japanese who looked for all the world like an editor."[4] The spirit of his description matches De Martino's, who remembers "a little, cleanshaven old man in a black kimono wearing, down over his eyeglasses, a Western style green bookkeeper's eyeshade."[5]

Though neither Kapleau nor De Martino met the oriental sage they had imagined, Suzuki's vision of Zen would change their lives. De Martino would go on to devote his life to the exploration of the connection between psychoanalysis and Zen.[6] Kapleau would return to the United States, go into business, and be chronically unhappy and sick. Until he rediscovered Zen. By that time, Suzuki, riding the postwar Zen boom, was in New York lecturing at Columbia University, inspiring luminaries such as the novelist Jack Kerouac, the poet Allen Ginsberg, and the music composer John Cage. If Kapleau had not found the oriental sage in Suzuki, he did not give up on the potential of Zen to solve all his life's problems. This is how he sets off for Japan a second time in 1953, searching for the enlightenment experience that Suzuki has told his American audiences is the end-all of Zen. Satori or bust.

Kapleau was not alone in getting on the boat to Japan in the 1950s. The poet Gary Snyder, the Dutch adventurer Janwillem van de Wetering, the New York musician Walter Nowick, and many others would all go the same way. Among these individuals, Kapleau is special because he wrote so comprehensively about what he learned in Japan. In 1965, he published *The Three Pillars of Zen*, a thick Zen manual that included speeches by Zen masters, koan commentaries, reports of private interviews between Zen masters and students, historical dharma talks by important Zen patriarchs, and instructions (with pictures) on how to properly sit while meditating. But the most important section of this book was the one titled "Eight Contemporary Enlightenment Experiences of Japanese and Westerners." This section contained eight autobiographical narratives that ended in enlightenment. Kapleau's own narrative was among them.

By all accounts, the decision to include these autobiographical narratives was a stroke of genius, greatly enhancing the appeal of Zen practice in the West. Judging from Kapleau's personal correspondence and published testimonies, the thing that most stood out for the readers of *Pillars* was these testimonies.[7] In the afterword to the thirty-fifth anniversary edition of the book, Bodhin Kjolhede, Kapleau's successor at Rochester Zen Center, where Kapleau had taught for many years after his return from Japan, describes the exhilaration of discovering that Zen could be practiced within a regular American household life: "We could hold on to our careers and families and still drink deeply from the wells of a great mystical tradition. It was Zen in a new package, stamped with an American brand name. We could have it all—or so it seemed."[8]

Kjolhede then shows that importing Zen was not so easy as some of Kapleau's readers imagined. Later, he adds: "Readers of the enlightenment accounts in *The Three Pillars of Zen* can be forgiven for idealizing awakening as a panacea for all of life's pain."[9] With this statement, Kjolhede points to one of the key features of the "Eight Contemporary Enlightenment Experiences," namely their obsession with the awakening experience as a solution to all of life's problems. It is there that Kapleau shows the immense influence Suzuki had on his way of understanding Zen. If for Suzuki koan indicated a universal experience beyond words, and if this experience could be found in Japan, Kapleau's life in a Japanese Zen temple must and will deliver the goods. And deliver it did.

In this chapter, I discuss the literary articulation of Zen enlightenment and mastery. In retelling the story of Suzuki and Kapleau, I focus on how they used koan to talk about experiences beyond words, and about the place where one can have these experiences. In interpreting koan, they present themselves as Zen masters and cast the reader as their student. In this sense, koan undergird their authority. They needed that authority because—this is an open secret—neither of them was an officially certified Zen master. Yet they spoke as masters, and they were able to do so because koan also structured their narratives through a specular relationship. They also use koan to make the Zen temple into a utopian space that is the opposite of capitalism, an egalitarian paradise where enlightenment, freedom, and joy could be found. What they said would lead generations of seekers to search, in America or in Japan, in the household or in the temple, for what they claimed to have found.

D. T. SUZUKI'S MIRRORS IN THE TEXT

I will discuss Suzuki first. After situating him in the larger history of modern Buddhism, I will examine how he uses koan in his work, first to characterize Zen enlightenment and then to portray the Japanese Zen temple as a utopian space. I have chosen to focus on one book, namely *An Introduction to Zen Buddhism* (1934), to do this. Readers interested in more can turn to the many available studies on this fascinating thinker.[10]

THE MAKING OF SUZUKI'S ZEN

Suzuki was there during one of the beginnings of Zen's coming to America, when Chicago hosted an event unprecedented in American history and momentous in its importance for American Buddhism: the 1893 World's Parliament of Religions. As its name implies, this event brought together representatives of a variety of religions. Among these representatives was Shaku Soen, whom we met in the introduction. Soen did not speak English and did not leave as strong an impression on the audience as the charismatic Sri Lankan Buddhist modernizer Anagarika Dharmapala. But in Chicago Soen did meet the right person in Paul Carus, an American publisher invested in reconciling science with religion, exactly the theme that Soen had talked about in one of his speeches at the Parliament.[11]

Suzuki was Soen's lay student. Under this master's tutelage, he had attained enlightenment. In an autobiographical account that would be published near the end of his life, Suzuki narrates this experience by drawing on koan, something he did throughout his scholarship as well.[12] Like Soen, Suzuki wanted to present Japanese Zen as a religion on par with, or even superior to, Christianity. But to do that, he had to get to know his audience. After the Parliament, he moved to the United States to help Carus with his publishing projects, mainly involving translating important East Asian texts such as the *Daode jing*, the Chinese classic of Daoism. In the process, Suzuki gained a deep familiarity with the methods and interests of Western scholars.[13]

The gist of what Suzuki learned was this: At the beginning of the twentieth century, Japanese Zen, as part of the Great Vehicle, or Mahayana, was not on the radar of Western scholarship. Instead, scholars had focused their attention on India, a region where, except in Sri Lanka, Buddhist monastic communities hadn't existed for centuries. Why, then, this interest in

India? An important part of the answer is the Protestant presupposition that the essence of Buddhism could be discovered by reading its original and earliest texts, just as the essence of Christianity was to be found in the Bible. What living Buddhists actually did and did not do was not as important.[14] That is why Indian Buddhism and the Pali Canon, the earliest collection of Buddhist texts written in a dialect of Sanskrit, became the focus of Western scholarship.[15] East Asia, an area that became Buddhist only later in history, was less interesting because it was not deemed authentic. Moreover, its Mahayana Buddhism, with its proliferation of Buddhist heavens, Buddhist saints (Bodhisattvas), and dazzlingly supernatural sutras, did not appeal to the Protestant mindset, which finds its origin story in the rejection of Roman Catholic imagery and ritual.

In his work, Suzuki undermined the philological prioritization of Indian Buddhism by proposing an evolutionary framework instead: earlier was not better, in the same way that an ape was not better than a member of the species *Homo sapiens*. A series of evolutionary adaptations separate apes from human beings, and likewise separate Indian Theravada from East Asian Mahayana.[16] The bottom line was teleological: East Asian Mahayana was the most superior form of Buddhism exactly because it came about later in history. Suzuki declares: "The so-called primitive Buddhism is the seed, out of it Far-Eastern Buddhism has come into existence with the promise of still further growth. Scholars may talk of historical Buddhism, but my subject here is to see Buddhism not only in its historical development but from the point of view of its still vitally concerning us as a quickening spiritual force in the Far East."[17] The syntax here quivers with contained energy, demonstrating the very point that Suzuki is trying to make: why study dusty tomes in a forgotten language when you can study Buddhism in the flesh, as it is practiced in East Asia?

But this line of reasoning wouldn't necessarily make Zen the best form of Buddhism. Other contemporary forms of Mahayana, let alone other schools of Japanese Buddhism, could make an equal claim to having evolved over time. How was Zen special? In *An Introduction*, Suzuki answers this with the astonishing claim that all other schools of East Asian Buddhism were in essence Indian due to "their metaphysical complexity, their long-winded phraseology, their highly abstract reasoning, their penetrating insight into the nature of things, and their comprehensive interpretation of affairs relating to life."[18] Zen, on the other hand, because it was simple and practical, was the only school that captured the essence of the East Asian mind.

Practical for doing what, though? To attain mystical insight. From his study of William James, the great American philosopher who gave a long series of lectures on the subject of mystical experience, Suzuki gained a vocabulary to elevate Zen above all other forms of Buddhism. James had argued eloquently that, underlying the variety of all religious expressions, was a more fundamental Experience. All things that one usually associates with religions, such as churches, rituals, and so on, were extraneous by-products accumulated over time. The essence of religion, however, was something accessible to any human being—if only you had the tools.[19]

Suzuki presented Zen as offering these tools. More than attempting to convince his audiences that Zen was compatible with science, like Soen had at the Chicago Parliament, he presented it as a method that could achieve what science could not. Instead of describing a flower, Zen would allow you to become one with the flower.[20] Moreover, the Zen idea that awakening, refigured now as James's experience, could be transferred from mind to mind, rendered the question of what came earliest redundant: texts were irrelevant when faced with the freshness of an experience that was at the same time ancient and universal.[21] Like James, Suzuki dismissed religious institutions as by-products of something much deeper. Zen Buddhists had it right from the start, because unlike their peers they focused on nonverbal experience and attacked institutional authority, dismissing everything, any concept to get at Experience (remember from the introduction that Bodhidharma had dismissed the idea that Wu's infrastructural zeal was netting him Buddhist credit).

But Suzuki wanted to do more than establish the primacy of Zen. He wanted to establish the primacy of *Japanese* Zen, and thus he had to account for the fact that Zen Buddhism thrives in China, Korea, and Vietnam, as well as in Japan. Practices in these countries differ vastly, despite Suzuki's essentializing claims about Zen. Suzuki solves this problem by claiming, again and again, that it was in Japan that Zen reached its full development. Only in Japan, Suzuki would affirm in the very title of one of his most popular monographs, *Zen and Japanese Culture,* did Zen become part of the fabric of society, and thus Japanese Zen was superior to every other iteration. Sometimes this slides into the assertion that only Japanese people can properly understand and practice Zen at all. Suzuki thus relocates the Protestant prejudice for the purest type of Buddhism from India to Japan.[22]

Within Japanese Zen, it was the Rinzai (C. Linji) school, with its emphasis on obtaining enlightenment through the arduous study of koan, that carried

Suzuki's preference, he himself being trained by a Rinzai master. Though the split between Rinzai and Soto is not hugely important for American Zen, I'll briefly repeat the ideological differences between these two factions of Zen here, because this will help us understand Suzuki better and because the very reason these schools disagreed was purportedly the usage of koan during meditation. I say "purportedly" because their history is complicated, with all kinds of political and polemical motives driving an ideological opposition that is presented as simply being about the best way of practicing.[23] Polemics in Zen, in Asia and America, are never just about practice, they are almost always about power and authority as well. Put differently, practice is polemics: when people decide to sit in meditation differently (as they do in Soto, where people face the wall, and Rinzai, where people face each other), this marks a distinction between them that is not as much a result of best practices being transmitted as it is the energy of the debate continuing to express itself in long-held silences. It's not as if there's evidence that says that facing a wall (which is what Soto practitioners do) gets you enlightened quicker than facing each other (which is what Rinzai practitioners do).

In any case, the polemics that Suzuki is engaged in here date back to China, to the Song dynasty. As mentioned in the introduction, under the influence of the Zen master Dahui Zonggao, the Rinzai (Caodong) lineage had started to use koan as a means of training Zen students. Koan were seen as tools to bring about awakening. The Soto lineage refused to do this because their interpretation of the doctrine of Buddha-nature implied that we don't need to do anything to achieve awakening. We're already awakened.

In *An Introduction,* Suzuki dismisses the Soto school in unmistakable terms:

> Whatever one may say against the abuses of the koan, it was the koan that saved Japanese Zen from total annihilation. Consider how Chinese Zen is faring these days; so far as we can gather it is more or less a mere name; and again notice the general tendency shown in the practice of Zen by adherents of the Soto school in present-day Japan. We cannot deny that there are many good points in Soto, which ought to be carefully studied, but as to the living of Zen there is perhaps greater activity in the Rinzai, which employs the koan system.[24]

Suzuki makes this point in response to the undeniable historical systematization of koan study: today still, students follow something like a koan curriculum. This seems to go against the freedom and vitality of the Zen patriarchs, and Suzuki thus affirms that koan do still possess that vitality. He suggests here that like Chinese Zen, which he earlier affirms has become fused with Pure Land Buddhist practices such as chanting Amida Buddha's name, Soto has let itself be compromised, and in doing so has lost its vitality. For him, Rinzai Zen is the supreme expression of Japanese Zen, and Japanese Zen is the supreme expression of the thought of East Asia and Buddhism at the same time: "in Zen are found systematized, or rather crystallized, all the philosophy, religion, and life itself of the Far-Eastern people, especially of the Japanese."[25]

THE FUNCTION OF KOAN IN SUZUKI'S WORK

For Suzuki, religious experience was beyond the power of language to express. In his writing, then, he only alluded to it. Koan were his means of choice to do so. As canonized Zen texts, koan fit the Protestant preference for older textual materials. As vague riddles whose ultimate meaning is unclear, they afforded Suzuki a freedom of interpretation that allowed him to cite them liberally in support of his Buddhist modernist theory of religious experience while still maintaining the impression that he was representing an ancient tradition. In speaking for this tradition, he cast himself as a Zen master and the Japanese Zen monastery as a utopia where koan defined daily life.

Let's take a closer look at how Suzuki does this. *An Introduction* continually cites koan, but Suzuki only comes around to defining the genre near the end of the book, when he engages in the polemics against the Soto school discussed above. For Suzuki, koan are "some anecdote of an ancient master, or a dialogue between a master and monks, or a statement or question put forward by a teacher, all of which are used as the means for opening one's mind to the truth of Zen."[26] Suzuki implicitly agrees with the viewpoint of the Soto school that we are already perfect: in addition to being an instrument, koan are "an artificiality and superfluity" that the strong masters of the Tang dynasty did not need. He thereby holds to the viewpoint (outlined in the introduction to this book) that the Song marked the decline of Zen, a teleology many scholars have since criticized.[27] Nevertheless, for our modern-day mind, koan are effective in that they destroy all rational ways of thinking.[28] Thus, through his discussion, Suzuki talks about koan as a flawed but ultimately effective instrument to break the duality of the mind, to destroy old thinking based on scientific or logical presuppositions, and to build up "a new order of things on the basis of Zen experience."[29]

However, koan are not just tools to access religious experience on the meditation pillow; they also stand in for this experience in Suzuki's prose. This creates a circular structure of authorization that constructs an influential version of the literary Zen master. That structure is as follows: Suzuki cites koan that he understands because he has had the experience that koan express. If his audience does not understand, that is because they have not had the experience Suzuki lays claim to.

Consider the third chapter of *An Introduction*. Like most other chapters, its title poses a basic question about Zen, namely "Is Zen Nihilistic?" In the first three pages, Suzuki seems to entertain the possibility that this is indeed the case, and subsequently cites eight koan, of which I only quote the first two:

> "I come here to seek the truth of Buddhism," a disciple asked a [Zen] master.
>
> "Why do you seek such a thing here?" answered the master. "Why do you wander about, neglecting your own precarious treasure at home? I have nothing to give you, and what truth of Buddhism do you desire to find in my monastery? There is nothing, absolutely nothing."
>
> A master would sometimes say: "I do not understand Zen, I have nothing here to demonstrate; therefore, do not remain standing so, expecting to get something out of nothing. Get enlightened by yourself, if you will. If there is anything to take hold of, take it by yourself."[30]

Suzuki explains these dialogues as implying that Zen is "nihilistic." However, shortly after entertaining this interpretation, he denies that it is valid and instead claims that "Zen always aims at grasping the central fact of life, which can never be brought to the dissecting table of the intellect."[31] This is a large interpretative leap from the materials themselves, which do not really "say" anything like that. What does it mean to say, like the master in the koan above, that "There is nothing, absolutely nothing?" Whatever it means, it seems a large interpretative leap to interpret this as relating to "the central fact of life," which is not intellectual. Suzuki's interpretative mobility in discussing the two koan relies on the ambiguity koan possess: you do not know what this koan means, so I will tell you.

Suzuki's authority to interpret koan partly relies on a hierarchy derived from koan themselves. In *An Introduction*, koan function as "mirrors in the text," a term the French literature scholar Lucien Dällenbach has used to describe a specific quality of inset stories, or *mise en abyme*. You are probably familiar with inset stories because they are everywhere in fiction. I'll give an example from hard-boiled space opera (a mixture of science fiction about outer space and detective stories). In one of this subgenre's most famous novels, *Leviathan Wakes* (part of *The Expanse*, now a TV series), a gumshoe named Miller is trying to solve the disappearance of a scion of a wealthy family, a woman named Julie. After fighting his way into a spaceship to escape a space station full of vomiting zombies, Miller collapses and falls asleep: "In his dreams, he was fitting a puzzle together as the pieces kept changing shape, and each time, just as he was on the verge of slipping the whole mechanism together, the dream began again. . . . The nearer he came to consciousness, the more he tried to postpone it. Imaginary fingers tried to complete the puzzle, and before he could make it all fit, his eyes opened."[32] Miller's dreams clearly are related to the main plot of the novel, but it's not immediately clear how. The "puzzle" seems to refer to the mystery of Julie's disappearance, and the dream could be read to imply that this mystery will never be solved. This is indeed one thing that becomes clear: by the end of the book, the reader has a good idea of how everything came to pass, but not the details of why Julie disappeared and exactly what role she played in the unfolding catastrophe. But the dream could also be taken to mean that Miller can only begin to make sense of Julie in his dreams, which is also true: as becomes clear, Miller is deeply in love with a Julie he has constructed in his imagination, a Julie who is very different from the real Julie. Finally, the dream could also be taken to be a vision of the future, when Miller, who has died trying to rescue Julie, will reappear in the dreams of the main character, James Holder, to point them toward the deeper mystery that caused the vomiting zombies to appear.

My point in this interpretative exercise is to show that an inset story, of which a dream is one example and a koan another, comments on the main narrative, but only vaguely so. It is and is not part of the story, and the reader needs to decide how to make sense of it. As mentioned, Dällenbach, who relies on the French highbrow *nouveau roman* for his examples, understands the relationship between inset stories and the main narrative as "mirrors in the text." As the term implies, he sees inset narratives as reflecting the main narrative, if we understand that reflection can also be refraction: from only one way of reading the text, we suddenly gain many more because we are forced to interpret the relationship between the inset narrative and the main narrative. However, when there's a deep similarity between the inset and main narrative, and when the same types of inset narratives are repeated, the interpretative possibilities become much narrower, and we become forced to read the text only in one way. One way in which mirrors in the text can condition a certain reading is by determining the relationship between author and reader.[33]

In the case of *An Introduction*, there is a deep resemblance between koan and the structure of the framing narrative. Let's look at that in more detail. Here's another koan quoted by Suzuki:

> Hyakujo (Pai-chang [Baizhang]) went out one day attending his master Baso (Ma-tsu [Mazu]), when they saw a flock of wild geese flying. Baso asked:
> "What are they?"
> "They are wild geese, sir."
> "Whither are they flying?"
> "They have flown away."
> Baso, abruptly taking hold of Hyakujo's nose, gave it a twist. Overcome with pain, Hyakujo cried out: "Oh! Oh!"
> Said Baso, "You say they have flown away, but all the same they have been here from the very first."
> This made Hyakujo's back wet with perspiration; he had *satori*.[34]

Here, the master's replies to the student's questions lead the latter to satori, the spiritual awakening that for Suzuki constitutes the ultimate goal of Zen practice. Note the violence accompanying this exchange: Baso can twist Hyakujo's nose exactly because he is the latter's social and spiritual superior, a position the tradition calls "enlightened."

Hyakujo's exchange with Baso is structurally the same as Suzuki's relationship with his reader. It has a master and a student speaking about something mysterious. The student asks commonplace, logical questions and gives commonplace, logical answers, whereas the teacher dodges those questions, instead resorting to nonverbal means to push his student toward awakening. Throughout *An Introduction to Zen Buddhism*, the reader is assumed to be asking questions of Suzuki like Hyakujo asks questions of Baso, an assumption reflected in chapter titles such as "What Is Zen?" and the already-mentioned "Is Zen Nihilistic?" Like Nansen lifting a hapless cat and demanding a word, Suzuki avoids rational explanations and delights in puzzling his audience. This hierarchy is made explicit when Suzuki tells his reader: "You and I are supposedly living in the same world, but who can tell that the thing we popularly call a stone that is lying before my window is the same to both of us? You and I sip a cup of tea. That act is apparently alike to us both, but who can tell what a wide gap there is subjectively between your drinking and my drinking? In your drinking there may be no Zen, while mine is brim-full of it."[35] While the reader "may" have had some taste of Zen experience, there is no doubt about Suzuki's claim to it. Koan and explanation, inset story and main narrative become reflections and reinforce each other's meaning, which turns Suzuki into the modern representative of the ancient Zen patriarchs.

Having assumed the position of a Zen master through this specular mechanism, Suzuki tells his readers what koan mean. As mentioned earlier, he understands Zen enlightenment as a universally available experience. Thus, he explains the exchange between Hyakujo and Baso as evidence that satori "is an experience which no amount of explanation or argument can make communicable to others unless the latter themselves had it previously."[36] Note how this statement explains very little. It states that a koan points to an experience that cannot be further explained. Koan are placeholders here for something that is beyond the ability of language to communicate.

Suzuki does not only tell his readers about the universal experience of enlightenment, but he also tells them where this experience can be best obtained. In a chapter titled "The Meditation Hall and the Monk's Life," Suzuki describes this "unique institution" that we can find in "most of the main monasteries in Japan of the Zen sect."[37] His discussion contrasts the Zen organization of life with capitalism: the monastery is a "solitary island of Zen" that must be protected against "the merciless tide of modern commercialism and mechanization [that] is rolling all over the East."[38] Despite the threat to this institution in our age, "[Zen's] guiding principles, such as the simplification of life, restraint of desires, not wasting a moment icily [sic], self-independence, and what they call 'secret virtue' are sound for all lands and in all ages."[39] Indeed, Suzuki suggests that the Zen monastery is a more rational way to organize the whole of society, asking:

Cannot society be reorganized upon an entirely different basis from what we have been used to see from the beginning of history? Cannot we ever hope to stop the massing of wealth and the accumulation of power merely from the desire for individual or national aggrandizement? Despairing of the utter irrationality of human affairs, Buddhist monks have gone to the other extreme and cut themselves off even from reasonably and perfectly innocent enjoyments of life. However, the Zen ideal of putting a monk's belongings into a tiny box is his mute protest, though so far ineffective, against the present order of society.[40]

Suzuki's portrayal of the Zen monastery is deeply utopian. Like Thomas More's imagined country, his Zen monastery is a "solitary island" protected from the "irrationality" of the surrounding world. This "irrationality" is tied up with capitalism ("the massing of wealth . . . from the desire for individual or national aggrandizement"), and in this way, Suzuki's utopia is similar to many other utopian narratives in the nineteenth and twentieth centuries.

Suzuki's monastery is protected not only from "the irrationality of human affairs" but also from the progression of time itself. In Suzuki's essay, Japanese Zen monasteries represent an ageless and unchangeable tradition, founded on monastic rules attributed to Hyakujo Ekai (C. Baizhang Huaihai), the eighth-century Zen master whom we met earlier when he was having his nose twisted by Baso. Hyakujo is most famous as the nominal author of a text describing Zen discipline, Hyakujo's *Rules of Purity*.[41] There, he prescribes a highly idealized Zen monasticism: in his monastery, monks do not worship Buddha statues, study scripture, or engage in ritual practices. Instead, everyone leads a simple lifestyle combining meditation and manual labor. But as Griffith Foulk has shown, these rules—of which it is highly questionable that Hyakujo even wrote them—were rarely practiced and need to be understood within the polemics the Zen school had been engaging in at least since the Tang dynasty, namely that it constituted a "special transmission outside of the scriptures, not relying upon words and letters," and could trace its lineage all the way to Shakyamuni Buddha himself.[42] When Suzuki thus bases his account of the Zen monastery on Hyakujo's *Rules*, he portrays the monastery as an ideal Zen space, not an actually existing one.

Suzuki's portrayal of monastic life cites koan as if they represent the contemporary reality of life in such a place. For example, when discussing the private interview with the master, Suzuki quotes a koan featuring the

Japanese master Hakuin Ekaku (1686–1768).[43] On another occasion, when talking about a Zen master's "long maturing of the sacred womb," the broadening of understanding after enlightenment, Suzuki quotes several koan describing the withdrawal of a master into the wilderness. Suzuki's portrayal of Zen monks is similar in kind. We read that "poverty and simplicity is their rule" and "to work [hard] is their religion."[44] Their Zen education does not come from books but from practice.[45] Like a commune, they are a "self-governing body" whose senior members have a character that "has been tested through many years of discipline."[46] Suzuki concludes, "The spirit of Hyakujo is ever manifest here."[47] The referent of this "here" is the contemporary Japanese Zen monastery, which is rendered virtually indistinguishable from the Zen spaces portrayed in koan.

Ultimately, Suzuki's Zen monastery is designed for enlightenment: "Taking it all in all, Zen is emphatically a matter of personal experience.... Therefore, everything in the Meditation Hall and every detail of its disciplinary curriculum is so arranged as to bring this idea into the most efficient prominence."[48] It is no wonder that this utopian Japanese Zen monastery generated immense appeal. It would not be long before Suzuki's readers would travel to Japan themselves in search of such transformative experiences. Many of them would presuppose that koan did indeed describe both the way of life in these places and the experience that could be gotten there.

PHILIP KAPLEAU: ENLIGHTENMENT OR BUST

As mentioned in the introduction, Kapleau was not unique among the many spiritual seekers who departed for Japan. But he was special in that he reported on his experiences with Zen with the attention to detail furnished by his experiences as a journalist. Published in 1965, *The Three Pillars of Zen: Teaching, Practice, and Enlightenment* remains a literary monument of American Buddhism, showing Suzuki's influence but also departing from him. If Suzuki's Zen was idealized and vague, Kapleau's was more down-to-earth. He provided his readers with authentic speeches by living Zen masters, verbatim reports of dialogues between students and their teachers, and practical instructions on how to sit in meditation. Suzuki sought to locate the essence of Zen and found it in religious experience. Kapleau showed his readers that they could access this experience themselves (he had), and that they did not need to go to Japan for it.

In an era when English-language resources on Zen were still scarce, its detailed reporting on actual practice would have made *Three Pillars* memorable enough. But what makes this book stand out in the history of American convert Buddhism is the inclusion of a section titled "Eight Contemporary Enlightenment Experiences of Japanese and Westerners." What was Kapleau's goal in including these? In the introduction to this section, Kapleau explains that he wanted to show his readers that the enlightenment experience was not only desirable but also possible. Noting that "in recent years stories of the enlightenments of ancient Chinese Zen monks have found their way into English," he objected that while these stories' goal was "to inspire and instruct modern readers, paradoxically they have the opposite effect," namely they impressed upon contemporary readers how vastly different the environment was in which these masters attained insight.[49] Any attempt to gain insight like theirs, Kapleau has his imagined reader go on, would be doomed because modern society is just too different from that of ancient China.

To alleviate such concerns, Kapleau decided to include accounts of Japanese and Westerners "living among us today, neither as monks nor unworldly solitaries but as business and professional men and women, artists, and housewives. All have trained in Zen under a modern master and realized their Self-nature in one degree or another. Their stories bear witness that what man has done man can do, that satori is no impossible ideal."[50] As if to counter the reader's other possible objections, Kapleau later adds that these individuals who found enlightenment did not possess paranormal or intellectual gifts: "If they were exceptional in any way, it was simply in their courage to 'go they knew not where by a road they knew not of,' prompted by a faith in their real Self."[51] After giving a comprehensive and clearly autobiographical description of the atmosphere during sesshin, a week of intensive meditation, Kapleau concludes the general introduction to the "Experiences" section of *Three Pillars* by emphasizing how congenial Zen, with its stress on self-reliance and personal experience, is to the American worldview, a statement I will return to at the very end of this book.

Kapleau's own autobiographical account is by far the longest of the "Eight Contemporary Enlightenment Experiences." Titled "Mr. P. K., An American Ex-Businessman," it shows Suzuki's influence in understanding the Japanese Zen monastery as a place where koan describe daily life and where enlightenment is the raison d'être. But because he is writing autobiographically,

Kapleau can contrast this utopian place with what he actually finds in Japan. It is only gradually that this tension is resolved, the narrative arc moving from despair and disappointment to joyous awakening.

The first entry in Kapleau's diary, dated April 1, 1953, is set in the United States. Kapleau complains about health problems and suicidal tendencies: "Belly aching all week. Doc says ulcers are getting worse . . . allergies kicking up too . . . Can't sleep without drugs . . . So miserable wish I had the guts to end it all."[52] From this world of suffering, Kapleau finds no release by attending Suzuki's lectures at Columbia University: "Why do I go on with [attending] these lectures? Can I ever get satori listening to philosophic explanations of *prajna* and *karuna* [wisdom and compassion] and why A isn't A and all the rest of that? What the hell is satori anyway?"[53] Despite not knowing what it is, Kapleau lets himself be convinced that satori is the solution to his ailing health and existential depression, a depression associated, through the "Ex-Businessman" title of the narrative, with capitalism. He asks an unnamed Japanese expert on Buddhism: "If I go to Japan to train in Zen, can you assure me I'll be able to find some meaning in life? Will I absolutely get rid of my ulcers and allergies and sleeplessness?"[54] Finding courage in the answers of his interlocutors, Kapleau departs for Japan, despite warnings from Suzuki and others that "Zen monasteries are too traditional and authoritarian for modern intellectually minded people."[55]

In Kyoto, Kapleau cannot believe how much Japan has changed since his visit right after the war. Asking himself why he has returned, he remembers "the unearthly silence of Engaku Monastery [where he met Suzuki with De Martino] and the deep peace it engendered within me."[56] With a friend, he asks around for a Zen teacher, and he receives a letter from Soen Nakagawa, whom Matthiessen would meet years later on his driveway. Nakagawa invites Kapleau and his friend to visit Ryutakuji, his temple in Mishima, Shizuoka prefecture. Almost immediately after their arrival, the two American visitors object to the daily ritual practice at the temple. Kapleau writes:

> What a weird scene of refined sorcery and idolatry: shaven-headed black-robed monks sitting motionlessly chanting mystic gibberish to the accompaniment of a huge wooden tom-tom emitting otherworldly sounds, while the roshi [Zen master], like some elegantly gowned witch doctor, is making magic passes and prostrating himself again and again before an altar bristling with idols and images . . . Is this the Zen of Tanka, who tossed a Buddha statue into the fire? Is this the Zen of Rinzai, who shouted, you

must kill the Buddha? . . . The Kyoto teachers and S——[Suzuki] were right after all . . .[57]

Here, Kapleau refers to two iconoclastic koan and contrasts these with what he actually finds in Japan. These koan are the Tanka Tennen's (C. Danxia Tianran) burning of a Buddha statue and Rinzai Gigen's (C. Linji Yixuan) famous injunction, "If you meet the Buddha, kill the Buddha." According to what Kapleau has read, monastic life should not revolve around ritual practice but instead should be a series of weird encounters with wild mystics. After Nakagawa prostrates himself in front of a statue of the Japanese master Hakuin, Kapleau's friend explodes, "The old Chinese masters burned or spit on Buddha statues, why do you bow down before them?"[58] Unfazed, Nakagawa replies, "If you want to spit you spit, I prefer to bow."[59] Later on in his training, Kapleau is surprised by the commitment required of him: if Zen experience is available at any point and any time, why should we strive to obtain it?

Like Matthiessen, Kapleau is tasked with solving the "Mu" koan, and he throws his full strength at it. Later, he would describe this koan as "an exceptionally wieldy scalpel for extirpating from the deepest unconscious the malignant growth of 'I' and 'not-I' which poisons the mind's inherent purity and impairs its fundamental wholeness."[60] This understanding is similar to Suzuki's idea that koan are tools to undo dualist ways of thinking. However, Kapleau does not realize this at the beginning of his koan study. His diary describes an egotistic quest for satori, which, once he gets it, will make his friends back in the United States jealous.[61] The seven-week intensive meditation period he sees as a "race," and those who have become enlightened are its "winners."[62]

Over time, Kapleau begins to win the race for satori. Jumping ahead a year and a half, the diary reports immense progress. Not only has he had great insights, but the health problems haunting him at the beginning of the narrative have completely disappeared, and meditation has become a nourishing experience. Here, Suzuki's assertion of Zen practice as a resistance to the diseases brought on by capitalism is literalized: Kapleau's body, damaged by his work as a businessman, is healed by his stay in Japan.[63] His perspective on ritual activities like prostration and chanting also shifts. Ritual is no longer an obstacle but "glows with the living Truth which these monks have obviously all experienced in some measure."[64]

The diary ends with a description of Kapleau's enlightenment. He achieves this under his new master Yasutani, whose Sanbokyodan school represents an eccentric form of Zen that, like Suzuki, focuses on the pursuit of enlightenment. Neither Soto nor Rinzai, the Sanbokyodan is in many ways a "new religion."[65] That this school did not conform to mainstream Japanese Zen practice is exactly what Kapleau finds so attractive about it. He loves the "homey" atmosphere and the absence of austere disciplinary punishments.[66] His new teacher is equally enthusiastic. Writing to Kapleau's sister Jean, he expresses great hopes for his new pupil, whom he wishes to "succeed in realizing true Zen as fast as possible, and return to America as the first pioneer of Zen for all the United States."[67]

Kapleau does not disappoint. Within this new environment and with this new teacher, he finally becomes one with his koan: "I completely vanished... I didn't eat breakfast, *Mu* did. I didn't sweep and wash the floors after breakfast, *Mu* did. I didn't eat lunch, *Mu* ate."[68] Shortly after, he finally attains an even deeper insight:

> "The universe is One," [Yasutani] began, each word tearing into my mind like a bullet. "The moon of Truth—" All at once the roshi, the room, every single thing disappeared in a dazzling stream of illumination and I felt myself bathed in a delicious, unspeakable delight... For a fleeting eternity I was alone—I alone was... Then the roshi swam into view. Our eyes met and flowed into each other, and we burst out laughing...
>
> "I have it! I know! There is nothing, absolutely nothing. I am everything and everything is nothing!" I exclaimed more to myself than to the roshi, and got up and walked out.[69]

Kapleau's commentary here corresponds to the koan he was examining: the "Mu" (meaning "there is not") that Joshu shouts out in the koan has become characteristic of reality itself. There is no separation between self and other, all is one and all is Mu. Kapleau describes feeling immense freedom and an overwhelming joy. This experience is authenticated by Yasutani as *kensho*, a type of awakening that is "seeing into one's nature." In solving, or rather becoming, his koan, Kapleau took a first step toward becoming a Zen master. For him, Suzuki's vision of Zen has proven accurate: enlightenment can be attained, and it can be attained through koan. The wisdom of the patriarchs has become available to an American ex-businessman.

Later in his life, though, Kapleau would articulate this foundational experience very differently. In the afterword to *Zen: Dawn in the West* (1979), after describing Suzuki as looking like an "editor," we only find a single sentence to describe his *kensho*: "My Mind's eye was opened to some extent."[70] What has happened to the overwhelming joy of the 1965 diary?

Kapleau's personal correspondence from the 1990s might provide a clue, as it contains some revealing comments on the reliability of (auto)biographical writing. In those letters, whenever Kapleau's students asked him to write or participate in an autobiographical or biographical project, he rejected (auto)biography in no uncertain terms. In a letter to his student Ann Kahl dated February 11, 1992, he states that he does not want to write another book. And even if he were to write one, "I wouldn't write an autobiography, given my strong feeling that autobiography is nothing so much as an egotistical attempt at self-elevation at the expense of facts. But what are facts? In Aldous Huxley's words, 'Facts are like a dummy on a ventriloquists [sic] knee: they can be made to say what ever [sic] you want them to say.' No, Ann, I'll take my chances."[71] Asked by another student whether someone could do a biography of him instead, he writes, "I firmly believe the statement of the person who said, 'Autobiography (or biography) is an honorable name for the dishonorable act of re-inventing the past.' So much for that."[72] Even a photograph is out of the question: "P.S. You asked for an autographed picture. When an artist said to the great Zen master Chou cho [Zhaozhou], 'I would like to paint a portrait of you,' the master replied, 'If it is a poor likeness, it will be thrown away. But if it is an excellent likeness, you might as well kill me and keep the portrait forever.' I feel the same way about photographs."[73]

Taken together, these statements demonstrate that by the 1990s at the latest (if not earlier), Kapleau believed that (auto)biography was by definition disingenuous. Even if an attempt is made to represent facts, these facts can be made to say whatever the author desires. And even if the facts paint a more or less accurate portrait of the person (as in Kapleau's reference to Zhaozhou), autobiography becomes a mask, a representation that replaces the original person.

These statements about autobiography in Kapleau's personal correspondence give us some background to understand the difference between the awakening account in *Pillars* and that of *Dawn*. In *Pillars*, Kapleau fit the diary into a narrative of Zen heavily influenced by both Suzuki and Yasutani. This narrative not only conditioned his expectations, but it also conditioned how Kapleau described his experiences: he focused on enlightenment, believed everything in a Zen space serves the goal of enlightenment, and referred to koan as the model of how Zen ought to be.[74] By the time *Dawn* was published, both Suzuki's and Yasutani's influence on Kapleau had waned. Suzuki died in 1966, and shortly thereafter Yasutani broke off ties with Kapleau over the latter's innovations in the Rochester Zen Center, denying that Kapleau had received Dharma transmission from him and was a legitimate master in his tradition.[75] Both of these personal developments begin to explain both why the account of the awakening experience in *Dawn* is so brief and why Kapleau became so dismissive of autobiographical statements: grown apart from his previous mentors, the narrative of his experience in Japan changed.

Most stories need a bad guy. The story of Zen coming to America is no different, and Suzuki has functioned in this role more than once. Starting in the 1990s (though critiques of him had surfaced long before then), Suzuki came under severe fire. Scholars, myself included, have described his ideas as complicit with Japanese wartime nationalism, and as portraying a misleading if seductive image of that tradition.[76] In his introductions to the recent reissuing of Suzuki's work, the historian of Japanese religions Richard Jaffe has forged a middle way between mere adoration for Suzuki's significant achievements and dismissing these achievements altogether. Jaffe does so by casting Suzuki as an innovator, passionate about adapting Zen to the needs of the modern world.[77] Suzuki certainly succeeded in this quest: he was without doubt one of the most influential Buddhist thinkers in the twentieth century.[78]

So, Suzuki was and remains a big deal. His worldwide audiences were mesmerized by the tradition that he portrayed, by the power of his unique writing style, and by his charismatic presence amplified by orientalist traditions of representation that cast him as the incarnation of ancient Asian wisdom.[79] Koan allowed Suzuki to cast himself as a Zen master who has the authority to tell his audience what the meaning of koan is: a religious experience called enlightenment that is universal to all humankind. The stories also allow him to create a place, the Japanese Zen temple, that eternally stands outside of the vicissitudes of modern life. It is there that this religious experience can be found; it is there that koan become reality.

Kapleau's autobiographical narrative showed how influential Suzuki's way of using koan was. Kapleau continuously struggles to reconcile what he finds in Japan with the koan he has read. He is shocked by Buddhist priests bowing to statues because that's not what people in the koan do. He sees Zen practice as a cure for the diseases of capitalism. He sees the only way forward as an overwhelming enlightenment experience, and his account of *kensho* in *Three Pillars* is decisively influenced by the idea that koan bring about an overwhelming transformation. The revision of this experience much later attests to this influence, as does his rejection of autobiography in his personal correspondence. Like Suzuki, Kapleau used koan to make himself into a Zen master, and koan deeply shaped his narrative.

Suzuki was an immense influence on my own path as well. In my native Belgium, as a twenty-year-old interested in Zen, his books were the ones I read first. With "satori," Suzuki seemed to be talking about that thing that I felt when, as a teenager, a poem I read suddenly exploded in my brain, an experience that became the reason for my majoring in literature in college. He seemed to have (and for all I know did indeed possess) regular access to something I desperately wanted. His work made me love koan: nowhere else had I found the meaning of life expressed so wittily.

All this is why I was so disappointed when I discovered that most of what Suzuki wrote was as modern as it was ancient, as Western as it was Asian. Acting out this disappointment, I wrote against Suzuki and against modern Zen in general. During my first years of graduate school, I summarily dismissed those aspects of Zen that had held such appeal to me before: enlightenment, meditation, koan practice. It took a while before I reached the middle ground where I find myself today, where religious experience is both real but also conditioned, where koan are tools to manipulate as well as enlighten, where meditation is both a waste of time and a good thing to do with your time.

In the year Kapleau achieved *kensho*, another tormented ex-businessman arrived in Japan. Like Kapleau, he was looking for the meaning of life, dreaming of enlightenment. He had read Suzuki with deep enthusiasm, drinking in the stories of the ancient masters and taking them as the essence of Zen. But his experience would be different from Kapleau's. Instead of meeting the patriarchs and seeing what they saw, Janwillem van de Wetering would always see the difference between the Zen of the classic koan and the Zen he encountered, first in Japan and then in America. His first memoir, *The Empty Mirror*, is the first memoir of Zen failure, a genre discussed in the next chapter.

TWO

FAILURE

*Janwillem van de Wetering, David Chadwick,
Natalie Goldberg, Shozan Jack Haubner*

In 1958, a young Dutchman rang the doorbell at Kyoto's Daitokuji temple. He had traveled a very long way to study Zen. His life thus far had been aimless, his business ventures a disappointment and his marriage a failure. During the Second World War, he had seen his native city of Rotterdam incinerated by German bombers, and his Jewish classmates deported to the concentration camps. Life had held no meaning until he had discovered, by chance, a slim volume in a London bookstore. Having opened the book, the young man came across the following interaction, paraphrased in his own, ever playful, style:

Gent: I worry.
Codger: Show me this I that worries.
Gent: I can't find it.
Codger: See?[1]

The man laughed out loud and decided that the Western philosophy he had been studying so far had not been worth his while. What he had been looking for all his life was waiting for him in Japan.

This is how Janwillem van de Wetering ended up seeking admission to a Zen temple. In his luggage could be found the work of the author who inspired this journey, D. T. Suzuki.[2] Despite Van de Wetering's high expectations, after being admitted to the temple he would spend only one year on his koan before giving up and getting on a boat back to Holland. "The whole Buddhist adventure now seemed one huge failure, and I wanted to leave," he would write fifteen years later.[3]

Among other Zen autobiographies of its era, Van de Wetering's reflection of his time at Daitokuji stands out. *The Empty Mirror: Experiences in a Japanese Zen Monastery* (1974) is the first extensive account of a Westerner going to Japan to study Zen and failing to obtain enlightenment.[4] If the venture itself was a failure, the book was not. It launched Van de Wetering's writing career. Though sales of *The Empty Mirror* amounted to virtually nothing in the Netherlands, the American edition made waves and would provide an influential example of how to write of Zen while not adopting the persona of a Zen master as Suzuki, Kapleau, and others had done.

Van de Wetering was the first to write a memoir of Zen failure, but he was not to be the last.[5] In this chapter, I treat three other books with the same theme: David Chadwick's *Thank You and OK! An American Zen Failure in Japan* (1994), Natalie Goldberg's *The Great Failure: A Bartender, a Monk, and My Unlikely Path to Truth* (2004), and Shozan Jack Haubner's *Single White Monk: Tales of Death, Failure, and Bad Sex (Although Not Necessarily in That Order)* (2017). This survey of memoirs discussing Zen failure shows how narrating failure can be used as a form of critique, and what role koan play in both causing failure and understanding it.

In these books, failure means to realize that enlightenment and eternal bliss are not guaranteed when one takes up Zen practice. Furthermore, enlightenment itself does not guarantee anything. Koan can generate misunderstandings about Zen and Zen teachers, and they do not always bring about an awakening, nor is that awakening always the overwhelming experience described by Kapleau. But koan can also help one come to terms with disappointment, offering a new narrative where the dark side of Zen has a place. This is how koan decisively shape even those autobiographies that refuse Suzuki and Kapleau's premise that Zen practice is modeled on or identical to koan.

In proceeding chronologically, the chapter shows an evolving understanding of Zen failure that is partly conditioned by events in American Zen, most notably the "Zen sex scandals" that started surfacing in the 1980s but continue until today. Written before these scandals, *The Empty Mirror* critiques the conception of koan and experience found in Suzuki. Instead of focusing on a singular successful and blissful "experience" that would be the same as the stories, this book describes "experiences," both banal and supernatural, that occur in Zen practice. Instead of seeing modern Zen Buddhists as copies of the ancient masters, Van de Wetering sees the difference between how he imagined Zen to be and how it is.

Thank You and OK! describes Chadwick's stay in Japan during the late 1980s. A student of both Shunryu Suzuki and his successor, Richard Baker (who would be embroiled in the first of many Zen sex scandals), Chadwick's account of Japanese Zen is clear-eyed, lacking the disappointment that characterizes Van de Wetering's autobiographical oeuvre. For him, it is a given that koan do not characterize how Zen works, and an enduring source of puzzlement that people keep wanting to get enlightened and want their lives to resemble koan. For him, failure is a source of joy, something that shows in the sense of humor that pervades this book.

The third and fourth parts of this chapter discuss Goldberg and Haubner, who both describe their coming to terms with the sex scandals related to their teachers. They ask, how and why can a person whom I loved and trusted have done such things? Their memoirs demonstrate how their understanding of their teachers is scripted through koan. For Goldberg, a classic koan series becomes the framework to understand the dark reality she's faced with. For Haubner, any challenge in life, particularly problems related to the sexual and mortal body, can be understood as a koan and can be solved by realizing that identity is fundamentally unstable. In the work of both these authors, koan have become a structuring device for the memoir as a whole. Their life story has become a koan to be solved.

WHAT IS FAILURE?

This chapter is about failure. But what does that word mean? Let's explore this term in the context of American culture. The historian Scott Sandage has argued that "failure" was not originally a term that applied to people, and I rely on his foundational work here.[6] The idea that people can fail is a relatively new concept, originating in the nineteenth century. It assumes that all individuals can be measured on a predefined scale. Today, some of these standards include getting married to a person of the opposite sex, having children, being wealthy, and so on. In some academic settings, it means getting an "A" grade. Anything lower can lead students to doubt their own capabilities and cause immense anxiety. To fail a course is to fail as a person.[7]

The insidious thing about the logic of failure is that it implies that individuals are entirely responsible for their own fate. Someone is a "failure" not because they weren't offered any opportunities but because they were lazy, stupid, inept, and so on. But closer analysis shows that failure is not a function of an individual person's capacities or "talent." More often, it is circumstances of race, sex, class, education, and random luck that decisively affect someone's success. For example, one study found that even one's surname matters when it comes to grades: people with surnames that start later in the alphabet tend to get lower grades, possibly affecting their future prospects (think of college entrance examinations, graduate school applications, and so on).[8] So failure is not always a reflection of our abilities or worth as a person. It is often a result of factors beyond our control.

If success is intricately connected to capitalist and patriarchal exclusionary ideologies justified by a rhetoric of meritocracy, describing failure can be a subversive act. In examining American twentieth-century literature, David Ball suggests that failure offers a counterpoint to American narratives of optimism, offering complexity instead of simplicity.[9] In the field of queer and gender studies, Judith Halberstam and Sarah Ahmed have paid particular attention to how notions of success always presuppose a gendered arrangement: I am successful and happy when I am a man married to a woman and have a family with biological children. To undermine this ideology, they suggest paying attention to failures in life and art, building a "shadow archive" (Halberstam's term) or becoming "feminist killjoys" (Ahmed's term).[10] In doing so, Ahmed argues, we can draw attention to the particular privileges that set up some people for success and others for failure, returning to the etymological root of "happiness" (another synonym for success today) as "happenstance," a sense that turns happiness into a possibility, not an expectation to be met.[11]

The four authors discussed in this chapter criticize Zen ideas of success and happiness. Such ideas include being enlightened, having a compassionate and selfless teacher, being morally upright, and so on. Apart from Van de Wetering, who would take his failure in a different direction (discussed in chapter 4), all of them value failure over success because failure destroys vacuous ideas of who we are. Failure thus leads to insight, even though the insights it generates might be uncomfortable.

The specific genre of these books, which is the memoir, supports the articulation of this critique. Memoirs are a type of autobiographical writing that has become increasingly common since the "memoir boom" of the 1990s, during which three of the four books I discuss in this chapter were published.[12] Before then, it was mainly famous people who wrote memoirs to explore their careers (think of the voluminous memoirs of British prime minister Winston Churchill). But with the "boom," we see ordinary people talking about their pasts. Often, the topics of these books involved deeply personal—and often traumatic—experiences: reports of childhood sexual abuse and drug addiction were (and remain) extremely common in the genre, leading to the designation "misery memoir."[13] Scholars have explained the "boom" as providing a type of citizenship, where the public is intimately linked to the private.[14] Memoirs provide a way to tell histories that have been obscured by larger metanarratives, but they conversely also are a way to create meaning when these metanarratives have lost authority.[15] Because the memoir often discloses shameful facts about the author's life, the reception is always uncertain: like the first offended readers of Jean-Jacques Rousseau's *Confessions*, the disclosure of very private things can be shocking.[16]

The memoirs of failure discussed in this chapter display these features to varying degrees. Both Goldberg and Haubner's books can be classified as "misery memoirs" in that they disclose a history of recovery from trauma, the trauma being the discovery that a trusted teacher did things that are wrong. All of them are written by people who do not claim to be Zen masters: they are written from a standpoint of not knowing, of wanting to make sense of things. They are the regular soldiers of Zen, not the Winston Churchills, and their writing is an attempt to come to terms. Their books are by no means glorious conclusions of lives already clear in their meaning. These people speak truth to power, sometimes very explicitly and against the will of their communities. Unlike Kapleau and Matthiessen, for whom Zen makes sense (even if that sense is nonsense), these authors write from a moment when Zen made no sense.

"ENLIGHTENMENT IS A JOKE": JANWILLEM VAN DE WETERING'S *THE EMPTY MIRROR*

There was no doorbell at Daitokuji. Ringing the bell, as described in the introduction to this chapter, was the first of many gaffes the young Janwillem[17] would make throughout his stay: "Later I found out that the bell was holy, only to be used during certain religious ceremonies. Visitors were supposed to enter without announcing themselves."[18] Cultural misunderstandings such as this lend *The Empty Mirror* its enduring appeal, and the most important of these misunderstandings is the idea that koan accurately describe life in a Japanese Zen temple. Unlike Kapleau's account in *The Three Pillars of Zen*, this tension between koan-inspired fantasies of Zen and Van de Wetering's own experiences in Daitokuji is never resolved by an enlightenment experience.

Van de Wetering would write about Zen in one way or another his whole life. As we will see in chapter 4, *The Empty Mirror* is not his only autobiographical engagement with Zen but the beginning of a prodigious career. After Japan, Van de Wetering would return to the Netherlands, but ultimately he would settle in Maine. He made money partly by smart investing decisions but also by writing a long series of best-selling detective novels that integrate Zen ideas, genres, and practices. He would never tire of investigating the question that drove him to Japan, but he would become disenchanted with the authority structures of Zen. Ultimately, he was a rebel against any type of authority.[19]

But back to Janwillem in front of Daitokuji. After some back-and-forth with a confused monk answering the bell, Janwillem is ushered into the temple and finds himself face-to-face with a statue that depicts, as the narrator informs us, "A Zen master who lived in the Middle Ages, one of the most spectacular characters from the history of Zen."[20] Despite the fact that Janwillem is unaware of this background, he feels "threatened by the willpower of the man."[21] Van de Wetering then tells us more about the Zen master in question, a roguish character who refused students and commissions, and who chose to live under Kyoto's bridges like a beggar.[22] At one point, the emperor sought his wisdom and was told beforehand that the master likes melons. This information proves to be true when the disguised despot encounters "a beggar with remarkable sparkling eyes."[23] What follows is a koan: "He [the emperor] offered the beggar a melon and said: 'Take the melon without using your hands.' The beggar answered: 'Give me the melon without using your hands.' The emperor then donated money to build a temple and installed the master as a teacher."[24]

The story of the beggar-master and his melons sets up a model for Janwillem's encounter with the Zen master of Daitokuji.[25] Janwillem is surprised, because he will actually get to meet the master, something that the books he has read about Zen did not mention as a possibility.[26] Janwillem again reflects on what this Zen master should be like: he should not like "long stories" and will prefer "methods without words."[27] Therefore, Janwillem expects a nonverbal treatment that might also be violent. Face-to-face with the master, he keeps his statements brief:

> "I am here," I said carefully, "to get to know the purpose of life. Buddhism knows that purpose, the purpose which I am trying to find, and Buddhism knows the way which leads to enlightenment." . . . To my surprise the master answered immediately. I had thought that he would be silent. When the Buddha was asked if life has, or does not have, an end, if there is, or isn't, a life after death, . . . he did not answer but maintained a "noble silence."[28]

This seemingly simple passage contains an important parallel: the very moment Janwillem starts speaking to the master, he is consciously repeating a scene he has read in books. However, the master refuses to conform to the role assigned to him and answers approvingly: "'That's fine', he said. 'Life has a purpose, but a strange purpose. When you come to the end of the road and find perfect insight you will see that enlightenment is a joke.'"[29] This answer does not complete the series of surprises: instead of being rigorously tested before he is allowed to become a student, Janwillem is readily admitted to the monastery, causing him to conclude, "Obviously the books which I had read about Zen were faulty, written by inexperienced writers."[30]

In *The Empty Mirror*, Van de Wetering never names the "inexperienced writers" who apparently so misinformed Janwillem about the reality of Zen practice in Japan. But, judging from his later writings, it is clear that one of these writers is D. T. Suzuki. In 1999, Van de Wetering would explicitly contrast the Zen master of Daitokuji with Suzuki: "When I tried to talk to

Roshi about enlightenment, the 'satori' I had been reading about in Dr. D. T. Suzuki's Zen guide, on the long ship's journey from Europe via Africa to Japan, Roshi said, 'What? Satori? Please? Where did you dig that up? Throw that out.'"[31] Like the scene in *The Empty Mirror*, the master here rejects the knowledge Van de Wetering has gained about Zen by reading. Although Janwillem is wrong that Suzuki is "inexperienced" (Suzuki did spend a good amount of time meditating, and his satori was confirmed by Soen), there is a vast gap between the latter's description of Japanese Zen and Janwillem's experience of it.

"Meditating Hurts," the second chapter of *The Empty Mirror*, provides another example of the contrast *The Empty Mirror* maintains between the Buddhism Janwillem has read about and what he experiences in the monastery: "The first meditation is forever etched into my memory. After a few minutes the first pains started. My thighs began to tremble like violin strings. The sides of my feet became burning pieces of wood. My back, kept straight with difficulty, seemed to creak and to shake involuntarily. Time passed inconceivably slowly. There was no concentration at all."[32] The books Janwillem has read do not mention this experience. In a hagiography of the Tibetan saint Milarepa, Janwillem finds "nothing about pain in the legs or back, the fight with sleep, the confused and endlessly interrupting thoughts."[33] Life in the monastery is tough: Janwillem sleeps some four hours per night, with an extra hour in the afternoon, meditates six painful hours in summer and more in winter, and spends the remainder of his time cleaning hallways and maintaining the monastery garden. This routine is not without results: regular meditation causes Janwillem to become "fully aware," able to "really see objects in [his] surroundings."[34] He even manages to instinctively solve a problem by improvising, something that his master considers a great accomplishment.[35] But what always remains beyond Janwillem's reach and drives him to despair is satori, the enlightenment experience Suzuki sees as the goal of Zen practice. He is supposed to gain it through solving the question contained in his koan, and then provide his master with the answer during a formal interview. Thus, Janwillem day after day lines up outside the master's room, goes in, bows to the master, and says nothing. In *The Empty Mirror*, he never finds the answer.

Janwillem also does not come to see the Zen monastery as a utopian space as Kapleau did. Instead, he constantly recognizes his own country. Very early on, he observes: "The newness of the exotic, mystical Far East had gone. Perhaps the people here looked different and sometimes wore outlandish clothes. . . . Even so, I couldn't rid myself of the clear and painful feeling that nothing had changed."[36] This comment follows a slightly traumatic experience: Van de Wetering finds a kitten in the garden and feeds it, only to see it bitten to death by the temple dog. He then finds out that people living near the temple use the dog to kill unwanted young kittens. This is the neighbors' solution to a moral quandary: as lay Buddhists, they are unable to kill the kittens themselves yet have no problem letting the dog take care of things. But Janwillem considers their behavior hypocritical and not in line with the pure ideals of the Buddhism he has read about.

Nor do the monks at Daitokuji act like the superhuman ascetics who populated Suzuki's temple. For instance, they do not take the monastic rules or the Eightfold Path very seriously. Whenever they like, they simply prop a ladder against the wall, put on civilian clothes, and rush off to the movies, a bar (a more challenging destination, since they might smell of liquor during the early-morning interview with the master), or a prostitute.[37] Most of them are only in Daitokuji for the job prospects it offers, anyway: after three years of being there, they are qualified to work in their local family temple. "The organization is similar to that of the Catholic Church," van de Wetering notes.[38] Later on, he will also compare Daitokuji to the "Free Dutch Reformed Church in Rotterdam," a comparison made when Janwillem sees the whole neighborhood enter the temple "neatly dressed" on a Sunday to attend a ceremony.[39] Gradually, the East loses its oriental flavor and becomes recognizable to Janwillem. Thus, throughout his stay he cannot find two things: he cannot find satori, and he can also not access the perfect place where this experience should take place.

Even the most important man of the monastery, the Zen master, does not live up to what Janwillem thinks he should be like. During the Second World War, he was conscripted and sent to Manchuria. To Janwillem's objection that killing is not allowed by Buddhist doctrine, he answers laconically, "I had to. If I had refused I would have been shot."[40] The master's life is filled with duties. Not only does he have to do koan interviews every morning, but he has to work in the garden with the others. In addition, he is the head of all nearby Zen temples and is responsible for lectures on varying topics. He does have two hobbies, however: watching baseball games and going to the movies, "but only when he could see a picture connected in some way with Africa; he liked animals and the jungle-lush, tropical vegetation."⁴¹ At one point, this activity leads to a conflict with his assistant, the head monk, when the master has no money but wants to go to the cinema anyway.⁴²

The contrast between Janwillem's experiences of Zen and the stories about ancient Zen masters reaches a climax at the end of the book. Janwillem attempts to cheer up a depressed American colleague called Gerald by telling him a Zen story.⁴³ The story goes as follows: A monk tries to solve his koan but does not succeed despite great efforts. He leaves the monastery and goes to live in a small temple. Over time, he forgets the koan and instead spends his days taking care of his new abode. But one day, the sound of a pebble sends satori surging through his being. Gerald, however, is not impressed by this story and tells two more recent stories: one describes a monk trying to solve the koan "stop the Inter-city train coming from Tokyo." He works on the riddle for many years, to no avail, and finally throws himself underneath said high-speed train. The second story is about a headstrong monk, whose master often punished him with a small hard cane. One day, the master strikes too hard, and the monk dies. No one is held accountable, because "the police know that there is an extraordinary relationship between master and pupil, a relationship outside the law."⁴⁴

At the end of *The Empty Mirror*, the gap between koan and reality remains unbridged. This gap, between everyday experiences and Zen Experience, is summarized by the title and the subtitle of the book. The subtitle proposes to describe "Experiences in a Zen Monastery," and the plural is significant here: Janwillem has plenty of experiences but no single Enlightenment Experience. The main title "The Empty Mirror" also signals this difference. To understand this, I need to briefly return to Suzuki. As the previous chapter showed, for Suzuki, the relationship between koan and his own descriptive prose (and, as we saw, between author and reader) is one of reflection, of mirroring. Koan point to an ineffable religious experience, and so does Suzuki's prose. Koan portray a Zen master and a student, and Suzuki likewise casts himself as a Zen master and the reader as a student.

Whereas Suzuki's mirror reflects, Van de Wetering's mirror is empty. Ironically, the title of *The Empty Mirror* is explained in a koan of sorts, one told by a priest who significantly does not belong to the Zen school but to the Tendai (C. Tiantai) school, which reveres the *Lotus Sutra* as the culmination of Buddhist teaching. This Tendai priest tells Janwillem about a court lady who wants to know the true meaning of Buddhism. To achieve her goal, she becomes the student of an old man who dwells in a dilapidated temple. She stays for three months but does not receive an answer to her question. When the master sees her disappointment, he pities her and promises to visit her in her palace. He asks her to collect fifty mirrors within one month and to await his coming. The master arrives and arranges the mirrors in a way so that all of them reflect each other's image. The lady sits down in lotus posture in the middle of this installation and concludes that everything reflects everything and is thus connected. This is deemed a meager but workable beginning by the master, who then leaves. The lady, after more practice, finally achieves the desired "sublime enlightenment." After this story is told to Janwillem and Peter (another American colleague living in the monastery), the following dialogue takes place: "'Those mirrors are empty', I said, 'there is nothing. Nothing reflects, nothing can be reflected....' [Peter] put his arm around me and pressed me against him. 'The empty mirror,' he said. 'If you would really understand that, there would be nothing left here for you to look for.'"[45]

The reflection stops because there is nothing to be reflected: there is no ideal reality to be repeated in our existences, and every experience of Zen and life is unique and different. In *The Empty Mirror* the "mirrors in the text" are not similar to the narrative that frames them: the masters and students are characters in stories that never define what Janwillem encounters. At the end of the book, Janwillem has come to understand that, even in a Japanese Zen temple, enlightenment is not guaranteed. He leaves Daitokuji as a student, not a master, and gets on a ship bound for his native Holland. The last sentence of *The Empty Mirror* describes him resuming a Dutch lifestyle: "I went into the bar and ordered a cold beer."[46]

"HOW MANY CC'S WAS THE ENGINE OF THE CAR?" DAVID CHADWICK'S *THANK YOU AND OK!*

David Chadwick's *Thank You and OK! An American Zen Failure in Japan* (1994) ends on a somber note. Chadwick's teacher and friend Dainin Katagiri (1928–1990) has passed away, leading Chadwick to reflect on the legacy of Katagiri and his own generation:

Transmission is mysterious. I felt that at [Katagiri's] ashes ceremony. Maybe his true Dharma heir is the whole sangha, everyone he got to—not like the traditional stories with one or more of us realizing the true light, attaining a perfect understanding, and the rest just plodding along. I think we're all just plodding along—and that is the true light.

So did Katagiri fail, and am I a failure because I can't remember what Buddhism is—and are the rest of us failures, as it seems, when contrasted against our early pure and simple expectations and the clear-cut enlightenment of the story books? . . . Anyway, it seems to me that all our endless failures are adding up to a magnificent success. It's just not what we had in mind. It's real.[47]

Coming at the end of his book, this statement aptly summarizes how Chadwick views the "story books" that portray enlightenment as the measure of one's success as a Zen Buddhist: these stories are in no way good representations of the messy reality of living a Zen life. Whereas, as we saw, *The Empty Mirror* ended in disappointment, *Thank You and OK!* is a very hopeful book. For Chadwick, failure only exists when measured against "our early pure and simple expectations," which include the expectation of an overwhelming awakening experience. Instead of such an experience, Chadwick's "endless failures" result in abandoning any preconceived notion of what Zen is supposed to be and, rather, seeing Zen masters and students for what they are: human beings with human foibles.

By the time Chadwick sets out for Japan, he is a Zen veteran. In America, he studied Zen with Shunryu Suzuki (1904–1971). Not to be confused with D. T., Shunryu Suzuki was perhaps the most famous Zen master in America. He so impressed Chadwick that, after publishing *Thank You and OK!*, Chadwick would go on to write a biography of his teacher, and to this day he maintains a website that maps Suzuki's heritage.[48] Despite his enormous admiration for Suzuki, by the time Chadwick goes to Japan, he has discovered that enlightenment is not quite what people make it out to be: in 1983 San Francisco Zen Center had been ravaged by the discovery of the sexual relations Suzuki's direct Dharma heir, Richard Baker, maintained with many of its students.[49] This same Baker called Chadwick a "Zen failure," and we can take that as an indication that if what Baker did is success, Chadwick does not want any part of it.

Chadwick did not always think this way. When he first came to Zen, his expectations were very similar to those of Van de Wetering and Kapleau.

His first encounter with Dainin Katagiri, the master whose burial ceremony was described earlier, exemplifies the type of superhuman expectations that Chadwick once had. Chadwick confesses that he expected Katagiri to be a kind of superman, an expert at everything.[50] However, he quickly discovered that this enlightened superman cannot even properly chop wood, an iconic Zen action that is the source of an oft-quoted verse by the legendary Zen hero Layman Pang, whose superpowers consist of "Drawing water and carrying firewood," a common Zen reversal that locates Buddhist supernatural powers (*siddhi*) in the ordinariness of everyday life.[51] With Katagiri not living up to the ideals of Layman Pang, the unrealistic expectations Chadwick had about enlightenment (who in the world is, after all, an expert in everything?) are shattered. Katagiri has no superpowers; he cannot even chop firewood.

For Chadwick, Zen masters are most admirable not when they behave like in the stories, but when they can embrace their failures. After instructing Katagiri in the proper way of handling a saw, which is "not to force it, to let the saw do the cutting," a colleague of Chadwick's gently berates Katagiri by telling him "you've just got to be a little more Zen."[52] In response, Katagiri bows and continues to repeat that he has to be more Zen, and it is this humility that Chadwick likes about him. The most moving scene in the book describes Katagiri breaking down when Suzuki announces that he will die soon: "Throwing his arms around fragile Suzuki, he [Katagiri] sobbed, expressing unreservedly the grief and love that the rest of us were trying so hard, like good little Zen soldiers, to keep inside."[53]

In attacking people who take themselves too seriously, Chadwick's primary target is himself. Trying to convince a foreign Zen priest, whose Japanese is better than his, to help him at the embassy, he gets the following response: "'You're a priest too, ne?' he said. 'Help yourself, ne.'/'No I'm not. I failed.'/'No more than I have—and don't give me that reverse arrogance trip. It's too easy an out.'"[54] Here, identifying as a "failure" is cast as yet another type of attachment that reinforces the ego. "Failure" is useful when it functions as a critique, but when it becomes something that one *is*, there's trouble. Chadwick also calls himself "the enemy of Zen" and characterizes his own meditative practice as "the zazen of demons."[55] He continuously undermines himself as a spokesman for Zen and never assumes the authority of a Zen master like Kapleau and D. T. Suzuki did.

Like Van de Wetering, Chadwick also deconstructs the orientalist separation between "East" and "West" that D. T. Suzuki relied on in much of his work.[56] When Chadwick has dinner with a party of Japanese businessmen, he finds that they flatly deny the possibility he could ever understand Zen. Just like a Japanese person cannot understand Christianity, they argue, Chadwick can never understand Japanese Zen.[57] This orientalism also appears in Suzuki's account of the utopian Zen temple, which is emphatically located in the "East," far away from the intellectualizing that so characterizes Suzuki's view of Western culture. Yet the Japan that Chadwick encounters makes such a distinction practically useless: Japan is different from the United States, but it is not more mystical and definitely not more "Zen."

In Chadwick's approach to Zen, enlightenment is not important. Emblematic of his attitude toward satori is the following passage, where he ironically describes his encounter with Japanese bureaucracy by parodying koan. When Chadwick attempts to validate his American driver's license so that he can drive in Japan, a clerk asks him countless minutely detailed questions, finally inquiring how much power the car had that Chadwick used to take his US driver's license test:

> Him: "How many cc's was the engine of the car?"
> Me: I spoke back from timelessness and without thought. I had come to Japan to study the teaching beyond words and letters, and here I had surely found it. "How many cc's does a big car have?" I heard emanating from my throat.
> Him: "2000 cc's."
> Me: "2000 cc's."[58]

Here, "the teaching beyond words and letters" that is central to Zen is found in telling the office clerk whatever he wants to hear. This dialogue is written like a koan, except that this koan expresses the opposite of what koan are usually taken to mean in the West: instead of Chadwick's final answer expressing his limitless freedom from conceptions, his answer expresses compliance with the ritualistic requirements of Japanese bureaucracy.[59]

Chadwick's treatment of the "Mu" koan, which Matthiessen, Kapleau, and Van de Wetering all attempted to solve, is perhaps the most emblematic example of how *Thank You and OK!* portrays Zen in Japan. Chadwick loves the "Mu" koan and suspects he's doing something wrong: he thinks it's supposed to be this tough, depressing, destructive ordeal, but for him, it's just a "poem" or a "tune" he hums throughout the day.[60] When he hears about how one person solved thirty koans in his first month, he feels he's losing a competition: "I felt like the football player who was kicked off the team because he couldn't meet the academic requirements."[61] In Chadwick's conflicted engagement with the "Mu," we can see the traces of Kapleau's view of this koan: it causes pain (remember Kapleau's description of it as a "scalpel"), and solving it is part of a competition.

However, unlike Kapleau, Chadwick is not encouraged to win this competition. Instead, his master tells him to simply stop doing the koan. Chadwick is confused because he didn't think the practice would ever have an end. And if it was to end, he assumed it would do so with some kind of transformative experience.[62] His teacher explains, but Chadwick can't understand his Japanese. The next day, he asks this same master to repeat his explanation in the presence of Jessica, who is more fluent in Japanese than he is. His master replies he has no idea what he said the day before. Then Chadwick asks, "Well, what do you think my practice should be? . . . If I don't do mu, what should I do?' He looked at me fiercely. 'Open your ears!' he yelled. 'I already told you!'"[63] Instead of the despondency that characterized Van de Wetering's getting back on the boat to Holland, Chadwick's account of Japanese Zen is fun. Koan are fun. Mu is fun.

In Chadwick's Japan, temple life and daily life, Zen and non-Zen are on the same continuum, barely separable. Some monks chain-smoke in the Buddha hall. Some burn plastic in the temple garden. A couple have anger management problems. A few are racist. All are mainly in the temple for the job prospects it offers. Unlike Van de Wetering, Chadwick is not shocked by this. There is no chasm separating koan and temple life because koan were just stories to begin with. The fierce master who told Chadwick to stop doing the "Mu" koan also gives him another piece of advice: Chadwick needs to get out of temples and zendos and just do Zen in daily life. His zendo will be wherever he is, wherever his journey leads. *Thank You and OK!* thus focuses not on Experience and success but on "the joy of continuing this bumbling unseen path of me as I am and us as we are."[64]

"A BOUNDLESS EMBRACE": NATALIE GOLDBERG

Chadwick thought of Katagiri as a good human being because he was able to face his own failures. Yet when *Thank You and OK!* was published, one of these failures had not come to light yet, and Katagiri would not face up to it while he was alive. It would be his other famous student, Natalie Goldberg, who would do so in a book titled *The Great Failure: A Bartender, a Monk, and My Unlikely Path to Truth* (2004).

Goldberg is one of the few people are both Zen autobiographers and creative writers. Originally from New York, she studied Zen with Katagiri in Minnesota. It was Katagiri who encouraged her to write and to speak about writing. The result was the immensely successful "Zen writing manual" *Writing down the Bones*. In this book, which has sold over one million copies, Goldberg tells her reader to write without censorship and without holding back: "Don't stop at the tears; go through to truth. This is the discipline."[65] "The discipline" here refers to both Zen meditation and creative writing.

Writing down the Bones shows the heritage of a particular type of Zen writing that is the result of the idea that Zen is about spontaneity, an idea that is the result of Suzuki's emphasis on personal and direct experience. This was also what the Beat Generation's Zen-inspired aesthetic was about. When the "King of Beats" Jack Kerouac adapted automatic writing in the 1950s, he gave it a deep Zen Buddhist flavor by using phrases like "No time for poetry, but exactly what is."[66] Whatever ends up on paper is beautiful, true, and expresses the Buddha nature within. As a manifestation of Zen modernity, this attitude ignores how deeply deliberate, sophisticated, and intertextual the Zen literary tradition is in East Asia, where knowing someone's mind implies decoding the complexity of their references.[67]

Even though Goldberg inherited this idea from the Beats, her published writing is much more polished than Kerouac's. Yes, spontaneous writing is the truth, but that truth requires regular commitment. It involves the discipline of sitting down to write, not just whenever you feel like it. This discipline allows you to see what the mind is like as it flows onto the page. This idea—that writing brings insight, that writing is Zen practice—is formative for all of Goldberg's fiction but nowhere more so than *The Great Failure*, where Goldberg uses autobiographical writing to look deeply at the dark side of her teacher, her community, and her own complicity in what happened.

The Great Failure opens with a bored audience. As the main speaker at a writer convention, Goldberg decides last minute to ditch her prepared lecture and instead presents her audience with a famous koan about the ninth-century Zen master Deshan Xuanjian (J. Tokusan Senkan). Before his career in Zen, Deshan was a learned scholar of Buddhism who set out, with a lengthy commentary on the abstruse *Diamond Sutra* on his back, to study Zen in the south. On the way, he stops to eat at an old tea lady's shop. But he gets served something very different than sweets:

> But the old woman, instead of setting out the provisions, inquired, "What's on your back?"
>
> "They are commentaries and teachings of the Buddha."
>
> "They are indeed! Well, if you're so learned, may I ask you a question? If you can answer it, the food is free, but if you fail, you get nothing."
>
> Our Te-shan [Deshan] with all his book learning thought this would be simple, like taking candy from a babe. He agreed.
>
> The woman then asked—and with her question I could feel my audience fading, that vital link between speaker and listener suddenly going limp—"If the mind does not exist in the past, and the present mind does not exist, and there's also no mind in the future, tell me with what mind will you receive these cakes?"[68]

As the comment indicates, at this point Goldberg is losing her audience. She forgets what she was going to say and can't even discuss creative writing, let alone Zen. Like Deshan, who is dumbstruck by the old woman's question, Goldberg is an expert left speechless.

The placement of the failed narration of a koan at the beginning of a memoir titled *The Great Failure* is programmatic. The "failure" here is not only Goldberg's own but also Katagiri's, whom she discovered was sexually involved with several of his students. *The Great Failure,* then, is a rare example of a Zen memoir narrating a sex scandal. Though such scandals have haunted American Zen since the 1980s, very few Zen students have published accounts of their coming to terms with such scandals as extensive as Goldberg's.

Failure is not the absence of awakening here, as it was in *The Empty Mirror.* But it is also not dismissing enlightenment, as it was for Chadwick. Instead, for Goldberg, failure is the very means of attaining insight. If human beings are always caught between the highs and lows, failure is a reset button that allows us to "drop through to a more authentic self."[69] Goldberg makes clear that she is not talking about failure in any ordinary sense: she is talking about Dogen's "boundless surrender." The book titled *The Great Failure* is then "a boundless embrace, leaving nothing out."[70]

This "boundless embrace" means that *The Great Failure* is also a biography of two people who have deeply affected Goldberg's life, for good and bad. In addition to describing her relationship with Katagiri, the book also portrays Goldberg's father, Benjamin "Bud" Goldberg. When Goldberg was a young girl, Bud sexually harassed her, a trauma that haunts her adult life.[71] She feels she has nothing in common with her father: Bud only cares about money and superficial things. The artistic pursuits of his daughter are an enigma to him.

Initially, Katagiri seems to be the opposite of Bud. As a Japanese person, he was Bud's enemy during the war. He is interested in art and philosophy and encourages Goldberg to write. His insights continuously baffle her: he tells Goldberg that the Cartesian "I think; therefore, I am" can be reversed in saying "I don't think; therefore, I am not."[72] After twenty years of trying to do Zen like Dogen did it, he realized that "there was no Dogen's Zen."[73] Goldberg's responses to these anecdotes echo the muteness of so many students when faced with an enigmatic action from their teacher: "I felt my legs buckle. I reached out for the back of a chair. Just us. No heaven Zen in some Asian sky out there."[74] Despite this ability to spark transformative experiences in his students, Katagiri is completely ordinary: he likes watching TV, drinks cheap wine, and wears a T-shirt from the school his children go to. Gradually, Goldberg comes to identify Katagiri as her ideal parent: "Roshi became my mother, my father, my Zen master."[75]

Goldberg's confrontation with the dark side within herself and Katagiri leads her to realize that she and Katagiri are not so different from Bud. This is because Goldberg's desires have shaped her perception of both father figures. She understands this phenomenon of seeing herself in others as the result of "projection," a concept from psychoanalysis that is commonly used in Buddhist writing to understand sex scandals involving teachers.[76] In exploring the lives of these two father figures, Goldberg is therefore also exploring herself. The description of projection in *The Great Failure* is worth quoting in full:

> In a healthy teacher-student relationship, the teacher calls out of the student a large vision of what is possible. I finally dared to feel the great true dream I had inside. I projected it onto this person who was my teacher. This projection was part of spiritual development. It allowed me to discover the largeness of my own psyche, but it wasn't based on some illusion. Roshi [Katagiri] possessed many of these projected qualities, but each student

> was individual. . . . Eventually, as the teacher-student relationship matures, the student manifests these qualities herself and learns to stand on her own feet. The projections are reclaimed. What we saw in him is also inside us. We close the gap between who we think the teacher is and who we think we are not. We become whole. . . . This projection process can also get more complicated if we haven't individuated from our original parents. Then we present to the teacher those undeveloped parts too. Here the teacher needs to be savvy, alert, and committed in order to avoid taking advantage of vulnerable students.[77]

Projection here is cast as something that is essential to the student-teacher relationship. A teacher reflects back an ideal version of who the student could be. This explains why, when Goldberg talks to other students, they have very different ideas about who Katagiri was, because they all saw a dream of themselves in him. One fellow student, for example, tells Goldberg that he most admired Katagiri's "unerring self-confidence," something she herself never noticed.[78] Yet all imagined Katagiri to be "something pure, untouched, celestial."[79] But as the carrier of that utopian dream, the teacher has a great responsibility. His students are vulnerable because they see him as a "flashy movie star."[80] And they are even more fragile if, like Goldberg, they come out of problematic families. Goldberg sees Katagiri as having failed to manage this responsibility well.[81]

But as I mentioned earlier, failure in *The Great Failure* becomes insight. Goldberg conveys this by paralleling her own story with that of Deshan, whose encounter with the old woman was only the beginning of his quest. When Katagiri's dark side is revealed, Goldberg tries to comprehend his actions by envisioning him as a patriarch from a koan, namely as Deshan's teacher Longtan Chongxin (J. Ryotan Sushin). Deshan's first enlightenment occurs when Longtan blows out a candle in front of him. After recovering from the tea lady's dharma assault that opened this chapter, Deshan asks her,

> "Who is your teacher? Where did you learn this?"
> She pointed to a monastery a half mile away.
> Te-shan visited Lung-t'an [Longtan] and questioned him far into the night. Finally when it was very late, Lung-t'an said, "Why don't you go and rest now?"

Te-shan thanked him and opened the door. "It's dark outside. I can't see."

Lung-t'an lit a candle for him, but just as Te-shan turned and reached out to take it, Lung-t'an blew it out.

At that moment Te-shan had a great enlightenment. Full of gratitude, he bowed deeply to Lungt'an.

The next day Lung-t'an praised Te-shan to the assembly of monks. Te-shan brought his books and commentaries in front of the building and lit them on fire, saying, "These notes are nothing, like placing a hair in vast space."

Then bowing again to his teacher, he left.[82]

After discovering the dark side of Katagiri, Goldberg wonders: "Did Roshi, knowing or not knowing, blow out our lights?"[83] Here, Goldberg attempts to understand Katagiri's behavior as the teaching device of a Zen master.[84] Katagiri is like Longtan, and in imagining him in this role, Goldberg casts herself and her fellow students as Deshan.

Goldberg's narration of Deshan's story above also mentions the iconoclastic act Deshan is best known for: shortly after meeting Longtan, he burns all the scholarly texts he hauled with him to the south. To Goldberg, Deshan's burning of the texts means two things: first, the burning symbolizes just how far Deshan's textual study has taken him: without it, he would be unable to understand what Longtan meant. Second, it indicates that "he still had a lot of maturation ahead of him. . . . He was still acting out, choosing this and leaving that."[85] Deshan cannot accept the good and bad of book learning. This is like Goldberg, who initially cannot square the good and bad of Katagiri. The Deshan koan anchor the autobiographical narrative and give it allegorical qualities: Goldberg's story of Zen failure is everyone's. She is writing an autobiography that describes a failure "greater" than any individual, a failure that envelops every single being.

As time passes, Goldberg learns to accept the darkness in Katagiri, and the flashbacks of the book start to highlight the less appealing side of her teacher. One such flashback describes a house party where Katagiri attempted to seduce her. This behavior leads her to suspect that he is in fact another man than her Zen master: "This couldn't be Roshi. This man was too creepy."[86] Because she has imagined her teacher as a holy superman, the younger Goldberg is unable to see that the Katagiri at the party is the exact same person. As a consequence of this disturbing and subsequently repressed memory, Goldberg also recalls intentionally keeping her distance from Katagiri and strictly defining her mode of interaction with him. Significantly, her experience fending off her father helps her do this.

Goldberg's coming to terms with these suppressed and painful memories gradually lead to a revision of the Katagiri who was the hero of her previous memoir, *Long Quiet Highway*. Instead of treating the unpalatable aspects of Katagiri as belonging to another person, she begins to see how one person can have two faces. In *Highway*, Goldberg described Katagiri as always and everywhere acting the part of the Zen master: "What amazed me was there was no difference in him. I'd known writers who were exquisite, deep, tender human beings on the page and monsters in person, rude, arrogant, alcoholic, undependable. There was a huge gap between what they wrote and who they were. I experienced Roshi as a whole, gapless."[87] But in *The Great Failure*, another Katagiri steps forward. After an exhausting car drive following a lecture, Goldberg drops Katagiri off at his home: "When I helped him carry his sleeping bag and duffel into Zen Center, he didn't look around or wave. I watched his back as he walked upstairs to his apartment. I had a glimmer then of the chasm between the Zen master and the lonely, insecure man."[88] Here, Katagiri is marked by exactly the type of internal division that *Highway* marked him as not having. In *The Great Failure* Katagiri is still a Zen master, but he is also a "lonely, insecure man." Comparing the two memoirs here shows that "projection" significantly affected Goldberg's memory of Katagiri. Likewise, whereas she once imagined Katagiri as the complete opposite of her father, through facing the darkness in both of them, she realizes that they are more similar than different. Katagiri's betrayal of her trust "was the same thing that happened with my father, different but the same."[89]

Goldberg does not only come to see that Katagiri is like Bud; she also comes to see that Bud is like Katagiri. If Katagiri also had a dark side, Bud also had a good, enlightened side. Despite his lack of education and his humble origins, Bud is a natural at meditation: when Goldberg leads him and her mother in a session, he asks afterward, "What's the big deal?," telling her he "didn't have a single thought" the whole time, a feat even veteran meditators would be envious of.[90] Goldberg again understands this side of her father through the Deshan koan. If Goldberg was Deshan and Katagiri Longtan, then Bud Goldberg is the old Chinese tea lady: "It was exactly right that I had talked about Te-shan [Deshan] at that conference. I was merely acting out his dilemma in another dimension. He had the tea-cake woman at the side of the road. I had Syl and Bud from Brooklyn, who were so enlightened they had no idea they were even awake. They were much too busy befuddling me, revealing my ignorance to myself."[91]

When Bud dies, Goldberg gains an insight into the nature of reality: "I know death will never scare me again. It isn't some foreign dark cave at the end of life. It is the most natural, ordinary thing. It is as though a hand turns over from palm up to palm down, or a leaf flutters and we glimpse its silver underside. It is almost as if nothing happens—the big emptiness is just there as it always has been."[92] Like the death of a Zen master, Bud's death imparts insights in fundamental Buddhist teachings, allowing Goldberg to glimpse the nature of all things as empty. Whereas at the outset of the book, Goldberg saw Bud and Katagiri as two opposites, by the end of the memoir these two fathers have converged: Katagiri turned out to also possess a dark sexuality. Benjamin Goldberg turns out to also be a Zen teacher of sorts. Katagiri's failure has allowed Goldberg to discover that they were never really separate from each other, and she was not separate from them because she continuously projected her desires and fears onto both of them.

In demonstrating that failure means seeing that there is no absolute distinction between self and others, *The Great Failure* moves beyond just the connection between Goldberg, Bud, and Katagiri, and speaks to the whole community attached to Minnesota Zen Center, where Katagiri taught. Most telling of this connection of student, teacher, and community is the way Goldberg describes an awakening experience. When she finally comes to terms with her teacher, it is by looking in a mirror, at her own reflection in an empty window:

> I was in a vast space. I wasn't myself. I was Katagiri Roshi, looking at Natalie. I experienced his love and admiration. I always thought it had been one-way, but he needed me as much as I needed him. . . .
>
> All of us in that small zendo across from Lake Calhoun had created something beautiful together. The love was equal; we all were part of the commitment and dedication.
>
> Roshi wasn't some piece of heaven that marched through our midst and then left. . . . I wasn't less than Roshi; we were all good enough, ample, sufficient. Standing on this zero spot, this level, steady view, I could step forth and speak. Unfettered, I could let go.[93]

The good and bad of the teacher have been absorbed within a self made more spacious by the experience of failure. Here, letting go means embracing everything, acknowledging how everyone's lives (note the use of "we") are so intertwined as to be nearly inseparable. Note how similar this conclusion is to Chadwick's idea that "all our endless failures are adding up to a magnificent success." But, different from Chadwick, Goldberg emphasizes that letting go of Katagiri as a perfect being means to finally "step forth and speak," even if Goldberg's revelations about Katagiri are unpleasant to others. She has come to believe that "silence protects no one. I have heard it often repeated: keep it in the family. That only continues the suffering."[94]

Goldberg's breaking the silence about Katagiri's dark side was not welcomed. During her research for the book, she notes, "I was very alone. People wanted to minimize these events."[95] As she has testified in interviews and in *The Great Spring*, a subsequent memoir, her entry in the "shadow archive" of Zen alienated many of her former readers and made Minnesota Zen Center a place where she will never return.[96] Reviews of the book have been mixed. The reviewer in the Buddhist periodical *Tricycle*, for example, expresses being bewildered by Goldberg's naiveté, saying that Goldberg's surprise at Katagiri's behavior is "quaint, if not disingenuous," considering how well-documented previous scandals in American Zen communities are.[97] Yet many books continue to present an uncomplicated hagiographical picture of "flawed" American Zen masters like Katagiri. Goldberg's misconception that her teacher was a supremely ethical being is far from unique, and her account at least has the merit that it openly acknowledges how the projection mechanism can prevent Zen students from clearly evaluating their teachers' behavior. More than that, it shows how projection is perhaps an essential component of the "work" Zen masters do.

"THE KOAN OF LIVING IN A BODY": SHOZAN JACK HAUBNER

I wrote earlier that *The Great Failure* is fairly unique in narrating the history of a Zen sex scandal in a memoir format. To my knowledge, only one other memoir does something similar: Shozan Jack Haubner's *Single White Monk: Tales of Death, Failure, and Bad Sex (Although Not Necessarily in That Order)*

(2017) relates the discovery of the scandal of a scope that far exceeds that surrounding Katagiri. Haubner's teacher Joshu Sasaki was accused of sexually abusing hundreds of women who studied with him, and Haubner's task of explaining both how and why Sasaki could behave this way is as daunting as Goldberg's. *Single White Monk* shares many similarities with *The Great Failure*, such as the use of projection to comprehend scandals and the comparison between father and Zen master. However, Haubner views failure as being closely linked to the body. Our bodies are the reason we are unable to act as perfect moral beings. However, they also are the gateway to enlightenment. Haubner explores this tension by examining how his male body can transform into a female one and how life transitions into death. Ultimately, the body becomes a symbol of the union of opposites, a dark koan that shatters any illusions about Zen practice.

If Goldberg was a well-established Zen author by the time she published *The Great Failure*, Haubner is a comparative newcomer. He is a former Zen priest (*osho*) in Sasaki's lineage, trained at Rinzai-ji Zen Center in Los Angeles. Originally from the Midwest, Haubner is a white, straight man in his mid-forties who grew up in a Catholic family. In early adulthood, he drifted to Los Angeles, where he tried to make a career writing for Hollywood, without much success. In LA, he met someone he calls his "mentor," who introduced him to Zen practice and Sasaki. At Rinzai-ji, Haubner made the acquaintance of singer-songwriter Leonard Cohen, who would write the preface to Haubner's first memoir, *Zen Confidential: Confessions of a Wayward Monk* (2013). Haubner quickly became one of Sasaki's closest aides but left Rinzai-ji after Sasaki died. According to Haubner's Twitter account description, he is currently "at large" and also "available for parties."

Haubner's published memoirs stand out because of their bawdy sense of humor and the abundance of sexual and scatological content they feature. This is a conscious move on his part. As he announced in *Zen Confidential*, "too many Buddhist books focus on the lotus of enlightenment, as it were, and skip the muck from which it arises."[98] In speaking truth to power, in smashing popular fantasies of Zen as "a kind of balmy, glassy-eyed minimalist aesthetic and little more," Haubner does not hold back.[99] If the Goldberg method consisted of not censoring while writing, Haubner takes this to the next level: his books are full of bodily fluids and sexual intercourse. The ultimate purpose of this full disclosure goes beyond correcting popular views of Zen: ultimately Haubner aims at destroying any duality, particularly the duality male-female and self-other. He does this by always returning to his body, because that body resists and undermines ideas of who he thinks he should be.

In trying to describe how his teacher could have abused his power for so long, Haubner also uses the term "projection." But he goes further than Goldberg in recognizing that if one's experience of the world is at least partly configured by unreconciled and unacknowledged conflicts within the self, *any* encounter is an encounter with oneself. He develops this theory of projection in the introduction to *Single White Monk*: "In these pages, I am both protagonist and antagonist. I like to be the center of attention. Put another way, I'm self-centered, a self that I am trying to kill off in every scene."[100] Haubner sees his "self" as being projected everywhere. It is present both in the protagonist and the antagonist. That mystery is "the koan at the heart of this book."[101]

This koan of how to unite black and white, good and evil, is articulated through the human body. Further in the introduction, Haubner provides a deeper explanation of the aforementioned quest of "killing off" himself: "In every chapter I'm trying to shed skin, get down to the bone, let you contemplate death in its many forms with me, like the Vedantic sadhus who meditate in charnel grounds beside smoldering corpses."[102] This statement is worth unpacking a bit. Haubner here compares writing with corpse contemplation. This famous Buddhist practice, traceable to the earliest Buddhist sutras, entails visiting charnel grounds to mindfully view the decomposition process of human bodies. However, not all charnel bodies were made equal: female bodies were specifically recommended for this practice, to pierce male sexual fantasies.[103]

So an exploration of death and sexual desire is central to Haubner's quest for awakening. But, dwelling a little more on the sadhu passage quoted before, we cannot identify him definitively with the male "sadhu" observer. The phrase "let you contemplate death in its many forms with me, like the Vedantic sadhus who meditate in charnel grounds beside smoldering corpses" does not make clear whom we should equate with sadhu or corpse, and this is exactly the point. Haubner is both male sadhu and female corpse, and so is anyone else. His goal is to dismantle comfortable identities such as Zen/Not-Zen, male/female, straight/queer, and alive/dead by showing how his own body does not fit into these categories.

To describe the deconstructive force of Haubner's body, we need to understand some more of his background. A chapter of *Zen Confidential* titled

"A Zen Zealot Comes Home" describes Haubner's conflicted feelings about his father's job: Haubner Sr. has built a very successful business producing custom-made rifle barrels. Due to a work accident, Haubner Sr. lost "the top half of his right index finger. (Yes, his trigger finger.) After several medical mishaps, that digit is now missing. In its place is a curiously malformed combination of flesh and scar tissue that bears a striking resemblance to another typically less visible part of the male anatomy. 'My pecker,' he calls it, waving the stubby appendage up and down in a suggestive manner."[104] Haubner Sr. thus associates his penis with his trigger finger, and phallus with pistol. Through another common utterance of his father's, "We Germans think with our hands," Haubner then associates Haubner Sr.'s mangled "pecker" hand with his conservative and individualist worldview (thinking with hands = phallic thinking = making and using weapons), which does not accept anything from anyone. For example, the very idea of begging for food, a Buddhist practice, is revolting to Haubner Sr.[105] Instead, one takes what one can get, through violent means if necessary. Such violence Haubner sees as being passed on in a paternal lineage from man to man in the family, in the violence fathers inflict on their children.[106] Psychologically, the Haubner men are completely isolated, like the basement shelter Haubner Sr. built and keeps stocked with provisions for the time when "the shit hits the fan."[107]

So Haubner was raised to behave like a phallus, which shoots but does not receive, which penetrates but is not penetrated itself. Paired with this phallic ideology is Haubner's desire to succeed, just like his father did in building his own business. But Haubner's body prevents him from becoming like his father. As a teenager, he is not physically strong or good at sports, earning him the nickname "dirt monkey" from his teammates. Later on, he fails at being a scriptwriter in Los Angeles (his dream career) but stumbles into discovering Zen. At Zen, too, he is a failure, because his sexual desire keeps undermining his lofty spiritual ambitions as a Zen priest.

One chapter, appropriately titled "Jumping the Wall," demonstrates this dynamic. It begins with Haubner smoking a joint and reflecting on power. He has just been made head monk, and the responsibilities are freaking him out. Doesn't this position of power, with all the stress it gives him, allow him to bend the monastic rules a bit? Like the rules prohibiting drugs? Extending this reasoning, Haubner shortly afterward sets out for paid sex. When the visit turns out to be a disappointment, he concludes, "You have to do the right thing, only you're not built to: such is the koan of living in a body—male in my case. My inner Ethel [conscience] is not the answer. Nor is an erotic masseuse. But what the answer is, I don't know."[108] Haubner here sees the body as a koan because his sex drive undermines his desire to do the right thing. The body is a container for two things that seem very different, a desire to behave ethically and a desire for sexual fulfillment.

If the body and its desires constitute a koan, solving this koan involves letting go of a stable sexual identity. For Haubner, who has consistently failed to be a successful heterosexual, this means opening up his body to penetration. Haubner's Zen mentor, who is gay, is the person who suggests this solution:

> "You gotta learn to bottom," he told me.
>
> "Come again?"
>
> "You're an angry young straight white dude, man. You think the world belongs to you, and so you just try and ram your way through it, grabbing whatever you want. You have to learn to take a dick. Otherwise, you'll become a dick." He saw the look on my face. "What I mean is, you gotta open your heart and let the big bad world in."
>
> To his horror, before we went out the next three times I put on a black dress, wig, and heels and transformed myself into . . . what, I still don't know.[109]

In his typical facetious manner, Haubner responds to the suggestion of figurative penetration by cross-dressing. This puerile response suggests that at this point he holds on to his phallic identity: if he is to be penetrated, he has to dress like a woman. The message implied is that it is women who are penetrated and men who do the penetrating. Dismissing this charade, his mentor warns Haubner, "You need to learn to listen. There's a true woman somewhere inside you, but you keep speaking over her."[110]

It is important to pause here and reflect on the Zen antecedents for the formulation "true woman." Haubner is modifying a phrase mainly associated with the ninth-century Zen master Linji Yixuan (J. Rinzai Gigen). In the opening section of the standard edition of the *Record of Linji*, Linji talks about "the true person without rank" (*wuwei zhenren*). Linji adapts this term from the Daoist classic *Zhuangzi*. For Zhuangzi, the "True Man" was an ideal person, which in later Buddhist works came to stand for an enlightened being.[111] Linji's initial treatment of this term is typically irreverent:

The master, taking the high seat in the hall, said, "On your lump of red flesh is a true man without rank who is always going in and out of the face of every one of you. Those who have not yet confirmed this, look, look!"

A monk came forward and asked, "What about the true man without rank?"

The master got down from his seat, seized the monk, and cried, "Speak, speak!" The monk faltered. Shoving him away, the master said, "The true man without rank—what kind of dried piece of shit is he!" Then he returned to his quarters.[112]

One can see immediately why this scatological passage would appeal to Haubner, who liberally uses excrement in his books as well (*Confidential* starts with a story of Haubner cleaning temple toilets). Linji here suggests that the "true man" is present within everyone, if only we would see it. At the same time, this true man is not to be revered as higher than us (hence the shocking dismissal of this person as a "dried piece of shit"). The "true man" is us, our true self.

Returning to Haubner's interaction with his mentor, we can see that something equally specific is meant here: the "true woman" whom Haubner is speaking over can be identified with his true, nongendered self, before identifications as "male," "female," "straight," and "queer." Ultimately, these distinctions do not exist. But then why does Haubner use the image of a "true woman"? I think it's partly because he wants to contest patriarchy in the Zen tradition: Buddhists throughout history have often treated the male body as the neutral, unmarked default, and the feminine as an inferior deviation that needed to be regulated and controlled.[113] By seeing our true nature as female, Haubner reverses the hierarchy that would elevate male bodies above female bodies under the pretense that everyone is ultimately equal (a dynamic I return to in chapter 3). If everyone is equal, then "female" is as good a symbol as "male," he is saying.

Haubner's "true woman," his true self, ultimately becomes a character in the book. She first manifests herself as a figment of Haubner's imagination, appearing in dreams of sexual fulfillment: "And when I wake up I always feel incredible, not even loved, but like love itself, like the woman I need is inside of me."[114] But this woman also steps out of Haubner's dreams to urge him to confront both his master's behavior and his own. She tells him: "This Sangha is full of violent men. And you're one of the worst."[115] To understand this, he needs to "Face [his] past," more particularly an incident in Atlanta, where Sasaki sexually assaulted one of his assistants, a woman called Lizzie.[116] Unfazed by the assault, Lizzie tells Haubner that he's too uptight about how he sees Sasaki:

> She [Lizzie] points at the trailer. "You ever met anyone who showed you more love than that old man?"
>
> "No."
>
> "And yet you draw all these lines in the sand around your relationship with him. That's why you're still stuck. But instead of pushing through, you step back and write about your Zen failures, and you publish, and you get the world to affirm you, and so you never really pass through these deep dark places that you pretend you pass through on the page."
>
> "This is not about me."
>
> "Well if it isn't, that would be a first. Honestly, the best thing that could happen to you is Roshi [Sasaki] slapping you upside the head. This practice ain't for wimps."[117]

This painful incident is tied up with the question of liminality, with borders and openness. To access his full self, beyond gendered and sexual identities, beyond right and wrong, Haubner has to let go of the patriarchal borders that define him, and the violence with which these borders are maintained. The image for doing so is, again, sexual: he is urged to "push through," a masculine image of penetration and transgression that shows that awakening cannot be definitively identified as feminine. As with Chadwick, this pushing through implies that Haubner cannot hold on to the idea that his experiences are "failures," as if that is all they ever could be. Haubner has to let go of all ideas of who he is and what awakening looks like.

A chapter titled "Expiration Date" again emphasizes that awakening involves getting rid of egocentric ideas of who you are. It does this by describing Haubner's sick body. What was medically described as an attack of pancreatitis felt like "my body was pregnant with its antithesis, as though a howling death baby was clawing its way out of me."[118] Notice that in encountering what feels like the moment of death, Haubner's body gains feminine features, it becomes pregnant, and gives birth. This is a key idea in this chapter because pancreatitis turns Haubner into a "patient," someone who has to accept everything coming to him, someone who receives and who has lost the phallic power he once thought to possess. It is telling that the only mentions of Haubner's penis in the chapter are of it being manipulated by others, first the monastery cat (clawing at it while he hangs vomiting over the toilet) and then a nurse in the hospital. Here, femininity is associated with penetration again, and Haubner's body forces him to abandon his male phallic identity. The only cure for his mysterious ailment is again to surrender, to allow penetration. Haubner drops his defenses, lets the "demons" of this disease in, and he recovers.[119] In the words of his mentor, he has "let the big bad world in."[120]

Haubner is not the only patient in the book, nor is he the only one whose masculine body starts to show feminine features. The longest chapter of *Single White Monk* documents the end of Sasaki's life. Unlike the physically strong and verbally infallible masters of koan, Sasaki's interactions with Haubner in *Single White Monk* are defined by his centenarian body and aging mind. Classic Zen literature describes Zen masters as strong heroes or "great men" (*dazhangfu*).[121] If we think back on the koan we've discussed so far in this book, it's not hard to see the many forms this rhetoric takes: slapping people in the face, meditating until you lose your legs, focusing on a koan until you break through, always having a snappy response ready, and so on. Masculinity is imagined here as being a warrior triumphing over adversity using verbal wit and physical violence.[122]

You need this background to understand how radical Haubner's portrayal of his teacher is. Sure, Chadwick portrayed a crying Katagiri, but the Sasaki of *Single White Monk* is of a wholly different level. After a visit to the hospital that would initiate the end of Sasaki's teaching career, Haubner describes his teacher as unable to speak but incessantly spitting, moaning, and "making a bird sound."[123] This is a Zen master who is very different from someone like Linji, who always has a ready answer to a student's question. Physically, Sasaki's body is nothing like that of the patriarchs in koan: "Roshi's age had reached numerical digits normally associated with a full-blown Fahrenheit fever. He had collapsed discs, heart stents, legs that no longer worked, savage arthritis, unremitting sciatica pain, a mouth full of dental implants, and a penis that was buried mangina style in a flab of old man crotch fat like the largely useless organ it was supposed to be at this age."[124] Sasaki is here cast as someone sick and dying, a man whose penis has withdrawn into his body.

We read how Haubner takes care of Sasaki by changing his diaper and feeding him through a plunger tube that goes straight to his stomach. While doing the latter, Haubner clogs the tube. Due to the pressure "a stream of goop backfires out of the G-tube valve in an explosion of green."[125] Recovering, Haubner spots what looks like a piece of flesh lying on the floor and concludes that he has "castrated my Zen master."[126] Explaining things to Lizzie, Haubner renames the piece of flesh "the aborted fetus of the patriarchy" (she clarifies that it is vomit from the temple cat).[127] In describing the aging body of a Zen master who can no longer take care of himself, Haubner is showing that deep inside, his teacher is not masculine or feminine either: he carries a "fetus," has a mangina, and is castrated by his student.

Yet it is exactly this disabled dying man who only a short time before sexually assaulted his students. Like Goldberg, Haubner attempts to read his behavior as a Zen teaching, another koan. Instead of a dying man, he sees Sasaki "manifesting completely in the present moment, which happens to be perched right between life and death."[128] Looking at his teacher after the plunger incident, he finds himself longing back to Sasaki's dharma talks. He opens his laptop to listen to one of Sasaki's videos, but in the process forgets that he had logged in to a live webcam session of a woman masturbating. The resulting audio thus mixes Sasaki's words with hers:

Completely dissolve your self. I need 100 percent!
Oh yeah baby, I need it, give it to me.
Your ego too big!
It's so big. Put it in me.
They are both in their own ways getting excited for the cameras. Their voices become indistinguishable. Moaning and shouting. Teaching and tricking. Love and lust. I can't tell them apart.
My koan still. I shut the laptop lid.[129]

This passage encapsulates how Haubner approaches koan and failure. Because we have bodies, we fail to be upright human beings. Because we have bodies, we are not in control. Seeing that means seeing that our bodies are ultimately neither masculine nor feminine, not alive or dead.

Haubner's quest to abandon any fixed notion of who he and his master are is resolved at the end of *Single White Monk*. In an afterword that directly follows the long chapter that describes the sex scandal and its aftermath, Haubner writes that he considered cutting this so-called "scandal chapter" because so many of his fellow students found it objectionable. In fact, Haubner (this name is a nom de plume) claims to have been the main author of the public apology issued for Sasaki's actions in the Buddhist periodical *Tricycle*: "I believed that if we faced the absolute worst in our teacher, it would bring out the best in us."[130] But this turns out not to be true, as some of his friends and colleagues continue to frame Sasaki's sexual violence as a teaching: what Sasaki does might be incomprehensible or unacceptable from an unenlightened perspective, but it must be assumed it is for the benefit of all, done out of compassion, not self-interest. Others object that speaking about these things as Haubner does "desecrates the Dharma," or that Haubner is taking out his deep misogyny by projecting it on his teacher.[131]

Looking for a solution to the question of whether or not to publish the scandal chapter, Haubner takes part in a shamanistic session powered by the hallucinogenic drug ayahuasca. After what he describes as "an experience of hell"[132] that leads to death-like oblivion, Haubner is told by the shaman's female assistant: "I feel you were very tight at the monastery. I feel you worry about what the others think and you become tight and try harder and harder but don't feel. It goes back to your father. And his father. And his father. And you brought your father and his father and his father to the monastery with you. And you tried to be man-monk. But you stopped feeling. Now you feel again. The plant, the Mother [ayahuasca] says, 'Now you feel again.'"[133] The symbolism here is quite obvious: encountering the "Mother" (the woman inside him) has healed Haubner's patriarchal past. His phallic behavior was tied up with presuppositions of what others would think about him, again indicating that for Haubner success is ultimately hollow. Instead of continuing to try to be a phallic man who tries to look successful, Haubner resigns from the temple. Instead of writing a new chapter to replace the "scandal chapter," he publishes the scandal chapter anyway and admits to the reader his need for companionship: he cannot do things alone anymore and needs to connect with another. In the final pages of *Single White Monk*, he imagines a blissful future with a wife and child, lying in bed and "mov[ing] on to the next koan together."[134]

In an email to me, Haubner looked back on the scandal chapter as a way to atone, not only for his actions but also for his teacher and the community as a whole. He explained it was a way to interrogate Zen ideals of perfection by making public a personal journey of failure:

> The notion of spiritual perfection is so deeply pernicious and pervasive and laughable, yet it carries on. Partly because it motivates people, and that's

actually a beautiful thing. But when you fixate on the teacher's perfection or on the supremacy of your tradition or method of practice, you start building this weird wall around yourself. I don't know if I had all this in mind when I was writing the Roshi essay [the scandal chapter] you speak of, because mostly I was just writing from a broken heart, and sharing that. I met with an ex monk recently. He said, Maybe you wrote what you wrote because you were confessing for Roshi. He never did it, so you did it.[135]

In speaking out, Haubner both confesses the darkness in him, his teacher, and his community but also moves forward in critiquing the ideological foundations ("the notion of spiritual perfection") that allowed the scandals to happen in the first place. As we have seen, *Single White Monk* centers around breaking down the "weird wall" around Haubner by confronting him with his mortal and sexual body. He is not a phallic master in control of his destiny. He is a failure whose body leads him to face the darkness in his master and himself.

The four memoirs discussed in this chapter revolve around two questions: "Am I doing this right?" and "Is my teacher doing this right?" For American Zen practitioners living far away from Asia, this question was crucial, but even for those who went to Japan, the question remained. Sometimes, they found answers to these questions in koan, but just as often, koan, or at least common ways of presenting koan, were deeply misleading. Inasmuch as they talk frankly about the process of making sense of Zen without reaching a clear conclusion, all these books are critical interrogations of what constitutes success in Zen. Even though these authors reject the idea that koan accurately describe what Zen life is like, what enlightenment looks like, or how a teacher is supposed to behave, they still rely on koan to tell their stories. That's how powerful koan are.

The earlier novels discussed in this chapter, *The Empty Mirror* and *Thank You and OK!*, both critique the privileging of enlightenment experiences over everything else, and the usage of koan as a prescriptive narrative of what Zen should be like. An added dimension to this critique is the destruction of orientalist fantasies surrounding Zen and Japan. Though Japan is fascinating to both Chadwick and Van de Wetering, it is not a country where Zen is present everywhere. Nor is the Zen temple a special place populated with iconoclastic dadaists. The Zen temple is a place like another, and the people living there are not superior to those in other countries. Their merits and foibles are the same as those of any other human being.

The Great Failure and *Single White Monk* continue this line of criticism but focus on understanding the figure of the flawed Zen teacher, and how to hold together the good and bad of any individual. Goldberg does so by reframing herself, her teacher, and her father as figures in a series of koan. For her, writing is a way of experiencing failure, and thus growth. Haubner also sees writing as an investigation of failure, but his work focuses on the body as the site where the contradictions of being human are located.

Due to the nature of the failures Goldberg and Haubner discuss, the sexuality of their teachers is also more explicitly discussed in a way that Van de Wetering and Chadwick would not (although Van de Wetering would have his say on this much later, as discussed in chapter 4). They also explicitly address the American Buddhist community in speaking out. For Chadwick, it's almost an unspoken given that monks and masters can misbehave. But Goldberg and Haubner feel strongly that they need to break the silence before things can mend. The reception history of these two last books shows that narrating failure remains an intervention that provokes resistance.

It is often said that analysis can obscure enjoyment. For me, this has not been the case with these memoirs. Digging into them was a pleasure that started with my discovery of *The Empty Mirror* in 2007, one year before Van de Wetering would pass away. Here was a way of writing about Zen that did not buy into the narrative of success. You could meditate, and if you didn't get anywhere, you'd know you weren't alone, because Janwillem spent one whole year in the best temples of Japan and he got nowhere. Chadwick's book I instantly liked because he was funny and down-to-earth. Haubner because he is hilarious. Goldberg because of her straightforward honesty.

In looking closely at these books, they've held up. There are all kinds of subtle details in the writing that you'll only get when rereading them, details that contain a clear message about how failed Zen is as profound as successful Zen. I've learned more from them than most "introductions" to Zen Buddhism that circulate continuously, and that's because the Zen they teach comes from a place of vulnerability: these are students, all of them, not teachers. They don't completely get it as well, nor do they claim to. But the few bits of insight that they have been able to gather, they share, and I find that not only very moving but also very practical: this is my specific situation, this is how I fucked up, this is what worked. I believe wisdom always has to be rooted in an individual and specific experience of the world falling apart. That's when you're really able to ask questions of the Zen patriarchs, instead of taking their enlightenment for granted, and assuming that your teacher will be a carbon copy of them. This critical interrogation does not dismiss koan, but it critiques naive approaches toward them. Koan can help you read reality, they tell us. But beware that they don't blind you to it.

THREE

THE TWO TRUTHS

Myoan Grace Schireson, Claire Gesshin Greenwood, Zenju Earthlyn Manuel

INTRODUCTION: WHAT'S YOUR TRUTH?

The Sixth Patriarch of Zen, Huineng (J. Daikan Eno), one of the towering characters of classic Zen biography, became a Zen master in spite of ethnic stereotyping. In *The Platform Sutra*, a medieval text in which Huineng recounts his life, we learn that when he initially arrived to study at the monastery of Hongren, the Fifth Patriarch, the latter expressed his disbelief that a "hunter" could ever achieve enlightenment: "If you're from Lingnan, then you must be a hunter. How could you ever achieve buddhahood?"[1] Hongren here correlates ethnicity and performativity in a way that today would be called racist.[2] Huineng, however, was unphased: "Although people may be from north or south, there is fundamentally no north and south in the buddha-nature. Although this hunter's body is different from Your Reverence's, how can there be any difference in the buddha natures [within]?"[3] Huineng (or whoever is ventriloquizing him)[4] here has recourse to the doctrine of two truths, which can be summarized as follows: although in everyday, "provisional" reality, there are apparent differences between people (e.g., people from the North look different than people from the South), ultimately those differences are insubstantial because we all share a universal

Buddha-nature inside. Our eyes deceive us, because they only see difference, but ultimately, we are all the same. This means that even a hunter can become a Buddha.

Later in the story, Huineng again uses the two truths doctrine to dismiss individual differences in favor of a reality where no distinctions exist. Hongren invites his followers to compose a verse demonstrating their insight. Shenxiu, Hongren's foremost student, writes the following verse:

> The body is the bodhi tree;
> The mind is like a bright mirror's stand.
> Be always diligent in rubbing it—
> Do not let it attract any dust.[5]

While publicly praising this poem, Hongren in private tells Shenxiu that it lacks insight. He then instructs Shenxiu to write a new poem, but the latter is unable to do so. It is the illiterate Huineng who will instead respond with a poem that Hongren sees as demonstrating true knowledge:

> Bodhi is fundamentally without any tree;
> The bright mirror is also not a stand.
> Fundamentally there is not a single thing—
> Where could any dust be attracted?[6]

As we can see, Huineng denies that awakening (bodhi) or the mind could be compared to anything, or that Zen study or practice is needed. If nothing exists at all, why polish or study anything? Note that in the process of denying differences, Huineng eliminates the body from his verse: Bodhi, as he says, is "without any tree."[7] His verse pleases Hongren, who will secretly turn this Zen Cinderella into the next Patriarch. The rest is invented history.

What's your truth? Do you privilege difference in approaching others, or do you think in terms of ultimate sameness? When thinking in difference, does that imply a hierarchy of better and worse? And when focusing on identity, does that imply for you that everyone should also follow the same rules and overcome their differences in the process? In this chapter, I look at how the two truths appear in the autobiographical writings of three Zen Buddhist women. They investigate the question of whether to privilege difference or sameness by interpreting classic koan, and they all reach very different conclusions. They use koan to imagine who they want to be in a variety of situations and how they should act when faced with androcentrism and racism. A central image that encodes the differences among them is the ritual of bowing. The three positions they take are the following: Don't Bow, Bow First, and the Inner Bow.

I first look at two white Zen women who have spent significant time in Japan. A section of Grace Schireson's *Naked in the Zendo: Stories of Uptight Zen, Wild-Ass Zen, and Enlightenment Wherever You Are* (2019) presents her fierce struggle with the Zen establishment in Japan, as exemplified in the title of one chapter: "Don't Bow!" Inspired by koan, she asserts her identity as a woman, as an American, and as an elderly person, even while she is also aware that, ultimately, these distinctions do not exist. Her interactions with Japanese monks are centered around an awareness of her individual body and its needs, needs that she implores her readers to heed as well. In *Bow First, Ask Questions Later: Ordination, Love, and Monastic Zen in Japan* (2018), Gesshin Claire Greenwood articulates the opposite position: as fiercely as Schireson, Greenwood often ignores her own needs to conform to the requirements of the monastic environment. Being a woman Buddhist in Japan for her is putting the ego aside and working as hard as possible within the rules of the discipline. In doing so, Greenwood gradually becomes someone else, the ritual activities working through her to mold a new person. Rather than being tools for insight, for Greenwood koan are distracting. Yet koan still provide her with a role model: Greenwood imagines herself as an old woman by the side of the road hitting male monks over the head when they ask her questions about Zen.

The third author I look at in this chapter is Zenju Earthlyn Manuel. *The Way of Tenderness* (2015) and *Sanctuary* (2018) are both autobiographical reflections on the intersection of Buddhism, race, gender, and sexuality. Manuel's version of bowing is the "inner bow," an expression of respect from the deepest roots of one's being. Instead of seeing the universal as the foundation for Zen practice (with the particular as something to be transcended), Manuel sees the particularity of the racialized, gendered, sexualized, stereotyped body as what makes awakening possible in the first place. Therefore, Zen practice should be tailored to the unique needs of specific groups. Mainstream American Zen practice may present itself as universal but is in fact tailored to white men. Manuel pushes her critique of American Zen much further than do Greenwood and Schireson. In doing so, she moves away from koan as a way to understand Zen and herself. To make this clear, I examine the single koan that appears in *Sanctuary* and frame it within her broader thinking.

DON'T BOW: MYOAN GRACE SCHIRESON

Myoan Grace Schireson is one of American Zen's most respected teachers. After a traumatic childhood, she studied Zen with Shunryu Suzuki in San Francisco and now teaches in his lineage. She is also a clinical psychologist, a grandmother, and an important Zen feminist. Part of her importance consists of her strong response to the Zen sex scandals (see chapter 2). She does this by using her background in psychology to understand how the Zen teacher-student relationship can go wrong. To prevent future abuse, Schireson organizes, at the Shogaku Zen Institute she helped found, an annual teacher training program.[8] Paired with her feminist engagement in the past is a historical interest: her previous book recovered, for a broad audience, the often-forgotten lives of Zen women in East Asian history.[9] This project has afforded her a broad knowledge of koan that feature women, and this knowledge is on display in her memoir, *Naked in the Zendo*.

Like Haubner's work, Schireson's book consists of short vignettes. Although the stories in *Single White Monk* were arranged in "no particular order," *Naked in the Zendo* proceeds chronologically, to describe the evolution of "how the mind may reflect itself."[10] Because Schireson is a seasoned Zen master, it should be no surprise that every story ends in success: as Schireson herself indicates, she is moving teleologically toward more awareness, a skill the book emphasizes as extremely important. In displaying her growing awareness, Schireson is unflinchingly honest, portraying the poverty and domestic violence she experienced as a child in a detached, matter-of-fact way: "My father died when I was six, leaving my mother unprepared to cope financially," one chapter starts.[11] Another goes as follows: "Mother picked up a plastic attachment to the vacuum cleaner and threw it at me.... Her aim was better than expected at twelve feet, and the hard, angular object struck me just below the right eye. With the immediate pain and blood, my attitude instantly shifted from defiant to needy."[12] This way of writing recalls the attitude of Goldberg and Haubner: the writing must be uncensored for the mind to appear on the page. But it also shows Schireson's psychological background in details like the clinical description of her shift in attitude.

Schireson's straightforward discussion of painful events paired with psychological analysis also appears in her discussion of her experiences in Japan, which contains the most extensive discussions of sameness and difference. Sameness is emphasized in an episode of *Naked in the Zendo* titled "Losing and Finding My *Ki*," with "ki" referring to the East Asian equivalent of "pneuma" (C. *qi*), the idea that the body is sustained by an energy that is cosmic and individual at the same time. Her elderly body beleaguered by the winter cold and her stomach unable to digest the monastic fare, Schireson faints on the meditation pillow. But afterward, she climbs back on. She explains that her determination was inspired by a famous koan featuring Wuzhuo Miaozong.

We'll take a closer look at this koan, because it's a really special one. Like Schireson, Miaozong was one of a kind. A disciple of the famous Song dynasty master Dahui Zonggao (Daie Soko), Miaozong lived during the Song dynasty and was one of the first nuns to be included in an imperially sanctioned Zen lineage history, *The Outline of the Linked Flames*. Published in 1183, *The Outline* collected the exemplary lives of the school's patriarchs. As Miriam Levering, the scholar of Chinese Buddhism, points out, "There are no 'matriarchs' in Ch'an's [Zen's] highly mythologized history. . . . Thus, at the beginning of the Northern Sung (960–1127), Ch'an represented itself as an almost exclusively masculine preserve."[13]

Given this "masculine preserve," it should be no wonder that when Dahui decides to give Miaozong sleeping quarters next to his own, this causes some of his male followers, including a monk named Wanan, to protest. Dahui responds to Wanan's criticism by pointing out that Miaozong has "outstanding merits" best experienced in a Dharma interview. Wanan thus agrees to take the role of student in an interview with Miaozong:

> When Wanan entered he saw Miaozong lying naked on her back on the bed. He pointed at her genitals, saying, "What is this place?"
>
> Miaozong replied, "All the Buddhas of the three worlds, the six patriarchs, and all the great monks everywhere come out of this place."
>
> Wanan said, "And may I enter?"
>
> Miaozong replied, "Horses may cross, asses may not."
>
> Wanan was unable to reply. Miaozong declared: "I have met you, Senior Monk. The interview is over." She turned her back to him.
>
> Wanan left, ashamed.
>
> Later Dahui said to him, "The old dragon has some wisdom, doesn't she?"[14]

In her reading of the koan, Schireson sees Miaozong as persevering over obstacles, as driving forward no matter what happens: "Like Miaozong before me, my perseverance at this temple could help or hinder women who came to practice after me."[15] Miaozong's battle with Wanan, Schireson reflects, both inspires and makes possible her own practice as a woman Zen Buddhist in modern Japan. Schireson sees Miaozong and herself as engaging in a struggle with the Zen patriarchal establishment, and this is a struggle that they must win. In "the land of the samurai," climbing back on the pillow after fainting gains her the respect of the monks: "Just like Miaozong, my fainting and remounting my cushion had created for them an image of female strength."[16] No matter male or female, all can sit on the pillow. Ultimately, then, this vignette demonstrates sameness, the ultimate truth.

Ultimate sameness also gets Schireson into trouble, though. Schireson practiced intensively with Joshu's Mu in Japan, but the result she obtained was different from that of Kapleau, Van de Wetering, Matthiessen, or Chadwick. In trying to become "Mu," she loses the ability to distinguish between men and women. In the middle of sesshin, an intense meditation session, she is told to go bathe. Unlike men, women have to bathe during intense meditation periods because of the prejudice that "women smell like fish when they don't shower for a few days."[17] Therefore, Schireson frantically runs to the bathhouse to make sure she can make it back to the meditation hall in time.

But she meets with unexpected adversity. With her shaved head and towering height, Schireson is mistaken for a man by the bath attendant. Oblivious to the mix-up, she is directed toward the men's bath, entering a room full of astonished, naked men. Schireson, however, finds herself unable to identify what, exactly, the problem is: "Becoming Mu, going beyond conceptual thought, putting all my mental constructions between the floor tiles, had erased my ability to identify man and woman."[18] Having exited the men's dressing room, she returns to mutely face the attendant, refusing to budge until the former understands her predicament. Here, Schireson's struggle with Mu leads to the insight that gender difference is an illusion: men and women are the same. However, she also recognizes the need to insist on the provisional truth, the existence of difference, in order to navigate the practicalities of life. And so she stood her ground, patiently awaiting her rightful place in the proper dressing room, until the attendant finally understood.

As a white elderly woman in Japan, Schireson quite often has to insist on the fact that she is different. In doing so, she often stands up against monks who tell her what to do. As mentioned earlier, her attitude toward Japanese Zen can be largely summarized as "Don't Bow." This is what one of her teachers, Keido Fukushima, shouts at her. At an advanced age, Fukushima has been suffering from Parkinson's disease and has trouble speaking. Schireson, for her part, is recovering from knee surgery, a testament to the toll that years of cross-legged meditation had taken on her body. Despite the pain coursing through her legs, she musters the strength to bow to her teacher during a private koan interview. However, to her surprise, he forbids her from doing so.

For Schireson, this prohibition against following etiquette is again one grounded in the body: "Clearly Roshi's own compromised physical experience had affected his awareness and his teaching style."[19] For her, this was already visible in the care he took to make sure Schireson got appropriate food in the Japanese temples where she stayed, a stark contrast to an unnamed "American Zen teacher" who attributed her physical and digestive problems to "practice failure."[20] She stopped practicing with this teacher because he would not pay attention to her individual situation, and she put "Don't Bow!" at the center of her practice. For her, this phrase means to never ignore bodily pain to conform to ritual requirements.

Schireson applies "Don't Bow" when she is suddenly slapped and shoved by the head monk while reentering the Zendo. The monk does this without cause and despite the rule that forbids hitting "Western women."[21] This violence activates Schireson's childhood trauma mentioned earlier. Figuring out what to do in response is hard. Schireson cannot tell her teacher because that would violate an unspoken rule in the Zendo.[22] But she also realizes she needs to stop the bully because he will abuse other people. To solve this issue, she calls to mind Linji's famous maxim, as translated in D. T. Suzuki's *Essays in Zen Buddhism*:

> If you encounter the Buddha [as merely a mind object], slay him; if you encounter the Patriarch, slay him; if you encounter the parent or the relative, slay them all without hesitation, for this is the only way to deliverance. Do not get yourself entangled with any object, but stand above, pass on, and be free.[23]

I find it significant that Schireson uses violent rhetoric to think about responding to violence. This represents how strongly she asserts herself as an elderly, white, American woman in Japan. The question that Linji's maxim provokes, a question that becomes Schireson's "personal koan," is, "What does a feminist do to stand up for herself and other women in this abusive situation?" Her answer? "I would let my body decide what to do."[24]

The next time the monk attempts to impose his will on her, she is ready. She is sitting in seiza, an "easier" meditation position where the buttocks rest on the heels. But the monk wants her to sit cross-legged, even though she has permission from her teacher to sit however she likes. Schireson answers his request by shaking her head "no." This position, she tells her reader, was inspired by her mind and body acting freely within the moment, spontaneously. Pressured to sit in the same way as everyone else, to take a beating like everyone else, Schireson refuses to conform.

Schireson's actions are made possible at least in part by her position as a white woman in Japan. Another episode, where Schireson finds herself condemned to "Death by *Seiza*," makes this even clearer. Attending a service honoring Shunryu Suzuki's son Shungo, she is one of two women and the only white person in a gathering where everyone is required to sit in seiza for a long time. To make herself more comfortable, the other woman, an elderly Japanese nun called Shunko-san, takes out a bench for support. Upon noticing this, the monk in charge of the ceremony promptly directs Shunko-san to sit on a chair instead. Schireson comments: "I understood the embarrassment that she faced being seated in a chair, differently from all the other male monks. . . . The entire history of the Zen nuns' practice weighed on me in that moment, when past, present, and future became fused."[25]

Schireson asks Shunko-san to lend her the bench and then shakes her head when the same monk asks her to sit in a chair as well, contesting the male pecking order. She concludes: "This is a feminist's dilemma—how to find your authentic place in a male-dominated environment. Do you follow the lead of women who have survived through submission? Do you risk your precious place for a single statement of equality?"[26] Shunko-san has chosen submission, whereas Schireson takes the risk of doing the same as the men in the gathering. But this is complicated by how she does it: for her, a bench is fine, because it does not visibly separate her from the men. For the monk, a bench already indicates a slight difference, one that he insists on enlarging by putting her in a chair. As in the previous case, where the monk hit her, Schireson explicitly invokes feminism as a guiding thread in her actions and bases this feminism on the actions of her woman Zen ancestors. In so doing, she actively resists the pressure from monks wanting to put her in (what they think is) her place.

Schireson's experiences in Japan teach her to put her own body first, and this is how she negotiates difference and sameness, male and female, Japanese and white. This is how she acts as a Zen feminist, and this attitude takes bravery: sometimes it involves standing up to custom and authority when it would be easier to just follow along. For Schireson, this bravery is partly inspired by the koan she has read, and partly by her liberal feminist ideas. Her core practice of putting the body first means that ritual requirements are negotiable: the body is not, as in so many ascetic traditions, tortured into them. Schireson asks her reader: "Do we glorify teachers who can sit seiza and full lotus—mistaking good joints and balanced musculature for spiritual accomplishment?"[27] For her, the answer to this question is clearly "no." Everyone has their own body, and listening to what that body says is a way of cultivating broader awareness. This is what being "naked in the zendo" means: dropping all pretense of who you are, including the pretense of being a "good" practitioner, and experiencing "vast awareness in the middle of everyday life experiences."[28]

BOW FIRST: CLAIRE GESSHIN GREENWOOD

For Schireson, the body needs to be in charge, even if that means not bowing. Claire Gesshin Greenwood's approach to Zen in Japan is different. Although Greenwood recognizes that sometimes resistance is necessary, she often conforms to the ritual requirements of Zen in Japan. Enlightenment does not involve asserting your individual needs but in finding freedom while following the rules.

Greenwood, a fresh voice in American Zen literature, shares a profound affinity with Schireson through her deep engagement with feminist perspectives and psychology. However, their paths to Zen unfold in contrasting ways. Whereas Schireson embarked on her training in the United States before venturing to Japan, Greenwood's journey took an inverse trajectory. She mainly trained at Aichi Senmon Nisodo, a nunnery in Nagoya where she studied with the internationally renowned nun Shundo Aoyama. Eventually, Greenwood ordained as a priest and then as a teacher. During her time in Japan, she maintained a blog that became the basis for *Bow First, Ask Questions Later*, the memoir I focus on here.

Currently, Greenwood is back in the United States and has completed a master's degree in East Asian studies, as well as a degree in counseling psychology, making her a practitioner-scholar, an increasingly common phenomenon in postmodern Buddhism.[29] In addition to her memoir, she also published a vegan cookbook based on the monastic fare she prepared in Japan.[30] As we will see, her experience in the monastery kitchen was a turning point for her study of Japanese Zen, and in doing so she is in good company: as we will see in chapter 5, the medieval master Eihei Dogen also experienced an awakening when interacting with a cook.

Like *Naked in the Zendo*, *Bow First, Ask Questions Later* is a journey of discovery and of adjusted expectations. The opening chapter is titled "Welcome to My Tea Shop, Here's a Hot Poker for You." There, Greenwood tells her reader that she does not want to be the traditional teacher

> who sits on the highest chair in the *zendo*, the meditation hall, and has private meetings with students to test their understanding of reality. On the other hand, I relate a lot to the Zen story about the old lady Zen master who runs a teahouse, making delicious tea for unassuming customers and responding to anyone who asks her about Zen with a hot poker. She's just trying to do her thing, make her delicious tea, run a teashop like old ladies do. Why does everyone have to bug her with questions about *samadhi* and relative and absolute realities? Why don't they just drink their tea?[31]

Here, you might recognize the character of the nameless old tea lady who also greeted Deshan in Goldberg's *The Great Failure*. This lady appears in a good number of koan and is the inverse of the Zen master as a "great man" (*dazhangfu*). She is a liminal figure, a trickster who stands in between the official patriarchal Zen (she is not a man and not even a nun) and a Zen that would be practiced within lay, family life (she often lives alone, and is no longer capable of bearing children). She is acceptable to mainstream masters (who sometimes explicitly identify as elderly women, as Linji's teacher Huangbo famously does) but, as a powerful female Zen presence, is also attractive to women practitioners.[32]

In chapter 2, I discussed how the old woman's interaction with Deshan allowed Goldberg to come to terms with her parents. Like the old woman, Bud and Syl Goldberg's down-to-earth attitude revealed to her that she still had much more to learn. But Greenwood uses this koan differently from

Goldberg. The old woman who beats annoying monks with the phallic fire poker represents Greenwood's rejection of utopian and gendered fantasies about what Zen practice should be like.

Greenwood finds that too many people come to Zen misguided by "a dream of Zen, a dream of enlightenment."[33] Her memoir details her own journey of waking up from the dream of enlightenment when she discovers that Zen transmission (and with it the certification of enlightenment) is a largely formal and administrative affair, signifying "the progression and completion of certain benchmarks in training, both spiritual and psychological."[34] Instead of acting like a superhuman sage, her Zen master falls in love with her, and she is forced to leave the temple where he teaches.

If enlightenment is not what Greenwood thought it was, the remaining chapters of her book describe a quest to understand what enlightenment does mean. Early on, Greenwood entertains a provocative hypothesis in a chapter appropriately titled "Enlightenment Is a Male Fantasy." While hulling rice, Greenwood concentrates on a koan:

> Xuefeng is working in the kitchen, picking sand out of the rice. His master asks him, "Are you sifting the sand and removing the rice, or sifting the rice and removing the sand?"
> Xuefeng said, "I remove the sand and rice at the same time."
> His teacher responds, "What will the great assembly eat then?"
> Xuefeng overturns the bowl. His teacher says, "One day you will study with someone else."[35]

However, exactly because she focuses her attention on this koan about hulling rice, Greenwood botches her own task of hulling rice. The next time, she foregoes focusing on the koan and focuses on the work at hand.

This experience inspires a reflection on the labor needed to sustain monastic practice. Greenwood realizes that there are significant differences between what men and women typically do in temples and monasteries.[36] Most of the practices that are hailed as quintessentially Zen (meditation, koan interviews, etc.) "were all made possible by women's work, by the women who cooked, cleaned, and organized the schedules of those men."[37] For Greenwood the deconstruction of enlightenment, which she calls a "male fantasy," is intimately linked with exposing how women's work makes the career of Zen men possible.

Despite the clear role division in Japanese Zen, ultimately "there is no such thing as women's practice or women's Zen."[38] This is what Greenwood discovers during the most harrowing period of her life at the nunnery, when she was tormented by suicidal thoughts. A chapter titled "Die Standing" portrays Greenwood working in the kitchen, which is the most physically strenuous job in the monastery, involving constant labor. The temperature is unbearable: "It was about thirty-five degrees Celsius every day in the kitchen, which I believe in Fahrenheit is 'really fucking hot.'"[39] She works like this every day five months per year, three years in a row. She wakes up at 4:00 a.m., goes through the day with barely any rest, and sleeps in a small room shared with five other women. The women she works with constantly scream at her for not doing things exactly right, and her Japanese is not good enough to understand anything of the Dharma talks: "So from my perspective, 'Zen practice' was just work, being reprimanded, and listening to hours of incomprehensible Japanese."[40]

After three months of this, Greenwood starts "thinking about dying all the time."[41] Desperate, she calls an English-speaking psychologist and is told to leave the monastery immediately. Though she thinks this is sound advice, she won't do it. The advice that saves her life comes from a French nun who tells her, "Gesshin, you have to fight. It is like being on a crowded bus when dirty men keep trying to touch you. You have to push them off."[42] Greenwood then starts to visualize pushing the suicidal thoughts away, and instead of the voice that advises her to kill herself, she gradually starts hearing the message "Just win everything."[43] This experience leads Greenwood to assert that the only way of practicing is fully committing to the tasks at hand, surrendering to what you are doing, whether it is cooking in a hot kitchen, sleeping in a tiny room, or listening to hours of incomprehensible Japanese. For her, this type of practice knows no male-female distinction.

In addition to piercing male fantasies about enlightenment, the old woman with the fire poker also symbolizes Greenwood's rejection of a "woman's Buddhism" that would be connected with nurturing, motherhood, and sexuality, the "narrative of women's Buddhism in some books I've read that women's highest spiritual potential is in the realm of relationships with family and children."[44] Greenwood does not find such a "woman's Buddhism" in Japan, where most women in the nunnery are fierce, celibate, and independent.[45] The idea, then, of "interpersonal, intimate relationships as a site of personal growth" does not exist in the Japanese Buddhist contexts she has experienced.[46] Greenwood's "just win everything" Zen implies triumphing over everything that's thrown at her and emerging unscathed. Buddhist women are the same as men: they are strong, determined, and die standing. As a category to examine the quality of Zen practice, gender is useless.

By the end of her book, Greenwood comes to see that enlightenment is ritual, but ritual is not just going through the motions as it is commonly understood. In Buddhist studies, some scholars following the "ritual turn" have seen Zen enlightenment as a performance.[47] This is what Greenwood concludes as well. Ritual is powerful, but it doesn't work its magic right away. One example is Greenwood's approach to Dharma combat: the classical stories of Zen are full of tales of such heroic interactions. *The Record of Linji* opens this way, with the teacher making a statement and then being challenged by several students in the audience. Linji, the ultimate Zen master, parries these challenges with his full arsenal of ambiguously poetic responses, invective, shouting, and slapping.[48]

Now it would be easy to believe that such spontaneous exchanges go on in Zen monasteries today, as Kapleau and Van de Wetering did in the 1950s. But such is not the case. Instead, Greenwood finds this fabled combat is "usually a rehearsed set of phrases, not something spontaneous," and the question asked by the master should be prepared in advance using literary allusion.[49] The same is true for koan interviews. Instead of epic mind games inaugurating dazzling insights, Greenwood sees such interactions as never diverging from a rather predictable template:

> I've narrowed down the teacher-student dynamic to an equation that goes something like this:
> Student/teacher: Absolute!
> Teacher/student: Relative!
> Student/teacher: Okay, middle way.[50]

Here, the master and student seem to just follow a preestablished pattern, where the master parries an affirmation of ultimate/provisional truth with the opposite truth until a balance between the two is reached. Greenwood's book thus does what scholarship on Zen has been doing for the past decades, namely deconstructing the idea that Zen is about spontaneity.

But at the same time, the templated interactions that define her life in the temple also transform Greenwood. She comes to understand that Zen transmission, instead of being a descriptive marker testifying to the attainment of immense insight, is instead prescriptive: "you grow into the role."[51] She understands this within the framework of the Japanese master Eihei Dogen's unity of practice and realization. This idea implies that there is no separation between inner and outer, between appearance and essence. She summarizes this idea in the memoir's title, *Bow First, Ask Questions Later*. The precepts she's taken as a nun are not absolute. Any power they have over her she herself has allowed them to have, and they constitute a fusion between community and individual.[52]

A beautiful image for this unity between practice and realization is how Greenwood's *okesa*, the traditional Buddhist robe, was made: the bolt was given to her by her sewing teacher at the nunnery, two European priests helped with the front "during a weeklong sewing intensive," and an old nun sewed the back of it.[53] This labor leads her to see that her practice is "a product of innumerable causes and conditions we can't see. It is aided by our parents, friends, teachers, community, donors, and so many others."[54] The *okesa* is her robe, and it is not.

For Greenwood, ritual ultimately becomes much more than drudgery. By both creating structure but also allowing freedom within that structure, ritual creates a framework wherein life can be lived. This is a similar conclusion to one reached by a team of religious studies scholars, who argue that the bad reputation ritual has in the West (due to the influence of Protestantism) is unjustified: for them, ritual is a fundamental way to organize the world, a way to suspend or reconcile its contradictions.[55] The opposite of ritual is not freedom but sincerity, "the belief that truth resides within the authentic self, that it is coherent, and that incoherence and fragmentation are therefore themselves signs of insincerity."[56] From the viewpoint of sincerity, ritual is bad because it forces us to behave differently in different situations and to adjust our behavior to external circumstances, which leads us to not be loyal to ourselves. But exactly this type of flexibility, which is the basis of relationship-building (I speak differently to my boss than to my children), is necessary for living in larger communities.

For Schireson, the ultimate guideline was to trust in the body and its awareness, and we can now reframe this as privileging sincerity over ritual. Greenwood is less sure that the body provides reliable guidelines. Instead, she trusts in the fact that the demands of the community on her will be effective, even if those demands include working in a "really fucking hot" kitchen for months on end without sleep while being plagued by suicidal thoughts. Ritual makes sense, even if it demands sacrificing your well-being. Difference needs to be sacrificed to sameness in order for an American woman to be transformed into an authentic Zen practitioner.

The differences between Schireson and Greenwood possibly indicate a generational difference between modernist Zen and postmodern Zen, between baby boomers and Generation Z.[57] Whereas Buddhist modernists focused on meditation, individual realization, and a disregard for ritual, more recently sanghas have begun to stress the importance of community and belonging, paying attention to the divisions, racial and gendered, that cut through communities. This is matched by a fourth-wave feminism that no longer sees the plight of Western women as universal but instead seeks to understand more subtle ways of resistance. In this sense, Schireson belongs more to the modernist Zen because she trusts in the individual as the ultimate authority. Greenwood, however, is more postmodern in that she is not sure that her ideals make sense in the Japanese environment she practices in. That postmodern Zen can take many shapes, though, is shown by the work of Zenju Earthlyn Manuel, whose approach to the two truths is different still from that of both Schireson and Greenwood.

AN INNER BOW: ZENJU EARTHLYN MANUEL

> If I were to define the way of tenderness, I would say that it is acknowledgment—acknowledging and honoring all life and all that is in the world, fully, with heart and body. This acknowledgment is wordless and is expressed in a deeply felt nod to everything and everyone—an inner bow to life, so to speak.
>
> —ZENJU EARTHLYN MANUEL, *The Way of Tenderness*

Zenju Earthlyn Manuel is an exceptional voice in American Zen Buddhist life writing: she is a queer Black disabled Zen Buddhist priest and writes from a position of multiplied marginalization that scholars have come to call "intersectionality."[58] Within the present study, Manuel is unique because she rarely uses koan. As I will show, this is because part of her project is to destabilize the type of Zen modernism that locates authentic Zen in Asia and texts. This Zen is the product of Asian teachers and white students, the result of colonialism and orientalism. Instead of koan, Manuel's books draw on a broader spiritual tradition that embraces her Black ancestry, indigenous religiosity, and Buddhist rituals beyond meditation across lineages and affiliations. She finds authenticity in each body that faces its unique challenges, challenges that are conducive to insight. When a koan does appear in her work, it encodes exactly the problem of being alienated from one's own body, of being divided into two, of being forced to wear a mask that hides her true self.

Like Schireson, Manuel believes in privileging the body and its unique needs. Like Greenwood, she is extremely sensitive to forms of difference beyond gender, notably disability, sexuality, and race. But she goes further than both of these authors in reimagining Zen as "the way of tenderness." For her, even the term "Zen" can be abandoned, and only the Way (C. *dao*) of being open to everyone and everything remains. This Way is grounded in the body and is expressed through an "inner bow" that conveys respect for tradition but also an awareness that not every space allows one to bow and that not everyone can bow. If Schireson didn't want to bow, and Greenwood did, Manuel's "inner bow" takes up an in-between position that is at the same time more radical than either: Manuel is famous for pioneering the idea of "sanctuary sanghas," separate Buddhist communities where people with shared experiences, particularly of exclusion, can come together for unique forms of practice.

Manuel's engagement with the two truths is very explicit. As Gleig points out in her study of Manuel, she does not dismiss the two truths model but points out that the common starting point is wrong: instead of starting from the abstract universal, the spiritual path should start with the specific situation of an individual practitioner.[59] Starting from the universal can "negate identity without considering the implications that identity can have for oppressed groups of people."[60] In *The Way of Tenderness*, Manuel documents how her own Zen teachers have shown this tendency to privilege the universal, and this was a Zen she could not relate to. This is all the more so because the "universal" Zen is in fact a very specific historical iteration. Convert Zen, she notes, was mainly shaped by "white men of European descent who were taught by Asian men."[61] Because this interpretation of Zen does not pay attention to the experience of Black practitioners who have been, among other things, on the receiving end of American racism, Manuel argues for the necessity of sanctuary sanghas, which only allow certain groups of individuals to participate. Such sanghas provide a space to "address the circumstances that are specific to who we have been born as, on our own terms, without interference."[62] Before we can realize our sameness, Manuel says, we need to know our differences.

As Gleig has documented, and as Manuel herself describes, white practitioners react strongly to such sanctuary groups, calling them, among other things, a return to Jim Crow.[63] Manuel's response to such accusations again draws on the two truths: "We are all in the same garden, but in different parts of it. Some plants need light and some need shade. Some are dying and some are not. We are in different parts of the garden because it is necessary."[64] Here, Manuel counters the problematic interpretation of the two truths doctrine that would neglect the particularity of groups suffering exclusion and violence by pointing out that multiplicity is what makes up oneness. Multiplicity should not be ignored to get at oneness. Samsara, our daily reality, and Nirvana, the ultimate reality, are not different realms but interpenetrate each other. For Manuel, the ultimate should never be an escape from the provisional.

Building sanctuary sanghas has many implications, including shifting what constitutes authentic Zen lineage. Adeana McNicholl has described how Manuel and angel Kyodo williams, another Black queer teacher, use "the wisdom of the ancestors of people of color" to "circumvent white male lineages."[65] Such ancestors include "Old women on the porches of the South that have never set foot in a classroom, African and Native American tribal elders."[66] Thus, williams's Zen lineage includes civil rights activists like Malcolm X, Sojourner Truth, and Muhammed Ali.[67] The same is true of Manuel, who protests, "Am I to let go of the shared historical past of slavery but continue to hold on to the uplifting shared histories or cherished lineages of the ancient spiritual communities of another? There is multiplicity in the spirit of oneness. This I knew in my bones."[68] Again, acknowledging how practitioners of color are different is necessary before there can be a discussion of sameness.

These innovations go a long way to resolve the problem of authenticity for Black Buddhists. Because authenticity has been "a central concept in African American literature and culture" and a source of much disagreement, Asian religions like Buddhism are often seen as a source of further alienation for Black Americans: why would you become a Buddhist, when you're already alienated from your African heritage?[69] Manuel's *The Way of Tenderness* reestablishes that connection by building a lineage of Black ancestry and by creating a separate space where the experiences of Black Americans are honored.

In addition to the creation of a Black lineage and the interpretation of Black tradition within a Buddhist framework, Manuel's stress on particular situations implies an emphasis on the body. Instead of trying to ignore her body as she is urged to do in the Zen Centers she visits, Manuel, who has suffered from arthritis since she was eighteen, understands the body as the site of awakening:

> The embodiments of race, sexuality, and gender are in fact the fires through which we must pass to awaken. The fire will not destroy us if we can see authentic interrelationship in its flames. Are these bodies really the enemy of the spirit? Do our struggles with race, sexuality, and gender belie a hidden denial of the body, a mortification of the flesh? Need we sacrifice our bodies in the name of spiritual attainment—hurting our backs and knees far too long in meditation? Why do we ignore the nature of our bodies, something we all share in common? What is this body?[70]

Manuel here uses the term "embodiment" for drawing together categories of discrimination that are vastly different, but the intersectionality of which she has experienced her entire life. The term "embodiment" is the English translation of a variety of French terms used by the phenomenologist Maurice Merleau-Ponty to point to how consciousness and experience always start from an individual body. If, as human beings, we are always embodied, our embodiment has two main aspects to it: like our two hands touching each other, our body is both a means of perception (it touches) and an object to another (it can be touched). The former leads to the possibility of the particular connecting with ("touching") the universal. For Merleau-Ponty, "the ground of our subjectivity is the ground of our intersubjectivity, . . . through our bodies we share a world."[71] However, the latter feature of embodiment—it being something that can be touched—also allows it to be objectified, and thus to be denied the shared world. Frantz Fanon developed this point in relation to racism.[72] For Fanon, Black people's relationship to their bodies is no longer one of sensation but is mediated constantly by the reifying narratives white people impose on them. Fanon's body is objectified as Black, and that's all it can ever be, pushed into a category and heaped with prejudice. He can never touch because his body is excluded from the community of humankind. However, Fanon also argues that the experience of discrimination can lead to solidarity among those who are discriminated against.

Instead of attempting to escape embodiments that are the target of prejudice and the source of pain, Manuel urges her readers to rediscover their individual bodies as "the ground of intersubjectivity," the only way of being in the world together with everyone else. Like Fanon, she sees reconnection with the body as a way of becoming whole. But she also acknowledges that there is a unique shared experience among Black people that also requires attention. Her term for the reconnection with the body is "complete tenderness," which is also the translation of her Japanese Dharma name, Zenju. As we have seen in the epigraph that opened this section, she defines complete tenderness as "acknowledgment—acknowledging and honoring all life and all that is in the world, fully, with heart and body." One does so by realizing that "within the seamless life shared between us, we cannot parcel out hate to some without affecting the whole of humanity."[73]

As an example of how complete tenderness works, Manuel describes how she and her partner wanted to order breakfast in a restaurant one day. The server, a person of color, ignores them for a long time and then serves a brown person who had arrived later than them. Manuel describes the anger and humiliation she feels but then sees the only way forward as acknowledging everything, without directing her emotions at any one single person. Complete tenderness is acknowledging the painful histories that lead to this moment of suffering but also seeing beyond, to what Manuel calls "multiplicity in oneness," a feature she sees as so fundamental that it is synonymous with "nature."

Manuel's "multiplicity in oneness," her version of the two truths, maintains a focus on the particular body that suffers objectification. In doing so, she proposes something different from an interpretation of the two truths doctrine that neglects the particular embodied experience in favor of an ultimate reality where particular bodies do not matter. We can now examine the second part of the long important quotation above, where Manuel asks, "Do our struggles with race, sexuality, and gender belie a hidden denial of the body, a mortification of the flesh? Need we sacrifice our bodies in the name of spiritual attainment—hurting our backs and knees far too long in meditation? Why do we ignore the nature of our bodies, something we all share in common?"[74] Here, Manuel connects ascetic ideals with racism, sexuality and gender discrimination: disciplining the body also means disciplining the bodies of others. Making it an unspoken rule that everyone should sit meditation in full lotus or seiza for hours excludes those who are unable to do so.

We can recall here Schireson's description of "death by *seiza*" as an example of this intersection of gender, race, and disability. As elderly people, Schireson and the nun Shunko-san do not feel they want to experience "death by *seiza*."[75] Yet as a Japanese nun, Shunko-san feels she has to obey the monk, whereas Schireson, as an outsider and an American nun, does not feel subject to this authority.[76] The physical regime here, between those who can and cannot sit seiza for a very long time, thus implies a gendered, racial, and spiritual hierarchy. The monk successfully disciplines Shunko-san because she is Japanese but cannot impose his will on Schireson, who is American. Everyone at the assembly is supposed to endure pain to demonstrate their accomplishment, and to deviate from this scheme is to be subject to criticism.

If, for Manuel, one's particular embodiment is the pathway to awakening, a "fire" that will both burn us and also reveal an "authentic relationship," there can be no hierarchy between different embodiments. Everyone has a particular body and thus can access awakening in a similar manner. Therefore, it should be no wonder that what Faure calls the Zen "rhetoric of immediacy," the idea that enlightenment is available right here, right now, without needing any training, is particularly prominent in Manuel's book.[77] She tells her reader, "You cannot be trained or taught, at any cost, to walk this path [the way of tenderness]. It cannot be practiced. I repeat: It cannot be practiced."[78] Instead, it "simply rises up as an experience void of hatred."[79] Like Huineng, Manuel rejects cultivation. She sketches a form of awakening that is inherently social: tenderness means understanding the particular embodiments of others as well as those of oneself, and meditation is not enough: "We need the connectedness we once knew," she writes.[80]

As we have seen, for Manuel the lineages of women of color and civil rights activists are as authentic as the Zen lineages of her teachers. Manuel's eclecticism, which also shows in her drawing freely from a variety of spiritual traditions, resists the type of Zen that would only see Asian Buddhism and its canonized texts as proper Buddhism.[81] Manuel rejects the orientalist tendency in scholarship and in American convert communities to see Asian texts as the authentic representatives of the tradition. This explains why there are so few koan in Manuel's work. Koan, after all, locate authentic Zen in texts. The patriarchs featured in these texts belong to a lineage that is far away from the lineages closer to Manuel's heart.

It is significant that the single koan that does appear in Manuel's autobiographical work shows how ignoring differences can be disastrous. Manuel introduces this koan in *Sanctuary*, the book that followed *The Way of Tenderness*. She describes a Zen priest training session, where she is invited to share her "deepest loss." Her answer: "My soul." She explains:

> Trying to please my parents, my community, and the entire race of black people, I had separated from my true spirit. I spent so much time shaping myself into what was expected by others, to be accepted, to be seen as in the mainstream, I became a stranger to myself. I recognized the gap between my manufactured self and my soul, which I experienced as a kind of homelessness.[82]

The contrast with Huineng is instructive here. Whereas that Patriarch dismissed racial distinctions by pointing out the universal nature of Buddhahood, for Manuel, ignoring who we are in favor of the ultimate is a kind of death. In response to her answer, a fellow Zen priest recommends "case 35 of the Gateless Gate" to Manuel. This koan is "about a woman separated from her soul."

Manuel doesn't really summarize the koan itself, which consists of the Fifth Patriarch Hongren asking, "Seijo's [C. Qian] soul separated from her being. Which was the real Seijo?"[83] Instead, Manuel focuses on the folk story behind the koan, which goes like this: Qian is the daughter of Zhang and has a handsome nephew called Wang Zhou. Zhang promises his daughter to Wang Zhou, and both children live their young lives expecting to be married to each other. But Zhang changes his mind and matches his daughter with someone wealthy. Wang Zhou leaves the village on a boat, alone. But in the middle of the night, he is joined by Qian, and for six years they live happily together in another province and have two children. But Qian is saddened by leaving home inappropriately and wants to return to make amends for abandoning her father. Wang Zhou agrees, and they steer their boat to Qian's ancestral home. Having Qian wait near the boat, Wang Zhou knocks on the door first and to his surprise learns from Zhang that Qian has never left the house. She has been sick all these years. Wang Zhou then invites the healthy Qian to meet the sick Qian, and they fuse into one being. The story ends with Qian wondering "whether I'm the one who went away or the one who stayed home with Father."[84]

Within Chinese mythology, the story is reminiscent of a much more famous one, namely the Daoist sage Zhuangzi having a dream about a butterfly and, having woken up, wondering whether he's a butterfly dreaming he's Zhuangzi or vice versa. The Zhuangzi story, as the story of Qian, dramatizes radical uncertainty: we cannot definitely say who we are. Though for some, this might seem like a prelude to enlightenment, for Manuel this is a tragedy:

> This koan speaks to the task of bringing together the fragments and images we hold, the parts of ourselves we abandon, and the journey home.... I resonated with Ch'ien-nu [Qian] not knowing who she was. I could understand that the two places—one healthy and one ill—expressed the separation she felt in her heart after her father's broken promise.
>
> As a child, I experienced the broken promise of my Christian faith. My mother, father, and ministers told me about a love that included all beings. When I discovered there are people who hate others for the color of their skin, I became emotionally and spiritually drained and separated from my soul. I was both healthy and ill.[85]

Manuel here speaks of a life lived in estrangement. For a person like her, losing the self is not something wished for because she had to struggle so hard to find out who she was. In doing so, she found "home," a key concept in her thinking that lends *Sanctuary* its subtitle, *A Meditation on Home, Homelessness, and Belonging*. "Home" signifies an authenticity that was denied to the young Manuel and is denied to Black Americans in general. This loss of home and sanctuary is ancestral: elsewhere in the book, Manuel brings up the experience of African slaves being abducted from their homes and brought to America. For her, the act of "taking refuge" in Buddhism is not "leaving home" (*chujia* in Chinese) but coming home to a place where the fullness of one's identity is recognized, where Qian can marry Wang and still have a father.

As mentioned, Qian's dilemma is the only koan in *The Way of Tenderness* and *Sanctuary*. To talk about the path to awakening in more depth, Manuel instead deploys a variety of other stories. One example is "When Crocodiles

Die," a story Manuel wrote herself.[86] It takes place in Madagascar's Ankarana jungle. Mustafa, a dead descendant of the ancient Vazimba people, has been waiting for a ceremony to honor his bones. Another man, a hunter, has killed a crocodile and deeply regrets it. Mustafa tells this hunter that if he honors Mustafa's bones, he will revive the crocodile. So it happens, only it is the hunter who is transformed into the revived crocodile, and Mustafa rides him, singing the ancient and forgotten songs of the tribe. A small girl who can see ghosts resumes singing these old Vazimba songs, and the interconnection between human and nature is remembered.

For Manuel, "When Crocodiles Die" is about reaching home, which here is the interconnectedness of all beings. Like a koan, it talks about lineage and authenticity, about remembrance and interconnection. It is a riddle, because it's not entirely clear why the hunter must be turned into a crocodile and ridden by Mustafa. But it is not a story found in any classical koan collection. Like koan it is a fiction, honored not for its canonical status but for the wisdom it can contain. Manuel thus ultimately invites us to reconsider what stories American Zen honors, and whether there might be space for stories that do not take place in Asia. Ironically, the single koan in *Sanctuary* is thus used within a project that no longer sees koan as the most important literary genre of the living American Zen tradition.

In this chapter, I have described three different responses to the doctrine of the two truths, especially as it relates to gender, race, and sexuality. I showed how the dominant attitude in Schireson's book is of resistance to conform: the body goes first. In Greenwood's book, the body is submitted to the demands of the community. And in Manuel's articulation, individual bodies require separate communities, and it is by honoring our individual specificity that we can walk the way of tenderness.

Schireson and Greenwood often refer to koan to articulate their positions. Schireson sees herself as a contemporary representative of nuns like Miaozong, who fought hard for their place in the tradition. This attitude is also inspired by Linji's urging to kill the Buddha. Moreover, Schireson casts her awakening to Mu as an experience of degendering: she can't distinguish between male and female anymore. Greenwood thinks about koan when framing her ideas about female Buddhism and enlightenment. In the opening pages of her book, she imagines herself as an old woman beating people who ask her about enlightenment. Later on, she uses the formulaic Dharma exchanges that emulate koan to articulate how she is transformed through practice and how enlightenment is not one all-defining moment but instead adjusting your personal desires to the demands of those around you.

Manuel was unique among these three authors in that she only used one single koan and deployed it in a project that undermines the project of using koan and the Zen patriarchs as the basis of imagining what Zen in America should be. In the split woman Qian, she sees her own dilemma, and solving this dilemma means, among other things, honoring stories other than koan, and ancestors other than the Zen patriarchs.

To conclude this chapter, I want to contrast Huineng's famous old story with a less famous but more recent one. I do this to show that what was discussed in this chapter, namely the question of difference and sameness as related to gender, race, and disability, remains at the forefront of contemporary American Zen discourse. In October 2018, Zen teacher Ed Brown was, by decision of the board of directors, banned from teaching classes at San Francisco Zen Center. Among the reasons given for his dismissal, the board cited a letter describing a recent retreat where Brown seemed to mock sexual inclusivity (more specifically, gender-neutral bathrooms) and seemed to suggest (something belied by the audio recording) that he got an erection watching a female student's panties.[87]

Reaction against Brown's dismissal was powerful, with his daughter writing a strong letter protesting the decision, and David Chadwick voicing his support and drawing attention to the incident on his popular website cuke.com, where most of the debate is archived today.[88] I want to focus, though, on the Zen author and hardcore punk musician Brad Warner's response to the events. On his blog *Hardcore Zen*, Warner first referenced an earlier post he had made on inclusivity.[89] Zen, he argued, was meant to make people uncomfortable, and he suggested that Brown had made the person who voiced the complaints against him uncomfortable.[90] Warner further supported his argument by saying that measures such as those taken against Brown would be unthinkable in Japan, where, if you're uncomfortable with something, that is your problem, not the problem of the institution that has made you uncomfortable.[91] For Warner, Zen consists of adjusting to the practice, not adjusting the practice. In a follow-up post, Warner apologized to San Francisco Zen Center and took back many of the things he wrote in his initial response to the events.[92] In explaining his thinking, he distinguished between "real Zen" and "Zentertainment," arguing that whereas only the former is authentic, the latter is necessary to attract donors. He then claimed that San Francisco Zen Center's actions regarding Brown were directed to please those who came for "Zentertainment" and did not reflect how they act toward dedicated students.

For Warner, real Zen requires individual bodies to submit to the rules of the community. Zen has to be the same for everyone. That is an idea that is very similar to Greenwood's notion that Zen is found in obeying the demands of ritual, and it seems no coincidence that Warner wrote the preface to Greenwood's book, praising her as being "the real deal."[93] The things Greenwood did, Warner goes on in that preface, are not something that "most of the folks you see writing puffed-up fluff pieces for those slick spiritual magazines by the check-out stand at Whole Foods" would do.[94] As Warner's typically acerbic description indicates, there is an undeniable normativity here: Greenwood is serious about Zen, and people writing for the magazines for sale at Whole Foods are not.

Viewed through the lens of this chapter, though, we can see that there are many different ways of being serious about Zen. *Pace* Warner, Manuel and Schireson assert that individual bodies deserve our attention. For Schireson, Zen practice consists primarily of bodily awareness, and of following the body wherever it wants to go, even if this means not bowing. Activism for her is done for all women across the ages. For Manuel, the body is linked so deeply to identity that it ultimately implies a deep respect for anyone and anything, even while one fashions one's own sanctuaries within that larger community. For her, the universal is everyone's individual uniqueness.

The works of these three woman practitioners are all attempts at telling us what to do when our body or mind does not fit in. In doing so, they speak to concerns much larger than the rather provincial realm of American convert Zen. They speak to me because in fashioning my own identity, even a writerly identity such as this speaking to you, I've often wondered whether to listen to voices outside myself, or to try to find an inner voice that I was told ought to be there. When I think about things quietly, when the children are in bed, often the voice I hear is the voice of a family member, a cherished friend, or an author I love. "Where is my voice?" I've often wondered. And I've found that Schireson is right: we can trust our own bodies to guide the way. Greenwood is right: sometimes we should bite the bullet and follow great examples. And Manuel is right: we should make a home where who we are is recognized.

FOUR

DETACHMENT IN VAN DE WETERING'S *AFTERZEN*

I n August 2004, the Boeddhistische Omroep, the Dutch Buddhist broadcasting organization, screened *To Infinity and Beyond*, a documentary about the life and work of Janwillem van de Wetering. By that time, Van de Wetering had become famous worldwide as the author of crime novels that incorporated Zen Buddhist ideas. After Kyoto and many other travels, he had settled in rural Maine, where the entire documentary was shot against the lush background of forest and lakes. In the film, Van de Wetering does a mock performance of the *sanzen* interview, where a disciple recites his koan to the Zen master and is then supposed to answer it.[1] Only, in this case, Van de Wetering's Zen master is he himself, dressed up in a traditional gown and wearing a wig to make his head seem bald.

While jazz plays in the background, the "student" Van de Wetering bows down and recites the "Mu" koan in Japanese. Then the "master" Van de Wetering commands his student: "Tell me." In response, the student raises his arms, shrugs, and says, "Mu?" The master answers, "So, what you do [*sic*] in the hundreds of hours, sitting still, weeks? What you meditate on?" After looking down at the floor, the student Van de Wetering looks up, smiles, and says, "Well, about the cunt. The cunt. You know? [Makes gesture portraying female genitals]. Pam-pam? [Slaps hands together] You know, cunt?"

Smiling, the master replies, "That's a fascinating subject." The student, also smiling, mumbles, "Yes, indeed." The master then concludes the interview by ringing a bell.

If your takeaway from this scene would be that, for the older Van de Wetering, Zen is about sex, you wouldn't be entirely wrong. Near the end of his life (he would die four years after *To Infinity and Beyond* premiered), Van de Wetering's interest in Zen had culminated in an idiosyncratic vision of the tradition, one that I'll analyze through the comparative literary category of the carnivalesque. It is a vision that takes nothing seriously and again and again exposes authority figures as ordinary people with ordinary desires. In his last book, *Afterzen: Experiences of a Zen Student Out on His Ear* (1999), Van de Wetering sketches masters and students who take themselves too seriously. The only antidote to seriousness is comedy, and Van de Wetering employs the full arsenal of satire to destroy any illusions his audience might still have about Zen in America.

But that's not all there is to it. Van de Wetering's mock performance in *To Infinity and Beyond*, where he acts as both student and master, also points to the idea that all characters in his autobiography are projections of his own mind. *Afterzen* is an autobiography that openly admits its fictionality. One way Van de Wetering celebrates this freedom, which he calls "detachment," is by reimagining koan. Instead of reading koan to understand what authentic Zen looks like, he rewrites koan to better reflect (and also to make fun of) what he understands present-day Zen teachers to be like. In doing so, Van de Wetering also demonstrates his detachment from the idea that koan are somehow inviolable and sacred. For him, the distinction sacred-profane, like the distinction fiction-reality, is a duality that the truly free author transcends.

Afterzen's deployment of koan is very different from that of *The Empty Mirror*, where (as we saw in chapter 2) koan acted as a type of foil or counterpoint for the reality Janwillem experienced in Japan. Koan represented an ideal Zen world that Janwillem could not access, no matter how hard he tried. If one dominant sentiment in *The Empty Mirror* was disappointment, in *Afterzen* Van de Wetering has a great deal of fun. His free usage of koan builds his authorial identity as a "Zen student out on his ear," a rebel who will never claim the title of master because to be a master is just another mask one can get attached to. Instead, it's better to be your own master, and your own student.

CARNIVAL IN THE ZEN TEMPLE

Van de Wetering's usage of sexuality to satirize Zen masters and students fits the literary tradition of the carnivalesque. For the Russian literary critic Mikhail Bakhtin, the major theoretician of this tradition, carnival celebrates the inherently antihierarchical force of laughter.[2] The medieval European festival of carnival created a world that, for a short time, was upside down: the roles of kings and priests were played by drunkards and idiots, and everything holy, sacred, and serious was reduced to excrement, gluttony, and fornication. Those in power were no more than shitting, fucking, ravenous creatures who were not intrinsically better than anyone else. In portraying the ruling classes this way, Bakhtin argues, carnival was an inherently egalitarian celebration. It removed fear of the higher-ups and showed that it is seriousness that is to be feared (when people pretend not to have an asshole, you're in trouble). Carnival was a celebration of the earthly dimensions of being human, an annual ritual that opened up utopian alternatives to the hierarchical society that the feast took place within.

Language is key in the operation of laughter, and an important example is the combination of praise and abuse: in the vernacular of the Middle Ages, insults would also be terms of praise, and vice versa. For Bakhtin, this inseparable fusion of two opposites is "based on the conception of the world as eternally unfinished: a world dying and being born at the same time, possessing as it were two bodies."[3] This is contrary to "the culture of the ruling classes," which sees the world as hierarchical, a world where upper and lower can never meet. Today, such a combination of praise and abuse is found often in the reappropriation of abusive terms, such as the word "nerd."

In this chapter, I use the term "carnivalize" to indicate how Van de Wetering shows that Zen masters, both alive and dead, are very similar to most of humanity. They fornicate, defecate, make bad money decisions, drive drunk, gaslight, and long for sex. In shocking his readers and making them laugh, Van de Wetering clears the ground for a fresh vision of what Zen really is about. Like Bakhtin's carnival, in undermining figures of authority he dispels fear and allows for the imagination of new possibilities. His prose is filled with new word combinations of his own making that combine praise and abuse, words such as "Master Dipshit," "Jan-Buddha," and "Holy Monk Yesyoupay." This particular way of writing, one that cannot be found in his previous two memoirs, makes it impossible to take Zen seriously, and yet it also makes it impossible to completely dismiss it.

My exploration of *Afterzen* proceeds as follows: First, I will sketch how Van de Wetering rates Zen teachers. As I will show, he has come to understand that most good teachers (1) have a healthy relationship with their sexuality (they are not celibate, nor do they pretend not to be so); (2) have a sound financial sense (if they are not wealthy, they know how to provide for themselves and their community); and (3) are detached from their mask as master (this is just a role, one not to be taken too seriously). Bad teachers manifest to varying degrees the opposite of these three characteristics: they are sexually frustrated, which can lead to abusive relationships with students; they make bad financial decisions; they are power-hungry and deeply attached to their role as a teacher, and would in some cases even kill themselves or others to maintain it. Then, I will show how this framework affects how Van de Wetering approaches koan in *Afterzen*. Instead of koan acting as the script to imagine a present-day Zen master, a mechanism we have seen at work so many times in this book, Van de Wetering uses present-day Zen masters to imagine what the patriarchs were really like. Koan still convey insight, but that insight is more mundane than an overwhelming experience of awakening. It is simply to say, over and over again, that we should stop taking ourselves so seriously.

This attitude affects the writing of autobiography: instead of a rigorously factual account of an Important Life, you can make stuff up as you go along. Van de Wetering is here consciously violating "the autobiographical pact," the idea that an author of an autobiography is the same as the protagonist of an autobiography.[4] Usually, when it is revealed that a memoir is fictional, people are deeply shocked: just look at the general disapproval when it was revealed that James Frey's memoir of addiction recovery, *A Million Little Pieces*, was largely made up (the television celebrity Oprah Winfrey, who had promoted the book, was particularly infuriated).[5] But for Van de Wetering, shock (and laughter) are ways of bringing his readers to insight.[6]

Before I can get to *Afterzen*, though, we need to talk about Van de Wetering's second memoir, *A Glimpse of Nothingness* (1975). In this short book, Van de Wetering portrays how he returned to Zen after many years. Practicing with an American Zen master, he finally attained the satori that had eluded him in Japan. However, many years after its publication, Van de Wetering admitted that *Glimpse* was mostly fictional. Though the motivations for fictionalizing *Glimpse* were financial, this book was an important step for Van de Wetering to be able to write *Afterzen* many years later. Whereas at the time of publication, he presented *Glimpse* as a narration of things that really happened to him, at the end of *Afterzen*, Van de Wetering reveals openly his creative attitude toward autobiography. *Glimpse* also introduced the theme of the masquerade that would become more prominent in *Afterzen*.

SUCCESS AFTER ALL? VAN DE WETERING'S *A GLIMPSE OF NOTHINGNESS*

As you might remember from chapter 2, *The Empty Mirror* concluded with Janwillem leaving Japan, seemingly having given up on Zen. But Japan was just the beginning. Back in Holland, Janwillem is visited by "Peter," his American companion from the Daitokuji temple. Peter, who stands in for the American Zen teacher Walter Nowick, has established a Zen community in Maine and invites Janwillem to come to practice with him there. Janwillem agrees, and a new Zen adventure begins.

In *Glimpse*, Van de Wetering follows the conventions of Zen literature more closely than in *The Empty Mirror*. During the private meetings between teacher and student, "Peter" is in essence identical to the Daitokuji abbot in *The Empty Mirror*:

> The master is very different [from his disciples], a being of another kind. The master also inhabits an ever changing body of flesh but he is no longer human for he has found the way to freedom and has discovered the final point of that way.... When I faced the figure opposite I knew I had not changed masters. There was no difference [between Peter and the Zen master of Daitokuji]. The human form facing me, quietly, in deep concentration, vibrating power and peace, didn't differ from the form of the old master. At that moment I could've never said, "Hello Peter."[7]

In *The Empty Mirror*, the Daitokuji abbot was introduced in contrast with the Zen masters Janwillem had read about. But in *Glimpse*, Peter and the Daitokuji abbot and all other Zen masters don't differ at all. All are essentially the same, in that they have awakened to the nature of reality. This endpoint can only be experienced, not understood intellectually. In the preface of *Glimpse*, Van de Wetering already announced, "Who the master really is I wouldn't know. I could only describe his mask and costume and repeat some of the statements he made and try to recapture the sense of the conversations he had with me."[8] Of Peter, Van de Wetering can only capture his appearance and social interactions, but to describe the Zen master underneath, words fall short.

Peter embodies the ideal of Zen in other aspects of his behavior as well. Further on in the preface, Van de Wetering predicts with certainty that Peter will never read *Glimpse*, signifying his position as a Zen master who, in the phrasing spuriously attributed to Bodhidharma, "does not rely on words and letters." In *Glimpse*, "Peter" is just one mask, behind which is hidden the essence of all Zen masters who have existed throughout time. Later on, Van de Wetering tells us a Zen master "is free, and you are not."[9] Peter is in essence the same as the Zen patriarchs of koan.

Although I haven't been able to ascertain whether Nowick in fact read *Glimpse*, in *Afterzen* Van de Wetering gives ample testimony of Nowick in fact reading plenty of books, about Zen and not about Zen.[10] This divergence between *Glimpse* and *Afterzen* makes it even more likely that Van de Wetering's description of Peter in the former book is deeply influenced by the Zen modernist rhetoric of people like Suzuki. After all, the idea that all Zen masters are the same is an articulation of perennialism, which implies that religious experience remains essentially the same throughout time. In *Glimpse*, it is the Zen master who is perennial: behind his individual appearance lies the eternal essence of Zen. He has become one with the Zen tradition. Facing Peter, facing the Daitokuji abbot, facing Bodhidharma, it is all, essentially, the same. Van de Wetering therefore articulates the direct opposite position from that of *The Empty Mirror*, which was structured around the gap between how koan portrayed Zen and how it appeared to Janwillem in Japan. If we take *Glimpse* and *The Empty Mirror* to express what Van de Wetering actually believed, this reversal took place in only two years. What on earth happened to him?

Well, perhaps enlightenment happened. In *Glimpse*, Janwillem experiences the satori that *The Empty Mirror* lacked. Studying with Peter, Janwillem very rapidly cracks his koan, but this is not the overwhelming experience he has read about:

You kneel down.
The master looks at you.

You state your *koan*.

The master keeps looking at you. The silence becomes tangible, you can hear the silence.

Tension mounts, very quickly.

And then, for the first time, you are very close to him. There is no distance.

You say nothing, the master asks nothing. Who or what you are is paper-thin. The veil is torn.

The master smiles.

The silence continues and then he gives you the next *koan*.

You have a new question and you are in another world.

For a very short moment.

Later you will know that you have been there.[11]

The description here, using the metaphor of the torn veil to describe a nondual experience of "forgetting the self," is similar to the enlightenment experiences of Matthiessen, Kapleau, and many others described in this book, though it lacks the overwhelming joy of those accounts. It is partly the absence of such a strong emotion that leads Janwillem to doubt whether what he had was the real thing. Unlike Kapleau, he does not feel very different from before: "I had to admit that nothing had changed very much. . . . It was quite possible that I was merely imagining my improved sense of detachment."[12] So despite the shift to a perspective where Peter is the same as his Japanese Zen master, the awakening experience in *Glimpse* remains something of a disappointment.

The satori in *The Empty Mirror* is not only disappointing, but it is probably made up. Looking back on *Glimpse* over ten years later, Van de Wetering expressed his dissatisfaction with the book. He told an interviewer of a local Maine newspaper, "I'm sorry I wrote it. But it's an impossible book to kill. It's just been bought again by Ballantine. And in Germany it's just gone again into a massive printing. I wish I could take it away, but I sold the rights. It's an idealized version of some truth I saw at some point. A lot of the stuff in it is contrived. But I must have done it very cleverly, because it's been a successful book."[13] Van de Wetering does not specify what has been "idealized," but we can easily speculate that it refers to his casting "Peter" as identical to the Zen masters of koan and his accessing an, albeit less than ideal, awakening experience. This idealization might be the very reason for the book's commercial success, conforming largely (if not perfectly) to the narrative of the seeker who makes progress and gains Zen enlightenment after long efforts, dispelling the failure that characterized *The Empty Mirror*.[14] The reason for the difference between *The Empty Mirror* and *Glimpse*, then, is likely not so much satori, but Van de Wetering's awakening to the commercial potential of books describing Buddhist experiences.

The strange epigraphs of *Glimpse* support the argument that the book is largely fictional. The Dutch version has an epigraph from Robert van Gulik, the famous Dutch sinologist whom Van de Wetering deeply admired.[15] It reads: "If I tell others what I see, I do partly to impress, partly to subdue my own fear."[16] This seems an exceedingly odd epigraph for a book that purports, as its Dutch subtitle says, to describe "a first awareness of Zen," as it attributes the motivation for writing to insecurity: either one impresses people or one is afraid.

Van de Wetering's tendency to make up stories to impress is also attested by a passage in *Afterzen*. Van de Wetering meets an old Zen buddy of his and tells him he quit drinking because he didn't need alcohol anymore. His buddy's response reveals a lot about Van de Wetering: "He thought that was a silly way of putting things and probably untrue. 'Your wife confronted you. Told you either you quit or she left. Now you need a macho excuse. Always trying to impress the audience. Haven't changed much, have you?'"[17] Though, as I will repeat many more times, much in Van de Wetering's autobiographical work is made up, this passage strikes me as too revealing to be fake. It gives us an idea of how Van de Wetering came across to the people meditating with him in Maine, as someone who wants to present himself in the best possible light. I can imagine vividly that at some point this meant to him that he had to lay claim to the enlightenment so many sought, if only to provide a clear motive for his permanent move to Maine to study Zen with an American master.

The English version of *Glimpse* provides further hints of fictionality. It does not have the epigraph from Van Gulik, only a dedication, but it is equally intriguing. It is dedicated to "the Bangideon." This was what Van de Wetering called his daughter Thera when she was still in her mother's womb. The story behind it is as follows: When he was still living in South Africa, Van de Wetering was stopped by the police for speeding. The police officer apparently did not understand his long Dutch name, and wrote out the ticket for "Bangideon," a name Van de Wetering liked so much he promptly decided to name his future child this way.[18] "The Bangideon" is thus a distorted version of Van de Wetering's own name that is the result of a linguistic misunderstanding. The dedication "To the Bangideon" expresses Van de Wetering's love for his daughter but also covertly indicates fictionality and misunderstanding.

I now turn to *Afterzen*. In that book, a much more mature Van de Wetering is open about his creative approach to autobiography. It describes a philosophy of identity that presents detachment as the highest virtue. Near the end of his life, Van de Wetering stressed the importance of being free from ideas of who you are and from notions of what is real and what is imagined.

MASTERS AND MASKS IN *AFTERZEN*

Afterzen opens with the phrase "Koans are vastly overrated," and this statement in itself encapsulates how Van de Wetering felt about Zen when he wrote this memoir.[19] In chapter 2, we saw how Janwillem threw himself fully into the study of Joshu's Mu, but by the end of the twentieth century, Van de Wetering doesn't think koan are so important anymore. And it's exactly because he stopped taking koan very seriously that he has a lot of fun with them in this book.

The statement that koan are overrated is not Van de Wetering's, though. It's a guru called Baba who tells Van de Wetering this. The full opening passage of the book, which immediately contrasts Baba with Van de Wetering's own Zen teacher, is as follows:

> Koans are vastly overrated. A Hindu teacher, whom I will call Baba, an Indian (from India) in whites whom I met at the Boston airport during a long snowbound wait, told me that. But then he might have been overrated himself. There's a lot of competition in religion. Jealousy too. Jealousy is a fact of life. One of my Zen teachers told me that, shortly before his center collapsed and we, the disciples, were out in the big bad world again.[20]

From the opening of *Afterzen*, there is no suggestion of the mystical Orient (as in *The Empty Mirror*, which opened with the phrase "The gate of a monastery in Kyoto, the mystical capital of Japan"), nor of a transcendent experience (as in *Glimpse*, which opens, as we just saw, by declaring that it describes "an authentic experience").[21] Instead, what this first paragraph addressed to the reader describes is a struggle for power, one with winners and losers. This sets the stage for what is one of the major themes of *Afterzen*, namely the attempt to determine what good and bad teachers look like. Though perhaps he is "overrated," the Hindu teacher Baba is the first of three teachers Van de Wetering considers to be good individuals because they are not attached to their masks as teachers. They are not holier-than-thou but ordinary in their desire for sex and their concern for money, and do not pretend to be anything they are not.

Baba is above all a practical man, without much concern for authenticity. Although he never thought of pursuing a spiritual vocation in India, when he arrives in the United States and lives in abject poverty, he quickly discovers that white Americans hungry for spiritual instruction will follow anyone with the appropriate oriental trappings. Having acquired a white robe, toe-sandals, and a beard, Baba quickly moves out of poverty, acquiring a Jaguar and several sexual partners in the process. He is also a very practical person. During the traditional farewell ritual at his hermitage, Baba hands out cookies to graduating students. Asked whether he bakes these cookies himself, Baba declares he buys them at the supermarket.[22] Van de Wetering, who clearly relishes Baba's story, comments: "There was some slyness about him that I, coming from a trading background in the Holland city of Rotterdam, thought I recognized."[23] As we just saw, in *Glimpse* the teacher was the embodiment of the eternal essence of Zen. In *Afterzen*, the spiritual teacher is recognizable as someone who takes their role lightly.

The vignette of Baba demonstrates that masters should not get attached to their identity or they will, as the Dutch edition of the book puts it, "sleep with your girlfriend."[24] For Baba, identity is just a game, and that's how Van de Wetering thinks it should be. This point is made more elaborately elsewhere in the book:

> Whoever looks for his own nature is lost from the start. I can find something temporary—my personality—but who, including myself, cares about that? Mostly the personality is boring and irritating. As long as it is used as a polite mask, expressing a little loving kindness in daily dealings, as long as it pays bills, does the regular routine in a pleasing manner, the

personality will serve until the day the body, another not too important and temporary manifestation, falters and is no more. I'm not my mask.[25]

If identity is only a useful fiction, openly admitting to its fictionality constitutes one of the most important notions of freedom the book has to offer. And because one is not one's mask, even a spiritual teacher must remain practical, an ideal that is often proposed in Zen literature and a concern that in *Afterzen* translates into being able to earn and handle money. Hence the earlier reference to Rotterdam: as the main harbor of the Netherlands, this city represents business acumen, an association found throughout Van de Wetering's work.

The best example of an ideal teacher who does not get attached to masks but also knows how to manage money is "Roshi," Van de Wetering's Japanese teacher at Daitokuji described in *The Empty Mirror*. In the conclusion of *Afterzen*, Van de Wetering identifies this man as "Oda Roshi" (Oda Sesso, 1901–1966) and expresses his deep gratitude to this "superior man" and his teaching that "'all lessons are fun' including the debilitating Parkinson's disease that was making such a mess of his bodily functions."[26] Roshi is completely "detached" and therefore goes "all out without caring about any results."[27] At the same time,

> personal concerns must have been minimal anyway. He never owned anything except a few robes, and he never seemed to attach importance to his title. Roshi, schmoshi. Who is there to care? His body suffered from a serious version of Parkinson's disease, but his shaking hands didn't keep him from helping out in the kitchen after long meditations and a strenuous series of active get-togethers with his students. Being on his way out, he had less reason to be concerned with the worldly advice of his senior monks.[28]

However, when "Jan-Buddha" (a good example of Bakhtin's praise-mockery mix) declares during their first meeting that he thinks money is illusory, Roshi suddenly becomes very worldly and concerned.[29] He immediately inquires anxiously whether Janwillem has, in fact, the financial means to support his stay at the temple. Roshi's anxiety is such that Janwillem feels forced to take out his wallet and show the traveler's checks it contains, much to Roshi's relief: "I did need money, Roshi assured me, and I did need to let go, even of my all-important nothing."[30]

The exchange about money with Roshi is typical of Van de Wetering's characterization of good masters: whereas spiritually they might be very much aware that everything is an illusion, they attend closely to worldly matters. Those who do not possess these two qualities take themselves too seriously and are therefore bound to cause damage to themselves and others. Roshi's detachment is made all the more clear by his malfunctioning body, which here functions as a gentle carnivalesque element in the narrative: the master has a body too, and this body starts failing him as he ages. As we will soon see, Van de Wetering considers hiding bodily needs a disaster. Such secretiveness is caused by attachment to a mask like "Roshi." Roshi schmoshi.

The third teacher *Afterzen* portrays in a more or less positive light is "Rimpoche," a transparent reference to the famous Tibetan teacher Chögyam Trungpa, whose Scottish hermitage Van de Wetering visited repeatedly.[31] Janwillem learns about Tibetan Buddhism through his acquaintance Dazi-Kawa, a Tibetan monk whom he liberates from two Dutch ladies who kept him as a slave. *Afterzen* delights in the description of Janwillem's interactions with Dazi, which undermine the idea of the oriental sage. While Dazi stays with Janwillem, cultural misunderstandings abound, and they lead to a kind of comedy of manners. An example is when Janwillem invites Dazi to eat a raw herring, a Dutch staple. For Dazi, who has never seen a fish before, the herring seems like a "bird with slimy tail."[32] After he is told what he just ate, Dazi vomits over his robes. He desperately saves money, even after being hired by a British pop star as counsel. Whenever he is invited for something, he replies "Yes-you-pay" earning him the name "Holy Monk Yesyoupay" among Van de Wetering's acquaintances.[33] Despite this sarcastic portrayal of Dazi-Kawa, Van de Wetering also conveys respect for him: it is he who telephones Janwillem every time he is late for early-morning meditation, and it is through him that Janwillem gets in touch with Rimpoche.

Janwillem is deeply impressed by Rimpoche, not only by his knowledge of and insight into Buddhism—even though he was trained in the Tibetan tradition, he knows more about koan than Janwillem does—but also by his immense personal charisma: "Whenever Rimpoche talked to me," Van de Wetering writes, "my spine became alive with an electric current."[34] Earlier he had observed, "Women loved the mere sight of Rimpoche. Men were also attracted by his powerful aura."[35]

Like Baba and Roshi, Rimpoche does not take his role very seriously. Instead of being sanctimonious during their very first meeting, he tells

Janwillem he really liked watching the blockbuster film *Lawrence of Arabia*.[36] Van de Wetering is enchanted by the liberal atmosphere in the hermitage, where everyone freely smokes, drinks, and has sex. Van de Wetering characterizes it as "a spiritual version of the British sitcom Fawlty Towers."[37] Rimpoche is also economically savvy. He drives around the English countryside in a Rover bought by his students. When he invites Janwillem to become his student, Janwillem can pay extra for a Tibetan name.[38]

But Rimpoche's not taking his mask seriously also has a dark side: he sleeps with a lot of his students and is an alcoholic. Driving drunk, he suffers a traffic accident that leaves him partly paralyzed. When visiting India, Rimpoche gets so drunk at a benefactor's house that he starts making sexual advances toward the daughter of his hosts. After both Rimpoche and his disciple Jetsun are thrown out, the latter criticizes Rimpoche for his bad behavior. In response, Rimpoche tears up Jetsun's plane ticket, forcing his student to beg on the streets of New Delhi.

The examples of Baba, Rimpoche, and, most of all, Roshi, who all take their identity as a master lightly, contrast with another manner of exerting spiritual authority, one that takes this role very seriously. The book most forcefully articulates this position through a person called "Sensei," a pseudonym referring to Walter Nowick, the "Peter" of *The Empty Mirror* and *Glimpse*. *Afterzen* is dedicated to Nowick, but Sensei's alcoholism and his abuses of authority, combined with Van de Wetering's departure from the Moonlight Hermitage in Maine where Nowick taught, suggest that this dedication is highly ironic, another provocation. However, Sensei is not alone: *Afterzen* lists many more Buddhist masters who are to varying degrees permutations of Sensei.

Sensei was already present in the opening of *Afterzen* cited above, where he was unfavorably contrasted with Baba. This comparison continues during the rest of the first chapter. When Baba tells Janwillem that he "had really expected a little more" of koan, Van de Wetering reflects that these are like the words Sensei spoke to his students after a week of sesshin, except that Baba is not disappointed or stern.[39] Moreover, when Janwillem, who is still unaware of Baba's humble background but drawn to this "exceptional-looking man," struggles to find the right term ("Shrih Baba? Shrih Baba Maharaj? You have a title sir? Your Holiness maybe?") to address this white-clad sage, Baba declares that he doesn't care about honorifics.[40] Van de Wetering appreciates this answer, which reminds him of Bodhidharma's no-nonsense attitude toward Emperor Wu, described in the introduction of this book. The conversation then turns to hemorrhoids that are the result of excessive meditation, and Baba declares that meditation is not necessary. Nor is it necessary that Van de Wetering become his student. This, again, is the opposite of Sensei, who gets infuriated when Van de Wetering sleeps in the Zendo; who, when Janwillem decides to leave, tries to trick him into staying; who, when Van de Wetering insults the Buddha, kicks him out of the hermitage.[41]

The problem with people like Sensei is that, unlike Baba, they have identified with their masks. As we saw earlier, in the preface of *Glimpse* Van de Wetering already described "Peter" in terms of a masquerade. But whereas in *Glimpse*, the true nature of "Peter" stands apart from his masks, in *Afterzen* the problem with "Sensei" is that he identifies too closely with his masks. A fellow student called Jonathan warns Janwillem early in the book to be cautious of Sensei, as he reminds Jonathan of "Father Stanislas," the abbot of an Orthodox Christian monastery who had one of his disciples kicked to death for insulting him in public.[42] Father Stanislas, Jonathan asserts, "had been tricked by some demon to exploit his position of temporary power. 'Disciples make good slaves.'"[43]

Although Sensei doesn't kill anyone, the story about Father Stanislas anticipates the scene where Sensei and Janwillem definitively break off their teacher-disciple relationship. When Janwillem gives Sensei a ride, and Sensei berates him for leaving a Buddhist dictionary on the floor of his car, urging him to "Apologize to Buddha," Janwillem responds tersely with, "Tomorrow nobody has heard of Buddha."[44] Janwillem then explains that this is "a koan I made up to replace the 'Buddha is a shitstick' koan. A shitstick is still something, but in my koan the Buddha would be totally forgotten."[45] Though this idea is not unconventional in Buddhist historiography, where the Dharma will eventually be forgotten only to be rediscovered by the future Buddha Maitreya, Sensei responds to Janwillem's provocation by getting out of the car and severing his relationship with his longtime student.[46] In *Afterzen*, this reaction demonstrates how much Sensei is attached to his identity as a Buddhist, an attachment that is damaging to others.[47]

For example, we saw how *Glimpse* portrayed Peter as not reading books. As I mentioned earlier, this is not true of Sensei in *Afterzen*, but Sensei does not want to admit this. When during koan study Sensei can't find a koan that he needs, Janwillem looks up the koan himself. At a dinner party at Janwillem's house, Janwillem then presents Sensei with the koan and asks whether this is what he was looking for. Sensei, however, gets angry at Janwillem and warns his other disciples to stay away from books, after which he stomps out of the room, leaving Janwillem's wife in tears. Afterward, while cleaning out the room where Sensei conducts koan interviews, Janwillem finds a book open at exactly the page that explains the koan he presented to Sensei at the dinner party.[48] In trying to maintain a front of the ideal Zen master, Sensei deceives others and hurts the hospitality of one of his first students and his wife.

Sensei also causes damage by his sexual advances toward his students. Talking to Baba, Janwillem tells him that "sexual desire, first frustrated, later perverted" was one important cause of the destruction of Sensei's Zen community.[49] Sensei's abuses of authority make his students want to kill him. One chapter describes Janwillem refusing to lend a gun to one of his fellow students because that student wants to shoot their teacher.[50]

When teachers like Sensei take their masks too seriously, they prevent Zen communities from flourishing. *Afterzen* demonstrates this by showing how such people, unlike Baba and Van de Wetering himself, have no sense of practical matters. All of Sensei's projects on the Zen Center grounds demonstrate this ignorance. He plants trees that will not survive winter and raises livestock that becomes food for the Maine bears. Local geese kill the elegant swans he's bought to enhance the pond.[51] More than a decade before he published *Afterzen*, Van de Wetering already contrasted his own sound sense of business with that of his Zen teacher. He told a Dutch journalist that Nowick had tried to convince Van de Wetering to build his house upon Nowick's land. But instead, Van de Wetering built it on his own land "[b]ecause you do remain a Rotterdamer."[52] Whereas Baba was favorably compared to an inhabitant of Rotterdam, in this interview Van de Wetering characterizes Sensei by his lack of a Dutch sense of sound entrepreneurship. This is all the more ironic because the classical literature of Zen would lead one to expect that Zen Buddhists are extremely industrious and practical, something that Suzuki emphasized in his account of the Japanese Zen temple (as discussed in chapter 1). This proves to be true for Roshi, but not for Sensei.

Sensei is not the only one who fails to live up to this ideal of industriousness. Some of the most sarcastic passages of *Afterzen* are devoted to "Bobbie-san," an American who spent a long time studying Zen in a Nagasaki temple. After so much time in Japan, Bobbie's English is inflected with Japanese mannerisms, he has "practiced perfectly the thousand-and-one different

Japanese bows," knows all the Japanese characters and sutras by heart, and has finished koan study.[53] He is a Japanese Zen master in all but name, and his teacher will soon confirm Dharma transmission. When he shows up in Maine one day dressed in priest's regalia, Janwillem is beyond himself: "I was so excited I stuttered to my wife when I introduced the remarkable being. Sage Bobbie-san from Boston and Nagasaki. . . . I felt sure I was about to make a quantum leap, both in body and mind. A mystical dream come true."[54]

Yet Janwillem doesn't waste time "testing" this supreme being. The first night Bobbie-san stays at Janwillem's house, he is unable to locate any of the materials to build a fire in his room for warmth and cannot use the propane stove to cook breakfast. Despite having been "the chief wood chopper at the Nagasaki sodo," he destroys Janwillem's tools in the process of attempting to perform exactly this task.[55] Later on, this former "tractor driver at Nagasaki sodo" runs Janwillem's tractor into a gas tank, which then explodes.[56] Thinking koan discussion would be better, Janwillem and Bobbie get very drunk, Bobbie's pants catch fire, and the two men get lost in the woods.[57] However extensive his experience in Zen milieus might be, Bobby does not conform to the—gleefully cited—ideal that "'realized' Zen men are superbly practical."[58] Bobbie acts as the inversion of this ideal.

After staying with Janwillem for three days, Bobbie tells him, "It's all bullshit, you fool!"[59] He then says his role as a foreign disciple to a Japanese Zen master is part of a fashion trend among Japanese, to increase the prestige of Japanese culture. It's all about maintaining face. Bobbie then shares his experience attending a Zen congress, an event that turned into complete chaos because of organizational problems and delays. Anxious, all the assembled Zen teachers, waiting for their assigned rooms at the hotel, want to call home. But the phones are not functioning properly, and masters end up calling the wrong temples: "They were talking to monks with names and voices they had never heard of. 'Moshi moshi—hello hello' the maddened teachers were shouting at noncomprehending parties who, in desperation, hung up. The roshis dialed again, and got through to other wrong monks. 'Moshi moshi.'"[60] Unlike Janwillem, Bobbie doesn't think this scene is amusing. It causes him to have a mental breakdown, and he temporarily quits the temple. When he meets Janwillem, Bobbie's plans are to explore his sexuality, because he has never had sex before.

Twenty years go by, and Bobbie shows up again at Janwillem's house. His quest to have sex has failed. He sees himself as being "up in a tree." This is a reference to a koan that depicts a situation where you're hanging on with your teeth by the branches of a high tree, and someone asks you the meaning of Buddhism. What do you do? And what do you do if you're not even in a tree?[61] For Bobbie, being up in the tree is wanting to have sex, being down is complaining about not being able to have sex.

Bobbie's master faced a similar dilemma, and this ended in disaster. At the celebration of his fortieth year as a teacher, this master screams at the assembly of all his heirs, students, government dignitaries, and lay supporters: "I want to get m-a-a-a-a-a-rrried," and then starts crying.[62] After some time resting and sobering up, the master is declared fit again, and students line up for their koan interviews. But when the master doesn't ring the bell for them to come in, they get worried. When someone finally opens the door and looks in, he discovers that the master has hung himself, dressed only in his underwear. His last words are a calligraphy of the Chinese character for "dream." In response to Bobbie's tragic story, Janwillem gives him wisdom from Rimpoche: "You watch and laugh and cry and applaud and boo, but it really doesn't touch you because it's some other illusive ego identifying with some other nonsense."[63] However advanced in koan study one is, Van de Wetering is implying, you cannot overcome sexual desire, and by putting on the mask of a Zen master and taking it too seriously, you can do serious damage. Just look at the calligraphy left by the dead master: meant to be poetic, in the context of *Afterzen* it sounds pathetic because this teacher took his identity so seriously, he had to leave a final Zen poem even while his own Zen practice fell apart. "Why didn't he get married?" is the question Van de Wetering no doubt wants us to ask.

REWRITING KOAN

If you, like me, are both shocked and amused by Van de Wetering's portrayal of spiritual teachers in *Afterzen*, he's got another surprise up his sleeve. Almost none of these teachers are real. Instead, they are "collages, put together to carry certain ideas. The actors on this stage aren't linked too closely to my actual life."[64] Whether you buy that or not (I don't), there's something really interesting happening here: the fictionalization of autobiography, hinted at in *A Glimpse of Nothingness*, is here made fully explicit. In *Afterzen*, Van de Wetering is no longer writing autobiography as a factual report of events. He is doing something very different: he is liberating himself and the reader from the distinction fact-fiction. By saying that the characters "aren't linked too closely to my actual life," he leaves us hanging: How closely are they linked, then? Are they real or fake? And what does it mean for a character to be linked to a life?

Being detached from the distinction fact-fiction allows Van de Wetering to take koan for a wild ride. Make no mistake: koan remain important to him. Each chapter of *Afterzen* is structured around a koan and its solution. Moreover, despite all its irreverent descriptions of teachers dead and alive, *Afterzen* still contains the nostalgia for an imagined golden age of Zen that characterized *The Empty Mirror*, but here Van de Wetering has given up on discovering carbon copies of the patriarchs in his teachers. "There must have been a time when Zen study was fun," Van de Wetering speculates after elaborating on the problems of the Maine Center led by Sensei.[65] He then sketches an imagined golden age of Zen, which should be familiar to you by now: teachers are wacky good-hearted men committed to bringing their students to enlightenment. Janwillem cannot find such masters in the Maine Center. Moreover, he is bothered by the rote repetition of koan. Why doesn't anyone improvise on these texts, like his jazz heroes do with the standards?

If his teachers won't improvise, Van de Wetering will. His reinvention of koan is a liberation of the genre. The patriarchs of Zen no longer function as role models whose mysterious actions have to be understood. Instead, the patriarchs become conversation partners who haven't figured everything out either. They're flawed but human, inspired by the teachers Van de Wetering has met on his lifelong religious journey. This revision of the patriarchs means that Van de Wetering handles koan not as sacred scriptures that must be preserved word for word. Instead of reciting the koan exactly in Japanese, an act that he mocks during the scene discussed in the introduction to this chapter, he makes koan his own. He does this by proposing shocking and provocative interpretations of these texts, by retranslating them, and even by composing new koan altogether.

But, first, Mr. Van de Wetering of *Afterzen* (can I call you Jan?), what are koan? "They are riddles that are deliberately phrased obscurely. There are pieces missing. No Zen student, not two thousand years ago in China, not a thousand years ago in Japan, not today in the Maine woods or in a California valley or on an Arizona mesa, can make sense of any given koan until the teacher does some explaining first. And he won't. He wants you to squirm in stupidity."[66] In *Afterzen* koan are no longer gateways to awakening but unfair games that the student has no way of winning unless the teacher feels like he has squirmed enough.[67] But for a student who doesn't particularly like their teacher, there's a way out: one can circumvent the teacher completely by imagining what the missing pieces could be. This is one approach to koan Van de Wetering proposes in this book.

Together with his fellow students in Maine, Van de Wetering imagines the true story of a koan, spinning alternative and provocative interpretations of these classic commonplaces. Here is a famous koan featuring an aged Tokusan. We have met Tokusan several times already since he was bested by an old lady in Goldberg's *The Great Failure*. Here, we have him at mealtime, near the end of his career:

> There is a Zen monastery. Tokusan is the abbot, Seppo [C. Xuefeng Yicun] is the head monk, and one day the noon meal is late. Tokusan, holding his bowl, enters the hall. Seppo says, "I didn't hear the bell announcing lunch and the gong hasn't been sounded either. Old man with your bowl, what are you doing?"
>
> Tokusan is quiet. He lowers his head and returns to his room. Seppo now tells another monk, Ganto [C. Yantou Quanhuo]: "Tokusan may be great but he never understood the final verse."[68]

Solving this koan poses considerable trouble to Janwillem, and so he asks his friend Jonathan about it over dinner. Jonathan, who is a "natural" at Zen, explains this koan as Tokusan calmly taking in whatever happens and moving on to something else, perhaps a nap. Who would want to hang around in the cold dharma hall anyway? Ah, great, Janwillem thinks to himself: Tokusan is different from Father Stanislas (the man who had his disciple kicked to death) in that he can put his ego aside. Koan might be overrated, but here's a little bit of wisdom that's useful to Janwillem, whose ego, like my own, is "particularly vulnerable when it has the idea that it 'gets no respect around here.'"[69] The solution is to just go back to your room.

Janwillem wonders, though, what would have happened if Tokusan had gotten angry at the head monk: "'I'm sure, in reality, he did.' . . . Jonathan the Natural said he thought that, in the actual and unedited scene, short-tempered sensei Tokusan probably had roared insults at uppity monk Seppo before stamping back to his room, but reporting on everyday events accurately doesn't create usable koans."[70] The interpretation Jonathan proposes sees the koan as a deliberate fictional invention. What Tokusan did or did not do is not so important. The important thing is that the koan be "usable." This word is of course ambiguous: usable by whom? One possibility is: usable by teachers who want to maintain their authority as founts of wisdom. But that does not deny that koan do contain some nuggets of wisdom, some suggestions to lead a slightly better, 10 percent happier life. This understanding does not come in a sudden surge of insight but in a cozy conversation after a nice meal.

The task of explaining koan, so crucial for a Zen student wanting to attain mastery, becomes a game that Van de Wetering also wants to liberate from its routine. Though Van de Wetering continually reminds us that you're not supposed to talk about koan, Janwillem does so incessantly throughout the book. One of his interlocutors is "Ben," a former colleague of Janwillem. Despite having left the Zen community disgusted with Sensei, Ben still wants to solve the last koan this teacher assigned to him. That koan is Gozo's water buffalo: "He [Sensei] points at the small window above his head. He tells you that it's like 'Gozo's water-buffalo bull, passing by that window—his huge head, his big horns, his four feet go by, but that's it, the tail never shows up. What of that, eh?'"[71] Janwillem, channeling Baba, calls this koan "overrated."[72] Ben is simply missing a piece of the puzzle, which is that "tail" in the Chinese context means the ego. He explains that he's read about this in a Zen cheat book that contains all the answers to koan.[73] Although spiritual people might want to get rid of their egos, ultimately, they can never cut it off. They can only be aware that it's there, holding them back. In Janwillem's reading, the koan was a way for Sensei to apologize to his disciples for making such a mess of things because he still had a selfish ego and could not come to terms with it. After introducing Ben to what type of performance would embody such an understanding in the *sanzen* room, Janwillem says goodbye. But Ben wants confirmation that what Van de Wetering has told him is the real thing, the true meaning of the koan. Janwillem denies him this, saying he "made it up," and then wishing Ben, "Bless Buddha."[74]

It's not that Van de Wetering thinks koan are complete nonsense. But he dismisses the whole idea that insight into a koan can only come through a sudden overwhelming experience. In the case of Gozo's water buffalo, he reads the koan as a rather transparent type of communication from Sensei, an oblique way of telling Jan and Ben he's sorry for the abuses of power, for the sex scandals, for his alcoholism. You could certainly read this as a type of mind-to-mind communication from Sensei. In that case, the message communicated is the one that *Afterzen* returns to again and again, that masters have earthly desires that they need to acknowledge if they are to remain sane. But even if this was a mind-to-mind transmission, one that was well received by Janwillem, he has been able to receive this message by reading books about koan, something he is not supposed to do. It is only by not taking seriously the Zen mystique around "the koan" that Janwillem is able to understand the last lesson of his teacher.

And even that understanding, as you just saw, should be taken with a grain of salt. Like Baba, maybe Janwillem himself is "overrated" whenever he assumes the role of explaining koan. He therefore refuses any responsibility for his explanation of the koan and rejects the idea that he has any "certainty" about anything at all. He is not a master defined by certainty but a masterless student chasing a question. That he bids Ben goodbye by saying, "Bless Buddha" further shows that he takes nothing seriously: the phrase is after all a carnivalesque combination of sacred forms of greetings, between "God bless" and the East Asian salutation "Amituofo" (referring to a specific heavenly Buddha).

Van de Wetering's irreverent and carnivalesque approach to koan comes most forcefully to the fore in his reimagination of Joshu as a man who has sexual intercourse with an old tea lady. The koan is as follows, as narrated by Van de Wetering:

> A traveling monk asks the old woman "Which way to Mount Sumeru," she says "straight ahead," he goes straight ahead, and she sneers at his back, saying, "This fine monk goes the same way."
>
> The monk, feeling insulted, complains to his teacher Joshu. Joshu says he'll check the old woman out. He visits the tea shop, asks for the way to Sumeru, is told to go straight ahead, the story repeats itself. Joshu returns to his temple and tells his monks, "The old woman has been penetrated by me."[75]

The point, as Van de Wetering explains, is that the monk is an idiot. Who needs to ask for the way to a huge mountain? Wouldn't you just see it? But instead, we dawdle at tea shops, asking people for confirmation: are we really on the way to somewhere? Which is also to ask, is what we're doing really meaningful? But of course, it's not: the sun will eventually explode, the human race will be incinerated, and a billion years hence no one will remember that we were here. Joshu knows this and has fun.

But the version of the koan we have in *Afterzen* is a strange one. The last line, which mentions penetration, implies sexual intercourse. This sexual interpretation is reinforced by Sensei and by Janwillem's Japanese colleague monk Han-san, who tells him about Joshu: "pam-pam, with some old mountain lady—the old boy just loved it."[76] Joshu here is portrayed as someone who acknowledges his sex drive and breaks taboos because he sees that everything is ultimately devoid of meaning.

The Chinese of this koan (case 31 of the *Gateless Barrier*) does not seem to support such an interpretation though. The last sentence reads *taishan pozi wo yu er kanpo liao ye*, which literally translates as, "I have seen through the old woman of Taishan for you."[77] Nowhere in the Chinese, nor in the translations of Sekida and R. H. Blyth that Van de Wetering says he drew upon in writing *Afterzen*, does the translation "penetrated" occur.[78] It thus seems most likely that Van de Wetering's take on the koan is of his own making, using the Buddhist teachers he knows as a template to reimagine (and carnivalize) one of Zen's most famous patriarchs.[79]

In addition to commenting on and creatively translating koan, Van de Wetering also invents new iterations of the genre. One example is when he satirizes a master he calls "Dipshit," whose signature treatment of students is to answer all their questions with silence. In the past, Dipshit ran a very successful Zen center in the American Southwest. His center had dozens of monks and nuns, beautiful Japanese gardens, and well-stocked stores with his own calligraphy and Buddha statues made in Indonesia. However, when Janwillem returns to the place many years later, it's gone, the land sold. The only person left is a former student called Jim. Once known as Daizui, he was named after a Zen master who features in a koan that Janwillem instantly solves. Asked how he did that, Janwillem tells Jim it's good to get angry at koan, because it gets you the answer quickly. That answer may not be that useful "because real insights are never koan-produced," but it gets you to the next koan.[80] After spending some time together denouncing their former teachers, Janwillem and Jim invent the following koan:

> A monk inquired, "What is the meaning of Daruma [Bodhidharma] going out to preach Buddhism to the Chinese?" The abbot was silent. Another monk asked another teacher, "What was the meaning of the abbot being silent?" "Maybe he didn't know," the other teacher said.[81]

Silence is a commonplace answer in Zen. The great bodhisattva Vimalakirti is the expert on being silent, and his silence to the question of nonduality in Buddhism has often been referred to as a "thunderous silence," denoting its immense power. In the sutra that bears his name, Vimalakirti's silence contrasts with the clueless silence of one of his interlocutors, Shariputra. This means that there are two types of silence. Vimalakirti's is the silence that has the power of the elements in it. However, this is not the silence Dipshit has. For him, being silent is a simple trick to maintain his authority, another power game that hides the fact that he is fundamentally clueless.[82] As Jim tells Janwillem, Dipshit had sex with his students and used their money to fly around the world and to buy luxury cars. The koan that Jim and Janwillem invent about him exposes him as a fraud. It carries insight, but that insight can be very easily translated into words.

EMPTINESS AND FORM

Like Bakhtin's carnival, Van de Wetering's unmasking of Zen ultimately has a serious purpose: to propose a new vision for Zen Buddhism. It is the final chapter of *Afterzen*, which quotes the Heart Sutra in its title "Emptiness Is Form," that elaborates the fundamental teaching of the book, which analyzes how modern Zen has gone wrong and what Van de Wetering thinks is the proper approach to practice.

The wrong approach Van de Wetering calls "indifference." It is the result of Joshu's Mu, and constitutes "a particular risk Zen students face: the possibility of being absorbed by the shadow side of negation, a weakness I saw in several teachers and also in my own approach, preferring self-centered lazy indifference to a state of mental freedom."[83] Van de Wetering later elaborates that although such an approach makes you stronger in that you see reality as an illusion, it is also "an ideal trap" because it can lead to an attitude where nothing matters at all.[84] From this perspective, acting in deeply immoral and harmful ways is totally okay, because it's all fake anyway. Indifference becomes a thick shield to protect the ego from damage. But this anaesthetizing effect ensures that one also becomes insensitive to the damage one causes to others. Sensei and Bobbie's teacher are good examples of this. In the showmanship of dying like the old Zen masters and seeing reality as nothing more than a dream, Bobbie's teacher traumatizes his students (and leaves the temple leaderless). In manipulating his students for his own personal gain, Sensei is seemingly oblivious to the damage he causes. At the same time, Janwillem's response to these incidents also shows indifference, for example, when he quotes Rimpoche to Bobbie saying that tragic stories are just "some other illusive ego identifying with some other nonsense."[85]

Instead of indifference, Van de Wetering proposes a position he calls "detachment." If indifference was emptiness, detachment is form. When one is detached, one selflessly performs the duties allotted by karma. We know the world is an illusion but still participate in it out of compassion and joy. For Van de Wetering, this is true freedom. What such detachment looks like we can see embodied in Roshi and Baba. On the last pages of *Afterzen*, Van de Wetering repeats Roshi's assertion that "all lessons are fun" and repeats his assessment of Baba as someone who takes good care of whatever comes his way.

To better understand this distinction, Van de Wetering offers his reader one last vivid scene. Walking around in New York, Janwillem hears jazz playing. Following this sound, he bumps into a parade composed of exhausted schoolchildren and adults. They came to play, but now they are dragging themselves through the streets. But then, something happens. As if wondering, "why do nothing?," the drummer starts playing, and "all heaven burst loose as his mates got going around him."[86] Carried away by the music, Janwillem suddenly feels the spirits of Philly Joe Jones, Art Blakey, Max Roach, and his hero Miles Davis to be there on the scene. The joy of this occasion leads him to celebrate his study of koan: they put him into a hole, but on the other end of that hole were light and connectedness. His last words to the reader are: "Fall into the big hole of not caring, fly out on the cloud of detachment./The cracked mirror, the empty mirror, the mirror showing true motivations, no mirror at all, no handle no frame, free passage to now, to here."[87] This final scene becomes a metaphor for the book as a whole, which likewise was a carnival parade of different Zen teachers and students, all guiding Van de Wetering on his quest. No image is necessary anymore; no mirror is needed for the joyous embrace that concludes *Afterzen*.

As we have seen, there are important metafictional consequences of this vision. If one does not take the ego seriously, there is also no reason not to fictionalize it, to freely blend fact and fiction in both autobiography and koan. For Kapleau, the problem with autobiography was that it is always to some extent a misrepresentation. For the later Van de Wetering, this misrepresentation is no problem. If everything is a mask, one can freely drop referential frames like "reality" and "fiction" and write in "pure emptiness" but with compassion for all. For Van de Wetering, this is the closest to the spirit of the Zen masters portrayed in koan, a heritage he hails even as he reimagines it.

At the end of *To Infinity and Beyond*, the documentary about his life and work, Van de Wetering sits down in his office with the interviewer.[88] He's wearing sunglasses, a faded white T-shirt with the American flag on it, a worn-out pair of jeans. The jeans have tight suspenders that pull up the T-shirt so you can see his belly. When the scene starts, the interviewer characterizes Van de Wetering as someone who was confrontational at first but now has turned into a gentler person. Van de Wetering admits that this is possible, and then mentions a series of photographs that portray him at different stages of his life: when he was twenty-one, when he was forty-five, and when he was seventy-one. When his cleaning lady saw these pictures, she told him, "You know what the difference is? You stopped shutting yourself off. I like you better the way you are now." Van de Wetering agrees with this, suggesting that it was his lifelong quest that made him a nicer guy who is less rebellious. But he then adds that this wasn't the point of what he was doing, which was finding out what the deal was with the universe, and what lies beyond the universe, "to infinity and beyond." Other questions he contemplated were: "Why do we always phrase questions wrongly, is this because of our self-centeredness, that we can never see far enough? What comes after the end? Why are we always at the beginning? That's the sort of thing I'm interested in. And I believe that if you're doing this seriously, you become a nice guy. I wouldn't be surprised."

The interviewer then asks Van de Wetering how far he's gotten in solving these questions. Van de Wetering instantly retorts that this is a bad question: "Compared to what?" He explains that a question that attempts to measure "how far" someone has gotten is based on an egocentric obsession with comparison and competition. The idea that you could somehow measure your progress as if it were a contest is exactly what you need to get rid of to get a good answer. The interviewer then asks him, "How can one ask a question without asking why?" Van de Wetering likes this, adding that this is a "question you can start with . . . and end with at the same time."[89] To me, this statement characterizes Van de Wetering's entire oeuvre, where there is never an absolute answer but instead always the question.

In this chapter, I have discussed how Van de Wetering gradually arrived at a unique way of writing about Zen. Already in *A Glimpse of Nothingness*, the short book where Janwillem finally experiences satori, there is the idea that Zen is a masquerade and that autobiography can be partly fictional. In *Afterzen*, this evolves into the idea that the key to living well is not taking your mask too seriously. As a consequence, Van de Wetering derides teachers who cling too closely to their identities, and he praises those who treat their role very loosely. Likewise, he parodies old koan and invents new ones, without much regard for whether doing so is appropriate or not. He deploys these refashioned koan to articulate his authorial identity as a Zen outsider, a trickster of sorts who freely moves between fact and fiction, between sacred and profane, between self and other.

For what it's worth, I think Van de Wetering's cleaning lady was right. Despite the increasingly mocking tone in his work, the author Van de Wetering, as far as he appears in his work, does get nicer and nicer. Remember that *Afterzen* ends by emphasizing compassion. How is this seemingly cynical book compassionate? My guess is that Van de Wetering saw writing openly about the problems with his teachers as a compassionate act, aimed at improving American Buddhism. This is one continuity with *The Empty Mirror*, which, as we've seen, questioned the narrative that koan portray what Zen is really like in Japan. *Afterzen* extends and refines this critique. It extends it in providing an overview of a whole life lived engaging with Buddhism. It refines it in that Van de Wetering sees both the potential of koan and how they can be abused. Sometimes, they are "overrated" tricks that Zen masters can easily abuse, boring word games that lead nowhere. But they continue to fascinate him, and he treasures the insights he's gained by studying them. In the same magazine interview where he dismisses *Glimpse* as a fictional creation, Van de Wetering also talks about Japan, characterizing the "Mu" koan as a "a time bomb in me that went off later—it's still going off."[90] Its detonation can be heard in the conclusion of Van de Wetering's final book.

This was the first of two chapters in which I focus on a single author. The next chapter examines the work of Ruth Ozeki, which has a number of similarities with the Van de Wetering of *Afterzen*. Like him, Ozeki blurs the boundaries between fiction and autobiography, and she sees all her characters as part of herself. Ozeki, too, thematizes the mask as hiding our fundamental nature. But whereas Van de Wetering presents fiction as autobiography, Ozeki presents autobiography as fiction. Whereas Van de Wetering sees all characters as originating in his own mind, Ozeki sees characters walking into her mind. Whereas Van de Wetering is out to shock us, Ozeki's purpose is to amaze. Whereas Van de Wetering sees carnivalizing koan as tools to achieve these goals, for Ozeki, koan contain all of reality.

FIVE

INTERDEPENDENCE IN THE WORK OF RUTH OZEKI

> Hi!
> My name is Nao, and I am a time being. Do you know what a time being is? Well, if you give me a moment, I will tell you. A time being is someone who lives in time, and that means you, and me, and every one of us who is, or was, or ever will be.
>
> —RUTH OZEKI, *A Tale for the Time Being*

Nao is a teenager who moved back to Japan from California because her dad got fired from his Silicon Valley job. Life isn't easy for Nao: her dad continually attempts suicide, her mother is deeply unhappy, and she is violently bullied at school. Having dropped out, she plans to kill herself. The only light in her life is her great-grandmother, a Buddhist nun called Jiko, who teaches her meditation and the intricacies of Zen philosophy. To memorialize Jiko's life, Nao writes a diary in English, using a purple ballpoint pen. It is that diary that makes up half of the novel *A Tale for the Time Being* (2013), one of two books by Ruth Ozeki that I talk about in this chapter. My discussion of Ozeki's work will center around what Nao just started telling you in the quotation above: we are all connected to each other. Taking this idea seriously has radical consequences for the writing and reading of both Zen autobiography and koan. It means that an autobiography is not about one person but about everyone. It means that when we read a koan, we change it. All of us are coauthors of every book ever written, including koan collections. We wrote the *Mumonkan*, *The Blue Cliff Record*, *The Record of Linji*. We are Joshu telling an anonymous student to go "Mu" himself, and we are also that nameless student.

Ozeki is a Japanese American Zen Buddhist priest, documentary filmmaker, and award-winning author who has written four novels so far. Ozeki's grandparents were Zen practitioners, and she herself eventually became a student of the Jewish American Soto priest Norman Fischer, who teaches in Shunryu Suzuki's lineage.[1] *A Tale for the Time Being* was a first for Ozeki in many ways. It was the first book that gained her a global audience. It was the first book where Ozeki herself appeared in her fiction, as a character named "Ruth" who finds Nao's journal washed up on the beach. It was also the first book shaped by Ozeki's study of Zen, and, as a consequence, she had to adjust her previously realist style to depict the paranormal. Since then, she has continued to use Zen to write the short memoir *The Face* (2015) and her most recent novel (one that she has called a "companion piece" to *A Tale*), *The Book of Form and Emptiness* (2021). My discussion in this chapter will focus on *A Tale* and *The Face*.[2]

Unlike most people I discuss in this book, a lot has been written about Ozeki already. My approach is special in several ways. I treat her recent work as a type of Zen autobiographical literature, comparable to Kapleau's diary in *Three Pillars* or Greenwood's memoir of her time in Japan. As with my analysis of those texts, I focus on how Ozeki engages koan. In doing so, I show that *A Tale* and *The Face* constitute a sustained exploration of what the Buddhist doctrine of interdependence—the idea that everything is interconnected—means for writing and reading. Ozeki elaborates an expansive vision of being, time, and self. In her work, autobiography becomes a co-created work of author and reader. When we read a book, we change it, we intervene in it, we become part of it. Ozeki's autobiography becomes our autobiography as well. But this also means that Ozeki's autobiography becomes an autobiography of no one. Likewise, koan become representations of all of reality, but they are no longer just the property of Zen masters and their students, secretly transmitted in an exclusive lineage. All of us are in koan, and all of us are koan.

This might remind you of Goldberg and Haubner, who to varying degrees saw life writing as a form of Zen practice. As you'll see, though, Ozeki takes this one step further by mixing her autobiographical self with fictional characters such as Nao, to the point where it becomes impossible to distinguish where "Ruth" ends and "Nao" begins. If Goldberg and Haubner thought that any encounter was an encounter with the self, Ozeki expands the self to the point where you don't really know who she is anymore. She is not different from us. She's not the same either.

I first discuss *A Tale*. In an interview, Ozeki suggested that *A Tale* was a type of "performed philosophy," a fictional commentary on the work of the Japanese Zen Master Eihei Dogen (1200–1253).[3] In one essay of his massive oeuvre, Dogen was trying to tease out the consequences of the Buddhist doctrine of interdependence on time. Ozeki draws on Dogen to propose that we are time itself: the future, past, and present are all right here, in us, in everything. We are not contained by time as if time were something external, just like we are not just this individual being, but are connected to all other beings. This implies that we can never be completely present: we can never be "fully" ourselves (because we are Many), and we can never be only in the Now (because Past, Present, and Future are all intertwined). Ozeki demonstrates (or "performs") this idea by making all her characters float between absence and presence: they are never quite here or there, never quite dead or alive, never in the past or present. This has stunning consequences for the reality portrayed in this book, which is ensouled, weird, and flippy.

Time-being is but one of the ways Ozeki teases out the implications of interdependence on autobiography. In a lecture, Ozeki mentioned that writing autobiographically had become for her "a way to deconstruct the self."[4] This is connected to another one of Dogen's ideas, articulated in the "Genjo" koan, that studying the self means to forget it, which in turn means understanding everything. Riffing on this idea, *A Tale* explores the effects of memory loss on the performance of Zen mastery. Throughout *A Tale*, Ozeki also refers to quantum physics, which she reads as yet another koan.

A Tale was only the beginning of Ozeki's investigation into what interdependence meant for autobiography and koan. Her short memoir *The Face: A Time Code* further explores the implications of this doctrine on identity, memory, and authorship. *The Face* is a memoir inspired by the famous koan "What is your original face?" Ozeki attempts to solve this koan by looking into a mirror uninterruptedly for three hours. The book consists both of Ozeki minutely recording the seconds and minutes passing by, and the stories of her life as they flit across her mind's eye. A key symbol of this book is the mask. But unlike with Van de Wetering, for whom masks were social identities, for Ozeki, masks are the lines and contours of our faces. They are the eyes of our ancestors staring back at us, the scars of childhood, the marks of old age. Behind these masks, during the rare moments when we can see beyond them, there is no one and thus everything. In such moments, there is no name and no face, because one's name is everything, and one's face is the universe.

Now, before I get to the details, let me take you on a short detour to sketch an attitude toward time that, I argue, Ozeki critiques.

BEING AND TIME IN *A TALE FOR THE TIME BEING*

THE POWER OF NOW

Have you read Eckhart Tolle's *The Power of Now*? This classic of modern spirituality has one core idea: when we are in the now, there are no problems. Problems only emerge when we have some idea of what we want the future to be like. For Tolle, a lot of suffering derives from such utopian, future-oriented thinking, which removes us from the present and abuses anyone and anything in the name of something that, for him, doesn't exist.

Here's a contemporary example of the type of thinking Tolle resists. "Longtermism" is the idea that the future (and, therefore, survival) of the human species trumps any other goal. Advocates of this theory, among whom are some of the smartest and wealthiest people in our world, believe to varying extents that global problems like climate change and famine are minor compared to the possibility of human disappearance. They postulate a galactical presence for all of humanity in the future. Compared to the gazillions of humans who will exist in the future then, sacrificing a few million lives today is justified, because these are just small incidents that will not even matter in the larger glorious history of humanity. One exponent of this movement proposes that we shouldn't worry about global poverty because global poverty will never pose an existential threat to humanity. We shouldn't worry about climate change, but we ought to think about AI killing us all. In longtermism, every human problem today is measured against a galactic space future that doesn't exist yet (and may never).[5] In view of the deep problems of such future-oriented ideologies (of which longtermism is but one example), Tolle's idea to prioritize the present makes a lot of sense. He believes that as long as we keep our focus on the present, we will react appropriately to circumstances, with rationality but also with compassion. We will act on climate change and feed the hungry.

Like a Zen koan, *The Power of Now* is composed as a dialogue between a teacher (Tolle) and the students (us). Tolle tells us that his message is shocking to many: "Some people get angry when they hear me say that problems are illusions. I am threatening to take away their sense of who they are."[6] I want to further investigate that claim, which speaks to the connection of presence with identity. When we tell the story of our lives and dig deep into memories of the past and hopes for the future, are we not absenting ourselves from our lives in the present? In short, is autobiography an act of becoming present or an act of disappearance? And who is it that appears or disappears?

Tolle has some more to say about this, and staying with him a bit longer is a good way for me to flesh out the stakes of the question. Tolle's book is "spiritual," a term that because of its vagueness has become very popular to denote an alternative way of being religious. In the introductory religion course I teach, I often compare spirituality to a supermarket of religious ideas: we pick and choose from ideas and practices assorted in different aisles, labeled Christianity, Islam, Buddhism, and so on, but none of our consumer choices imply a commitment to buying everything in a given aisle. We're just shopping around for what we like, for what speaks to us.

The aisles that Tolle visits to build his own spiritual vision include the aisle of Zen. He tells his readers:

> The whole essence of Zen consists in walking along the razor's edge of Now to be so utterly, so completely present that no problem, no suffering, nothing that is not who you are in your essence, can survive in you. In the Now, in the absence of time, all your problems dissolve. Suffering needs time; it cannot survive in the Now.
>
> The great Zen master Rinzai, in order to take his students' attention away from time, would often raise his finger and slowly ask: "What, at this moment, is lacking?" A powerful question that does not require an answer on the level of the mind. It is designed to take your attention deeply into the Now. A similar question in the Zen tradition is this: "If not now, when?"[7]

Rinzai is here cast as saying, in essence, what Tolle is saying. Like Suzuki in chapter 1 of this book, Tolle is ventriloquizing this Zen master to say things he did not. In my view, *pace* Tolle, Rinzai's asking students to pay attention to the present moment does not necessarily mean that he understood the end of suffering to consist of holding on to the present moment.[8] Indeed, Tolle's imagination of "the Now" as some special place where all suffering ends insofar as one simply goes "there" strikes me as a perfect example of attachment, which for Buddhists is the very cause of suffering in the first place. For Rinzai, at least, "now" is not so simple as it is for Tolle.

I also disagree with Tolle's assumption, visible in the quotation above, that "the whole essence of Zen" is as follows: "who you are in your essence" is disclosed "in the now." The proposition that Zen has an essence and likewise that we ourselves also have an essence strikes me as doubly problematic. First, if the essence of Zen is being in the moment, then do you become not-Zen when you remember things or look forward to the future? Are you not being definitively not-Zen when writing a Zen autobiography or reading an ancient koan in a search for contemporary insight? If so, that would classify almost everyone I write about in this book as not Zen, a proposal that is ridiculous. Second, if our essence is disclosed during the present moment—an idea that I call, admittedly not very prettily, "pressence"—what can we do with the idea of no-self? And how is it possible to remain in that present, as Tolle claims we can?

I disagree with Tolle because before I studied Zen, I was obsessed with the work of the French philosopher Jacques Derrida, who is famous for exactly his critique of presence.[9] For Derrida, the attribution of self-presence is dangerous because it always implies a hierarchy. Plato, for example, speaks of a world of Ideas; a divine realm in which every thing is perfectly and uniquely itself. For Plato, these ideas, these ideals, are the source of the things of our world, and they are also superior to the things of our world. The idea, the divine essence, of a "horse" is far superior to any earthly horse you might ride. This might seem a banal bit of classicism when talking about horses. Its insidiousness becomes clear, however, once we think of ideas of (essential) "womanhood," "childhood," "Americanness," "Japaneseness," in similar ways, a critique elaborated by feminist thinkers like Judith Butler and postcolonial thinkers like Gayatri Spivak. Rather than presence or absence, Derrida understands all concepts as promising themselves, promising a presence that, however, they never obtain, always deferring this presence. We can never find ourselves because truly "finding ourselves" would mean that we could never change again. And that would mean we'd be dead.

I agree with Derrida. I think that, ultimately, it's a mistake to privilege the present as this utopian space where there is no suffering. In my own meditation practice, I've found that the present was interpenetrated with the past and the future. And I think autobiographical writing has to be the same way: writing down the now, this now, has to be writing the fullness of time. Awakening means losing the boundaries between then and now, us and others, being present and being absent. It should not be privileging the presence and my essence as something separate that will protect me, as a cocoon, from harm.

Deconstruction has often been accused of destroying without replacing. "If we can't have a present, then what do we get?" is a question we might ask Derrida across time and space. While we wait until he calls us back, we can turn to *A Tale for the Time Being*. That book posits the time being as an alternative to pressence. Instead of trying to be essential and present all the time, we can instead open our eyes to the fact that everything and all of time is already right here. It was us all along.

BETWEEN ABSENCE AND PRESENCE

As you might've guessed, *A Tale for the Time Being* is kind of complicated. Here's a stab at what it's about. It's a novel told by two alternating narrators who are both biographers and autobiographers. The first is the Japanese teenager Naoko Yasutani, "Nao" for short, who (as mentioned earlier) attempts to write a biography of her great-grandmother, a Zen nun called Jiko. She fails to do so because the description of her own struggles adjusting to Japan after moving back from the United States takes up all her time. These struggles include her father's suicidal tendencies and her classmates bullying her at school. The second narrator is "Ruth," a Japanese American moviemaker and author who shares some characteristics with Ruth Ozeki but also is clearly different from her.[10] Ruth has for years tried, in vain, to write a memoir of the last years spent with her mother, Masako, who suffered from Alzheimer's. Instead of finishing the memoir, Ruth finds, reads, and comments on Nao's narrative, which has washed up on the shores of the island in British Columbia where Ruth lives with Oliver, her partner. But Ruth also adds to Nao's story: as she researches Nao and her family on the internet, she acquires information that Nao is unaware of, involving both Nao's father and Jiko.

The book took Ozeki forever to write, something that she reflected upon in an article in the Buddhist periodical *Tricycle*. In addition to a wonderful meditation on writer's block, the piece is also remarkable because it identifies the source of the writer's block as Zen practice. Asking her teacher Norman Fischer about her inability to write, Fischer admits that he had anticipated this problem:

> I was shocked. I pressed him for an explanation. "You were such a nice writer," he said. "I was afraid Zen would wreck it for you. I've watched you getting so serious about your practice, and I wanted to warn you. Practice will ruin everything! It will change you so you won't be able to write in the same way anymore. Maybe you shouldn't practice Zen so much." He was smiling when he said this, so I knew he was joking—sort of. He shrugged and continued, "But I knew it was hopeless; it was already too late. You were in too deep already, and besides, I knew you wouldn't listen."[11]

Fischer's comment implies that writing, even fiction, is to some extent an expression of the self. Zen practice, he is saying, can significantly alter that writerly identity so that we cannot call forth the same stories in the same way we used to.

Ozeki eventually solved her Zen writer's block by entering into the novel herself, as "Ruth." She struggled with this for a long time but ultimately felt that she had to be in it.[12] But in a way, she was in her fiction all along: as an Asian American novelist, she felt she was always being read autobiographically. Whereas white authors have the privilege of their novels being read as separate from their lives, all the Asian American main characters from Ozeki's first and second novels were invariably associated with her, even while she had no such autobiographical intentions.[13] By writing an autobiographical novel where she is literally there as Ruth, but by making Ruth different from herself, Ozeki both supports and undermines such a reading. Yes, Ozeki is there in *A Tale*. And she's not. As Ozeki said somewhere else, she came to see *A Tale* as teaching the Buddhist lesson of no-self, showing that identity is a story we should not cling tightly to.[14]

As I will show, every character in the novel is fluid like Ruth. Nao, Oliver, Jiko, Masako are all in-between identities, floating between presence and absence, between present, past, and future. They are Ruth Ozeki and are not Ruth Ozeki. Ozeki thus generalizes her specific situation of being an Asian American author (and the racially specific readings of her work) to the condition of all human beings, the condition of interdependence, which is the reason that there can never be a stable self. We are unique expressions of the whole cosmos, which exists in us and through us. We are everywhere and nowhere all of the time. So not only is Ozeki there in *A Tale*, but we are there as well.

Ruth, for example, is the narrator of half the book, but even as a character she's only half there. She notes early on that, pronounced in Japanese, her name means either absence (*rusu*) or roots (*rūtsu*).[15] While reading Nao's diary, Ruth wonders: "Who had conjured whom? . . . Maybe she [Ruth] was as absent as her name indicated, a homeless and ghostly composite of words that the girl [Nao] had assembled."[16] In a striking reversal of ordinary assumptions, the autobiographical character (Ruth) imagines here that a fictional character (Nao) calls her into being, not vice versa. Ruth's speculations are all the more striking because she has absented herself from the rest of the world by withdrawing to an island. She is embarrassed by Nao's father becoming a recluse, a *hikikomori,* because she recognizes herself in him. Instead of being present, Ruth is continuously drawn away to the past, where she finds Nao calling her into being, giving her an identity as a reader at a time when, as a writer, she is struggling with putting words on the page.

As for Nao, she's a character. But she is not as fictional as you might think. Ozeki has repeatedly indicated that Nao had appeared in her mind out of nowhere, fully formed, and started speaking to her.[17] Like Ruth, Nao is as much an absence as a presence: one of the ways her schoolmates bully her is by acting as if she does not exist and telling the teacher that she is absent (*rusu*): "Yasutani-kun wa rusu desu yo. [Yasutani is absent!]"[18] This bullying culminates in a funeral for Nao that her classmates post on YouTube.

But look at that last quotation again: "Yasutani-kun wa rusu desu yo." It is meant to be doubly humiliating to Nao, not only by pretending she is invisible but also because the *-kun* added to Nao's last name implies that she's a boy, an insult borne out of the fact that she's physically much taller than her female "petite" classmates.[19] But literally, the sentence could also mean: "Nao (the boy) is Ruth [*rusu*]." *A Tale* fuses autobiography with fiction, making it hard to distinguish between fact and fiction.[20]

Here are some more examples of how characters fade into each other. Nao gets bullied by people singing the *kagome* children's song, just like her great-uncle Haruki was hazed by soldiers singing this same song when he entered the army. That same great-uncle Haruki wrote in French, just like Nao's diary is held within the pirated covers of the French modernist author Marcel Proust's *In Search of Lost Time*. As a Buddhist nun, Jiko has a shaven head, Nao shaves her head while cross-dressing, and the real Ozeki shaves her head when she becomes a Buddhist priest.[21] Nao's father, Haruki, attempts to commit suicide, and his uncle—also called Haruki—actually does commit suicide. The father Haruki writes emails on suicide using the English pseudonym "Harry," which makes him similar to Ozeki, who, as we will see, uses a pen name in her work. But "Harry" also makes him "any Tom, Dick or Harry" (which is to say anyone).[22] The multiplying similarities between characters and individuals across time and space create a dazzling web, blurring the boundaries between the novel's characters and even author and reader. We are all in this book.

This play with presence and absence extends to national, racial and gendered identities. This speaks to what Eleanor Ty identifies as a salient characteristic of Asian American authors like Ozeki, namely that they are "'unfastened,' mobile subjects in a global age."[23] Nao is neither American nor Japanese. She is bullied at school in Japan because her classmates think she is American, which for them means that she is also a disease. Nao feels alienated in Tokyo and desperately wants to return to California, where she grew up. At the end of the book, however, she ends up in Canada studying French. Likewise, Ruth's national identity cannot be fixed to Japan, Canada, or the United States. She lives on Cortes Island in British Columbia but longs for New York City. At the same time, Oliver judges that what Ruth says about her mother, namely that she "wasn't very Japanese," is also true of Ruth herself.[24] In addition to having no fixed national identity, Nao has no fixed gender identity either.[25] As mentioned earlier, because of her size, her classmates speak about her as if she was a boy. After being forced to have paid sex with a man named Ryu, and dressing up in his suit, Nao comments: "It's not such a big deal, anyway, male, female. As far as I'm concerned, sometimes I feel more like one, and sometimes I feel more like the other, and mostly I feel somewhere in-between, especially when my hair was first growing back after I shaved it."[26] Nao here sees her gender identity as fluid, not a given essence. In this way, the novel undermines the idea that characters have some kind of ready-made essence that can be recovered.

QUANTUM PHYSICS AND INTERDEPENDENCE

In addition to the way these characters keep slipping away, like beings half-seen in twilight, there's a lot of really weird and magical stuff going on in this novel. This is significant because in her previous two novels, Ozeki had not been writing magical realism. But there's plenty of it here. For example, despite their separation in time and space, Ruth directly intervenes in Nao's life, preventing her father's suicide and giving her the diary of her father's uncle Haruki, who died sabotaging the kamikaze war effort.[27] This is impossible within a linear conception of time: Nao writes her own diary long before Ruth actually finds it, and so Ruth should not be able to influence events in the diary. But she does. Likewise, Jiko intervenes in Ruth's life. In a dream, the Japanese nun gives Ruth insight into the true nature of reality (more on that in a bit).

Plenty of other spooky stuff happens. Web pages mysteriously pop up and disappear, never to be found again (OK, maybe that's not *that* weird). Nao meets the ghost of the kamikaze pilot Haruki.[28] Japanese birds never seen in America appear on Ruth's island. Nao's diary changes while Ruth reads it, and so on. All these elements work against commonsensical notions of time and presence: according to a material conception of reality, Ruth can only be present in one place at a time, and yet she is not. Nao cannot rewrite her diary while Ruth is reading it (it is dated before the Fukushima disaster, and Ruth reads it after), and yet that is exactly what happens: pages that were full of writing suddenly turn blank.

What is happening in this book? Much of it can be explained (sort of) through two complex sets of ideas that Ozeki sees as related: quantum physics and Dogen's notion of the time being. For Ozeki, both quantum physics and the time being are a way to explain how reality works. I'll talk about quantum physics first. Ozeki refers to the following concepts:

Superposition: although we might see a particle located in a specific spot, the next time we look the particle may no longer be there.
Entanglement: two particles that have come into contact with each other will continue to behave in a coordinated manner, even if they are light-years apart.
The measurement problem: our observation of a particle changes it.[29]

To demonstrate how these principles work, Ozeki introduces Schrödinger's cat, the famous quantum physics thought experiment (Schrödinger also being the name of Ruth's cat in the novel). Take a cat, put it in a box. Hermetically seal the box and arrange for toxic acid to be released when one atom in a piece of radioactive material decays. Though this will surely happen, it's not clear *when*. At this moment right now, is the cat alive or dead? We can never be sure, unless of course we open the box to check.[30] As long as the cat is inside the box, it is "both dead and alive, *at the same time*," much like electrons in an atom only collapse to a particular location when they are measured.[31] The act of measurement determines the situation of the particle and the cat. Until that time, though, nothing is certain. The atom might have decayed, it might not have decayed. The cat might be purring and alive, it might be dead. Poor cat.

That's quantum physics for you, and it's only really supposed to describe how things work at the particle level, not at the cat level—Schrödinger's undead cat is a joke of sorts, which makes me think particle physicists have an even weirder sort of humor than Zen Buddhists do (recall Nansen's treatment of another poor cat discussed in the preface!). Experts have speculated on the implications that quantum physics has for the macroscopic world, but thus far there is no agreement. Ultimately, quantum physics is, as an expert puts it, "a finger, pointing at the moon." This is a reference to how Huineng (whom we met in chapter 3) explained how an illiterate person like him could understand Buddhism. Huineng pointed at the moon. "Truth is like the moon in the sky. Words are like a finger."[32] Whereas the moon is reality, the finger is just a symbol pointing the way, and we should not mistake one for the other. *A Tale* is one interpretation of what the finger is pointing to, a commentary on the koan of quantum physics. The book suggests that human beings can behave as particles. This means that they can suddenly disappear and reappear (superposition), are connected to each other across space and time (entanglement), and change each other by observing each other (the measurement problem). Nao and Ruth drop in and out of existence, communicate across time and space, and change each other by "reading" (observing) each other.

Quantum mechanics is one finger indicating the truth. Another finger is the Buddhist doctrine of interdependence. Again, this is the idea that no single thing really and permanently exists because every particular thing depends on every other particular thing, so nothing has an independent essence. A lot has been written on interdependence, and the following summary is bound to be reductive, but here we go:

Interdependence—or dependent origination, as it's more often referred to in Buddhist studies—is the reason why the Buddha denied that a stable, unchanging self could ever be found. We exist in a universe of constant change, and we are a part of that change. Though we can fantasize that we are separate people who are somehow isolated from the world, this is nothing more than a fiction, convenient when seen as such but harmful when taken too seriously. Though I can tell you I am this person with these parents and siblings, writing this book and teaching such-and-so classes at such-and-so university, all these characteristics do not point to one single coherent self. This becomes especially clear when we go back in the past. What do I have in common with little Ben thirty-eight years ago? If we compare little Ben to Ben now (bigger Ben), apart from some physical features (brown eyes, brown hair [although I was more blond as a kid], prominent nose), we might find very little resemblance.

But we don't have to go back that far. Right now, this very moment, I am constantly changing: the oxygen levels in my blood, the cells of my body reproducing and dying, the microbiome in my stomach changing with every meal, the neural connections in my brain growing and fading. And you're changing too. If we take all of this into consideration, it becomes impossible to posit that there is something called "Ben," something permanent at the heart of this flux, a flux that does not stop at my permeable skin. If you do so anyway, you're imagining things that are not there. Sure, you can call me Ben, and I can call you Reader. But we need to be aware that these names are just conventions. An Indian Buddhist teacher called Nagasena famously compared the self to a chariot, the ancient equivalent of a car. When you take the car apart, where do you find its "car-ness?" It's simply not there. Instead, we have wheels, mirrors, engine parts, and so on. And even these parts are made up of their own components.

Everything depends on everything else. For example, Reader, I need you. If there was no one to write or talk to, this book would not exist; it would not have been written. I do not have a self, yes, but I do need others. This is what Ruth means when she speculates about Nao, "Who had conjured whom?" Nao, in turn, says to her reader, "Here's a thought: If I were a Christian, you would be my God."[33] We exist together. This is what emptiness means: we are empty of a permanent, unchanging self; we are not separate from an objective reality outside of us. Instead, we *are* that reality, or at least a single unique expression of it.

Now, as the scholar of Buddhist modernity David McMahan tells us, for early Buddhists interdependence meant that life was hell.[34] The doctrine entailed that the world was an unceasing source of suffering because human beings tend to thirst for the security of eternity: you will love me forever, we will be happy together, I wish this moment could last. But the moment does not last, the lover dies, and happiness changes into sadness. The best way to deal with the world, then, is to see it for what it is and escape it (or whatever it is that Nirvana means: it literally means blowing out a candle, disappearing). But in the modern era, particularly in the work of the Vietnamese Zen Buddhist Thich Nhat Hanh, interdependence becomes something to be celebrated because it gives us immense agency: if we are part of the constant change that is the world, we can also influence the world through our behavior. Every little bit truly matters because it affects everything else.

A Tale does not really take a normative stance on interdependence. In its universe, interdependence is simply the way things are. Characters constantly respond to each other, and they are constantly changing. Their bodies, mind, and identity are not fixed, but fluid. In some ways, this is really fantastic: Ruth can help Nao across time and space. In other ways, this is tragic because we will never be just ourselves, or be just in the now. Reality just won't leave us alone.

THE PAWA OF NAO

The very title of *A Tale for the Time Being* alludes to the notion that all beings do not have a stable, unchanging identity. The term "time being" refers to Dogen's notion of (keeping the order of the Japanese) being time (*uji*). As we will now see, Dogen takes the notion of interdependence one step further: it is not just that there is no separate self; there is also no present that is separate from the future or past. Ozeki quotes the following enigmatic passages from Dogen's discussion:

> Do not think that time simply flies away. Do not understand "flying" as the only function of time. If time simply flew away, a separation would exist between you and time. So if you understand time as only passing, then you do not understand the time being.
>
> To grasp this truly, every being that exists in the entire world is linked together as moments in time, and at the same time they exist as

individual moments of time. Because all moments are the time being, they are your time being.[35]

Reams of books have been written on Dogen's being-time, and I don't pretend to fully understand this extremely difficult passage contained within an extremely difficult text, but I do get the following: Normally, we conceive of time flying away, "time flies" being a common expression in the English language as well. This type of expression presupposes that time is separate from us, and indeed that is what the Cartesian conception of time common in the West and, now, globally is like.[36] This conception implies that there is an unchanging "I" (located in the mind) that is absolutely separate from time. This makes us time's prisoners. We long to spend "quality time" and can't wait for our work hours to pass by so we can go home. We are time's objects, its victims, because ultimately time leads to our deaths.

Against this widespread understanding of time, both in Asian Buddhism and in European philosophy, Dogen posits the notion of primordial time.[37] He does this because of a central paradox in Buddhism in general and Zen in particular: if we're always already enlightened, why do anything at all? That is to say, why do we have to work to attain enlightenment through meditation and so on if we are always-already enlightened?[38] To have to work to attain Buddha-nature is to presuppose that enlightenment is something that will come sometime in the future, but this goes against the idea that it is always right here. The term "Buddha-nature" encodes this understanding of enlightenment as the birthright of all sentient beings (and, for some, all of reality).

Inspired by an awakening during his stay in China, Dogen resolves this paradox by the astounding claim that each moment in time is connected to every other moment in time.[39] Time is not separate from us or happens to us; we are ourselves time. The whole history of the universe, from start to finish, is available to us right here, right now. This is how we are already enlightened, but this is also why we need to work for enlightenment incessantly. If enlightenment is no longer a finish line after which we take a break and drink some water and congratulate ourselves (a linear conception of time), there is never an end to our working toward enlightenment, even while we're already enlightened and have always been such.

In *A Tale*, this means that past, present, and future interpenetrate each other. As mentioned earlier, Ruth and Nao exist at different times and places, with Nao writing her diary before the 3/11 tsunami, and Ruth discovering Nao's diary years after. And yet Ruth is able to intervene in Nao's life.

As Nao tells Ruth (and the reader) from the very beginning, "You're my kind of time being and together we'll make magic!"[40] Instead of time progressing in a linear and inevitable fashion, Ozeki portrays time as modular units that are "linked together" (in Dogen's words) with everything else. Just as every individual expresses the universe in one unique way, so does one single moment express all of time. In that moment are contained all other moments, just like in one thing is contained all other things.

Telling "A Tale for the Time Being" expresses this idea as well: Nao and Ruth's story is just one story, but in this story are contained all possible stories. The wordplay of the title of the book combines this modesty (it's just a story "for the time being," merely provisional) and this ambition (it's "for the time being," which is to say everything). When we take into account that we ourselves are "time beings," the wordplay gains another level: *A Tale* is written for *us*. This type of game is characteristic not only for Ozeki but also for Dogen, who continuously turns canonical Buddhist terms on their head through tricky (or fake) etymologies, the point being that there is no "authentic" meaning to Buddhist scriptures since the Dharma can be found anywhere.[41] As we have seen, Ozeki plays with words across languages: Ruth means absence in Japanese, and if Nao is absent (*rusu*), she is also Ruth. But "Nao" herself is of course also a word game. Pronounced in English, "Nao" sounds like "now," as in "the power of Nao."

The wordplay of Nao's name indicates how much Ozeki's approach to the present diverges from accounts like that of Tolle. The present here is not a blissful and isolated place where no problems exist. Instead, the now, Nao tells us, contains a spirit: "In Japan, some words have kotodama, which are spirits that live inside a word and give it a special power. The kotodama of *now* felt like a slippery fish, a slick fat tuna with a big belly and a smallish head and tail that looked something like this: [here, a black-and-white illustration of a fish with the word NOOOW on it appears in the text]"[42] It is telling that when Nao wants to define now, she uses an image to supplement her description, which expresses exactly that "now" is constantly slipping away. It is always moving beyond words. Moreover, when capitalized NOOOW is also another word. Turn this book upside down. What do you see appear? That's right: "MOOON." Like the moon that the finger pointed toward, the now cannot be captured in words.

The "now" in *A Tale for the Time Being* can be extremely frightening. That same fat fish with NOOOW tattooed on it appears in Nao's stomach when her mother examines the scars from the bullying and decides to send Nao to do *more* things related to school instead of protecting her. Nao is speechless in the face of her mother's inability to comprehend the problem. Her fear draws her into the present moment, but that experience is anything but bliss. For Nao's father, now appears only at the moment of death: in an email correspondence on the topic of suicide, he claims that ending your life "stops life in time, so we can grasp what shape it is and feel it is real, at least for just a moment. It is trying to make some real solid thing from the flow of life that is always changing."[43]

"Now" also marks the end of Nao's diary. As her father makes a final attempt to commit suicide, Nao travels away from Tokyo to meet Jiko. But Sendai prefecture, where Jiko lives, is far away, and Nao gets stuck because she does not have enough money to get to the temple. Sitting alone on a bench in the station, she writes, "Nobody sees me. Maybe I'm invisible. I guess this is it. This is what now feels like."[44] After this sentence, the diary becomes empty, whereas before there were many more pages full of Nao's scribbled handwriting. Nao as a person disappears (her classmates' bullying finally worked), and time stops, replaced by the "now."

In these passages, Ozeki is saying things about the relationship of identity, language, and time. Language is the opposite of pressence, because words are time beings. As long as there is time, there is language. When there is no time progression, when there is only the now, there are no words. For Ozeki, *pace* Tolle, the now is the absence of presence, an absence that characterizes zazen and the apprehension of emptiness. It is to lose any idea of selfhood. It's like the BOOOM of a drum: "When you beat a drum, you create *NOW* when silence becomes a sound so enormous and alive it feels like you're breathing in the clouds and the sky, and your heart is the rain and thunder."[45] In the now, Nao is not herself anymore. She is everything.[46]

This is how what I call "The Pawa of Nao" critiques "The Power of Now." The "now" is not a comfortable refuge where all of our life's problems will disappear. Instead, entering the "now" can be an extremely frightening and dangerous experience because we lose our identity. The "now" is also not isolated from past and future but interwoven with it.

Take Ruth's encounter with emptiness, which is anything but blissful. Ruth meets Jiko in her dreams. Jiko "beckoned, calling her closer, and then Ruth was beside her."[47] Putting on the nun's glasses, the lenses of which "were too thick and strong" but which are nevertheless similar to her own, Ruth visually experiences the Buddhist void, which is "Nothing but a vast and empty ruthlessness." Note the wordplay in "ruthlessness": there is no "Ruth" in this void; she is absent. This ruthlessness is harrowing: "She screamed but no sound emerged. She strained into the vastness, pressing into a direction that felt like forward or even through, but without a face there was no forward, or backward, either. No up, no down. No past, no future. There was just this—this eternal sense of merging and dissolving into something unnameable that went on and on in all directions, forever."[48] Luckily, a "feather-light touch," which I assume is Jiko's, removes Ruth's fear and restores her composure.[49] Entering the "now," experiencing the vision mystics long for, is "terrifying beyond belief," as the scholar of comparative religion Huston Smith characterized his own mystical experiences.[50] It is a vision beyond conceptualization: there is no past, no future, no now, no Ruth.

In calling Ozeki's critique of pressence "The Pawa of Nao," I substitute the term "pawa" for power, because Jiko calls meditation a "*SUPAPAWA-*" that will help Nao survive.[51] But this power is not a peaceful solution for all of life's problems. It doesn't stop the bullying, and it doesn't prevent Nao's classmates from sexually assaulting her. All this "supapawa" does is to allow Nao to remain perfectly still, tricking her classmates into believing she's badly hurt. But this very Buddhist acceptance of her fate is also a submission to the violence inflicted on her.[52]

Ultimately, Nao decides to employ this "supapawa" for revenge. On the last day of school, she cuts off all her hair, and sits zazen all night. In the morning, wearing a hoodie, she walks into class, climbs on top of her desk, and shows everyone her bald skull. Then

> a gasp went around the room that sent shivers up my spine. The *supapawa* of my bald and shining head radiated throughout the classroom and out into the world, a bright bulb, a beacon, beaming light into every crack of darkness on the earth and blinding all my enemies. I put my fists on my hips and watched them tremble, holding up their arms to shield their eyes from my unbearable brightness. I opened my mouth and a piercing cry broke from my throat like an eagle, shaking the earth and penetrating into every corner of the universe. I watched my classmates press their hands over their ears, and saw the blood run through their fingers as their eardrums shattered.[53]

There's a lot going on here. Nao's emission of light is similar to that of the Buddha in the Mahayana sutras. In those sutras, though, Shakyamuni's illumination literally brings enlightenment to all sentient beings. Here, though, Nao is using this brightness as a terrible weapon. The shout that vanquishes her classmates has a parallel in that of Zen master Ganto. We met Ganto in the previous chapter of this book, when Seppo told him old Tokusan didn't have it together anymore because he showed up at the wrong time for lunch. Ganto lived to see the bloody and chaotic end times of the Tang dynasty, the twilight of the mythical golden age of Chinese Zen during which so many of the most famous patriarchs had lived and taught. Ganto was murdered by bandits who couldn't find anything in his humble abode to steal. But he went out with a boom, with a shout that could be heard for miles around.[54] Ozeki's reference to Ganto's death reinforces the idea that the power of now is a powerful and terrifying weapon, to be used with care. Meditation, or holding onto the now, does not solve all of your life's problems, nor does it necessarily make you a kinder individual. It's a powerful and sacred force beyond morality.

Recasting "now" as "Nao" is not a move of which only Dogen would approve. It's also something Derrida might have liked.[55] To indicate the infinite postponing of presence, he invents the term *différance*. Though it looks different from the standard French *différence*, it does not sound different (yes). Instead of prioritizing the spoken word (its phonetics), *différance* and *différence* are only distinguishable by their spelling. This is part of Derrida's project to destabilize the primacy of speech and thus presence in philosophy. He does this by emphasizing writing (and spelling). For Plato, whom Derrida identifies as one of the most influential examples of logocentrism, the ideology that emphasizes self-presence in Western philosophy, writing was a big problem. In the patriarchal and hierarchical system Plato represents and would go on to politically defend in *The Republic*, meaning needs to be authorized by self-presence. Writing, however, doesn't need an author's words to be present: we can read anyone's words at any time.

Here's another way of getting at Plato's beef with writing. Have you ever sent a text message that got completely misinterpreted, and you had to call the person to make your meaning clear? Plato would've hated text messages, the same way he disliked writing in general. Because putting something in writing implies that you can't control how people read your stuff. You can't be there to correct what you see as misinterpretations. Plato wants to control knowledge, to make sure that meaning is policed and that those lower in the hierarchy (women, slaves, non-Greeks) are excluded from participation.

Now, ironically, Plato had to write, and indeed his words escaped him and have been read, by Derrida among others, in ways that he surely did not intend.[56] That, for Derrida, is not an accident but the very nature of language: it stretches beyond, it disseminates meaning endlessly. Plato's writing can be endlessly reinterpreted, and this is a good thing because it is inherently democratic: everyone across time and space can read Plato and participate in the sharing of ideas, not just a bunch of Greek men at fancy dinner parties.

Ozeki draws on her knowledge of Japanese and English to free words from the idea that someone needs to speak them, be present with them. Nao as "now," but not quite. Ruth as *rusu*, absence, but not quite. "Pawa" as "power," but not quite. Written words for her can be as powerful as spoken words: Nao's diary can travel across time and space to be found by Ruth, and in reading Nao's narrative, Ruth transforms it. "The Pawa of Nao" is then something very different from "The Power of Now," in that, through Dogen, quantum physics, and the shadow of Derrida, this Pawa sees present, past, and future as interconnected, a vision that might be transformative but also deeply unsettling.

MASTERY AND MEMORY: JIKO AND MASAKO

I now want to turn to focus on two specific themes connected to interdependence: the way Zen mastery is portrayed in *A Tale* and the way it handles memory. For the first theme, I will talk a bit more about Jiko, the Zen nun of the story, because she's fantastic. Ozeki uses her to say things about Zen mastery that are worth hearing. Because—you guessed it!—Jiko is and is not a Zen master.[57] At the time Nao is writing, Jiko is 104 years old, suffers from arthritis, and is nearly blind. That this disabled nun is presented as a Zen master is in evidence everywhere. Jiko's last name (also Nao's), "Yasutani," is no doubt a reference to Yasutani Hakuun, the famous teacher of Kapleau who appeared in Matthiessen's driveway (as described in the introduction to this book). Sometimes, Jiko speaks in koan-like riddles. For example, when Nao tells her that the surfers she is watching keep falling down, she responds, "Up, down, same thing."[58] Nao reflects, "I know better than to argue with her, because she always wins, but it's like a knock-knock joke, where you have to say 'Who's there?' so the other person can tell you the punch line," a comment that could be easily applied to most classical koan and would fit the template Greenwood outlined (as discussed in chapter 3).[59]

When Jiko is dying, she composes a death poem as is the tradition for Zen masters. But instead of writing didactic verses aimed at instructing Zen students, this poem, consisting of a single character that means "to live," is directed at Nao and her father. She tells her grandson and great-granddaughter, who both have contemplated suicide so often: "For now . . . For the time being."[60] She uses her last moments, then, to emphasize to her family that they should live because they are not alone in their suffering. Their "now" has to be shared.

After finishing her one-word poem, Jiko continues to play with convention: "A lot of Zen masters like to die sitting up in zazen, but old Jiko lay down. It's no big deal. It doesn't mean that she wasn't a true Zen master. You can be a true Zen master and still lie down. The Buddha himself died lying down, and all that sitting-up business is just a big macho add-on."[61] Indeed, plenty of classic Zen hagiographies end with masters dying in the meditation posture, sometimes while conducting one final koan-like exchange. In further violation of convention, Nao gives Jiko some candy for the road to the afterlife: "Zen masters don't usually take chocolates with them to the Pure Land, since they're supposed to be so unattached."[62] Nao's description of Jiko thus casts her as a Zen master by drawing upon the conventions of the classical literature. But she also exposes the androcentrism of these conventions, their "big macho add-on." Jiko is not a Zen master who is an isolated "great man" but one who is deeply connected to those around her.[63]

Another example of the way the novel undermines conventions about Zen mastery constitutes one of the most hilarious scenes of *A Tale*, namely when Jiko acts like a Zen master but is only able to do so because she cannot clearly see her interlocutors. When she accompanies Jiko to the convenience store, Nao is stiff with fear that the girl delinquents hanging out in front will harass them. And indeed they do, spewing sexual innuendo and spitting on the floor. When Nao and Jiko exit the convenience store, and the harassing resumes, Jiko stops walking and bows deeply to the girls. And to Nao's complete amazement, one of the girls bows back. This girl is then berated by another girl, the "girl boss," who teaches her how to bow properly. After this exchange concludes with more collective bowing, Jiko asks Nao:

"I wonder what omatsuri [religious festival] it is today?" she said.

"Omatsuri?"

"Yes," she said. "Those pretty young people, dressed up in their matsuri clothes. They look so gay. I wonder what the occasion is. Muji [Jiko's assistant nun] remembers these things for me . . ."

"It's not a matsuri! They were gangbangers, Granny. Biker chicks. Yanki [delinquent] girls."

"They were girls?"

"Bad girls. Juvenile delinquents. They were saying stuff. I thought they were going to beat us up."

"Oh no," Jiko said, shaking her head. "They were all dressed up so nicely. Such cheerful clothes."[64]

A lot of things are going on in this droll exchange, which is a clear allusion to the koan format. Jiko is able to meet the girls, who are outcasts, with a gesture of deep respect that is returned. In doing so, she implicitly teaches that everyone is worthy, everyone possesses Buddha-nature. However, Jiko is able to do so because she is unable to see the girls as most other people would. Her near-blindness allows her to act like a Zen master when most other old women would have likely been terrified.

The encounter with the *Yanki* girls is Ozeki's way of exploring another complex consequence of the doctrine of interdependence. This is a perspective elaborated in Dogen's "Mountains and Waters Sutra," which starts with the stunning assertion by a Chinese Zen master that "The blue mountains are always walking; a stone woman gives birth to a child at night."[65] The relevance of this text to *A Tale* is playfully indicated from the start of the book, when Nao announces that "my coffee is Blue Mountain and I drink it black, which is unusual for a teenage girl, but it's definitely the way good coffee should be drunk if you have any respect for the bitter bean."[66] In several passages of the "Mountains and Waters Sutra," Dogen points out the limited nature of human perception. In our daily life, obviously we don't see mountains as walking. Nor do we see water as a palace. But to a fish or dragon, water is a palace, a magnificent place to dwell. To a hungry ghost (a kind of Buddhist vampire-zombie), however, water is "raging flames or pus and blood."[67] To my cat, a cast-off sweater is a king-size bed. No single perspective can encompass all this multiplicity, which is the result of the fact that everything is so deeply interconnected: to our ordinary senses, only one single aspect of an object is displayed, but that does not mean that other aspects are not there. It does not mean that water cannot be fire or a palace.

All these aspects of one thing are available at the same time if we have eyes to see them, if we eliminate our tendency to see things in a limited, egocentric manner. Read this way, in seeing the Yanki girls as "pretty young people," Jiko is neither deluded nor disabled. Instead, she is merely seeing another aspect of these girls, one that she honors. In doing so, she brings about a complete reversal of the hostile social scenario that would have ordinarily played itself out. Suddenly the girls are appreciated as beautiful, which is indeed what they are, and in return, they show respect for Jiko. Suddenly there is a festival in front of the convenience store.

If Jiko is Ozeki's way of shifting our perspective on what Zen mastery is, Masako is her take on forgetfulness and memory. Masako is the fictional representation of Ozeki's own mother, to whom the book is dedicated. Ozeki said of caring for Masako, who died of Alzheimer's disease, that it caused her to think about what forgetting means for the self, and we can thus read her description of Masako as exploring this connection.[68] As you may recall, Nao and Ruth's failed writing goal was to capture the memory of Jiko and Masako so their stories are not lost to time. From their perspective, forgetting is a tragedy. The history of how Nao's great-uncle Haruki subtly sabotaged the kamikaze war effort by crashing his plane into the sea or the horrible narratives that surfaced after the Fukushima disaster should not be forgotten. Forgetting precious stories is likened in *A Tale* to the gyres in the Pacific Ocean carrying along and gradually decomposing trash into smaller and smaller pieces.[69] This attempt to remember narratives that would otherwise be forgotten has been cast by some as one of the major investments of *A Tale*.[70] Read in this way, Masako's story is a sad one. She suffers from Alzheimer's but ironically hates forgetting: "Missing things upset her. Missing price tags. Missing memories. Missing parts of her life."[71] In this, she is similar to Ruth, who is deathly afraid of forgetting things and becoming like her mother.[72]

But forgetting can also be a blessing. In the "Genjo" koan (the "presencing," or "actualization," koan), Dogen writes: "To study the Way is to study the self. To study the self is to forget the self. To forget the self is to be enlightened by all the myriad things."[73] Unlike a contemporary viewpoint that praises "finding yourself" as the pinnacle of spiritual achievement, Dogen here claims the studying this self means forgetting about it.[74] Only then can we see that totality is contained within every thing.

Applying Dogen's idea to biography and fiction, *A Tale* presents forgetting, public and private, as an opportunity. Loving a good bargain, Masako is a regular customer at the "Free Store" on the island Ruth lives on, which she experiences as "heaven" because she can take anything she wants without paying.[75] Whenever Ruth's house is full of the clothes Masako brought from the shop, Ruth returns them, allowing her mother, who has forgotten all about these things, to find them all over again. Forgetting is a boon for Nao as well. Her classmates document in detail their humiliating bullying. They upload both Nao's "funeral" and their sexual assault of her on YouTube, afterward selling her panties to the highest bidder. Nao's school history, it seems, will stay with her forever, saved to the cloud. But at the end of *A Tale for the Time Being*, Nao's father, Haruki, writes a software tool called "Mu-Mu the Obliterator" that erases Nao's history from the internet, thus giving her the opportunity to start over.[76] "Mu-Mu the Obliterator" is of course named after Joshu's famous answer to whether a dog has Buddha-nature, an answer Ozeki here takes to mean "emptiness" in that Mu-Mu is a tool to delete a traumatic past. For Ozeki, then, koan can erase identity as well as construct it. Through Masako's joy in rediscovery and Nao's fresh start, Ozeki shows forgetting can be bliss.

THE INTERFACES IN *THE FACE*

If *A Tale* talked about interdependence using two semi-fictional narrators, *The Face: A Time Code* departs from a single person (Ozeki herself) and shows how within this single character is contained many others. It does this by documenting what happened when Ozeki looked into a mirror for three hours. She gradually discovers that she is not herself, just like "Ruth" and "Nao" also had no stable identity. "Ozeki" is and is not.

It should be no surprise that one inspiration for this painful exercise is Buddhist, related to a famous koan, where a student is asked, "What is your original face?" In the prologue of *The Face*, Ozeki tells her reader how as a young child she read an introduction to Zen Buddhism and was spellbound: "The crazy old Zen masters, with their staffs and whisks and comic antics, who were always slapping and cuffing each other, cutting off their arms and eyelids, and pulling each other's ears and noses, seemed to hold a key to my nine-year-old identity."[77] Ozeki therefore "read the koans earnestly, looking for an answer."[78] In doing so, she is performing in a very intentional and explicit way what all authors described in this book are doing: she is using koan to explore who she is. But, unlike the others, Ozeki's face itself becomes a koan, a riddle for her to decipher. The face staring back in the mirror is not fully her: it has secrets, of identity and ancestry, that Ozeki attempts to entangle as she looks on. In the process, she discovers a nonstop parade of others: "Hey Dad. How are you doing?" she says to her father, whose stern gaze still makes her feel fearful of disappointing him.[79] Later on, she sees her mother's smile in her own. To look at oneself is to discover endless associations and memories.

This division of identity, the poet Arthur Rimbaud's *je suis un autre*, also appears on a structural level. Because even though it seems only Ozeki is writing, there are, like in *A Tale*, two voices separated in time narrating this short book. The first is Ozeki in the moment, documenting her observations as the seconds tick by. The second is Ozeki after the experiment is over, delving deeper into insights generated by her moment-self.

Long after *The Face* was published, Ozeki explained the writing process of the book, which involved two different people who are nevertheless called "Ruth Ozeki." First she did the experiment "in the moment" and wrote down all her raw thoughts. Then she put these notes aside for a while and returned to them later to supplement them with mini-essays with distinct titles.[80] For example, an admission from her moment-self that she "preferred my Caucasian eye to my Asian eye" led to a mini-essay by Ozeki's after-the-experiment-self titled "optical orientation," on being the daughter of a Japanese woman growing up in America. It's these essays that are more worked on, more elaborate, compared to the rawness of the moment-self.

Perhaps unintentionally, *The Face* thus became a reflection of two types of Zen writing. There is the stream-of-consciousness writing that Kerouac and Goldberg advocated for, and which Ozeki is here trying. And there is writing as a sophisticated art, a cultivated expression that has less to do with the Beat Generation and its influence and more with elite Zen in China and Japan, the Zen of deeply intertextual poetry and long philosophical commentaries.

In addition to this structural feature, *The Face* thematizes the idea of identity as multiplicity through the symbol of the mask. An important passage in this respect is a reflection on Ozeki's experience carving actual masks for the Japanese ritual theater form of Noh. This reflection starts off with a memory of having sexual relationships with older men when she was fourteen years old: "These relationships never felt real, because the 'I' who was having them never felt real. That 'I' desperately wanted to be different from me.... That 'I' was the mask, and she was having the relationships."[81] Here, Ozeki is implying that there is a real "me" underneath the masks, but one that is repressed by a fictional "I." We will meet this maskless "me" in a bit.

After this recollection, Ozeki reflects on the *ko-omote*, the type of Noh mask worn by a male actor playing a teenage girl. Though the mask is expressionless, it can convey a range of emotions. Its production is fascinating: after being painstakingly wrought from age-old trees and carved for years, it is made to look older by a variety of techniques so it no longer looks new. Ozeki claims to have been an expert at one technique that makes a new mask look like it has been partly eaten by insects. Noh, then, is a complex play of presence and absence. A man plays a young girl. The mask seems old but is newly made. It is expressionless but conveys emotions.

Did you notice Nao in all of this? Like Ozeki as a teenager, Nao, too, has sex with older men. And literally, these relations are not real because Nao herself is fictional. Her classmates describe her as a boy, and she cross-dresses. And, as you will recall, Nao shaves off all her hair, as we will see Ozeki do in a bit. Nao is not only Ruth, then; she is also Ozeki. We cannot rigorously keep these identities apart, and that is exactly the point, because they interface with each other.

Ultimately the masquerade becomes a metaphor of what happens when we read and write. Ozeki describes the room where a Noh actor ritually readies himself for the performance. This is "a liminal space, silent, bound by certain rituals and full of magic."[82] The actor gazes at the mask, bows to it, puts it on, and becomes the character. Likewise, when an author puts on a mask, she is "transformed into the protagonist of her story, looking out through its eyes at her reflection in the mirror, made strange by the face of another."[83] This is what happens in *A Tale*, and it explains why there are so many connections between Ruth, Nao, and Ozeki. Ozeki's novels are autobiographies, and they are also not autobiographies.

But there's more. When we read novels, we read ourselves too: we put on the mask of a character to see ourselves in a new way. Like a Halloween dress-up, we look in the mirror and laugh at how funny we look. We experiment with thinking differently than we would usually do, absenting ourselves, even for just a moment, from our "real" identity. Putting on masks is yet another game with presence and absence, with being someone else, somewhere else, some other time.

Another example of such a mask is the name Ozeki itself, which is a pseudonym. She did not want to use her real name because she was afraid of hurting members of her family.[84] The decision to adopt a pen name, which she initially resented, ended up marking her freedom: "Ozeki is my face, the face I chose, a nominal face that keeps them safe from me, and me safe from them."[85] The name was in fact someone else's: she "stole" the name Ozeki from a Japanese man she met in Burma, who lost money she gave him because he had "a gambling problem" but is now a successful businessman in Japan.[86] The mask "Ozeki" is both authentic (it is her "face") and false (it is not her real name); it tells the truth, and it lies.

Ultimately, there is a real person behind the masks (Ozeki is not *that* postmodern), but that person cannot be found within the limits of a face. Early on in the book, Ozeki tells the reader that when she was young, she used her hair to hide from the world.[87] One of the most memorable scenes in *The Face* is therefore when Ozeki shaves off her hair as part of her ordination as a Zen priest.[88] Before doing so, she has her doubts: is this ritual just cheap orientalism, trying to mimic monks and nuns in Asia? Is it not outdated, not taking into account how shaving off women's hair has been used to humiliate them? Is shaving off her hair not completely disrespectful to cancer patients, who have no choice but to lose their hair? Tired of these thoughts, Ozeki decides to just get it over with. Afterward, she approaches a mirror:

> I remember feeling excited as I approached the mirror, and feeling some trepidation as well, but when I caught sight of my reflection and saw my skull for the very first time, I felt a powerful sense of recognition.
>
> "There you are!" I whispered. "Where have you been all this time?"
>
> It was like my face had opened up. There was no place to hide, but there was no need to hide, either, and this was a powerful feeling. Hair had become extraneous. In the shower, I didn't need shampoo and conditioner, because there was no longer any separation between my face and my head, or between my head and the rest of my body. I was unified, all one; it was a profound kind of liberation.[89]

In this awakening, there is no longer a face framed by hair. Ozeki is everywhere; she is no longer just a face. Earlier she had questioned why we put so much value on the face as representative of identity: "What makes a face so special? It's just an organizational device. A planar surface housing a cluster of holes, a convenient gathering place for the sense organs."[90] Losing her face, then, means losing her masks and gaining a body that extends endlessly.

Upon looking in the mirror and discovering her original face (which is not a face), Ozeki adds a phrase that by this point I'm bound to overinterpret: "where have you been *all this time*" (my emphasis). I've only so far discussed the main title of the book, *The Face*. But the subtitle, *A Time Code,* is equally important.[91] Not only are we other people, but we are other people across time and space. Time codes these resemblances into and onto our bodies, our faces. Ozeki sees her shaven head, her face unmasked by hair in the mirror, and with it she sees time.

The Face ends with Dogen's answer to the question of what he actually understood by studying Zen in China: "I have come back empty-handed.... What I know is this: that my eyes are horizontal and my nose is vertical. I can no longer be misled."[92] For someone who would go on to write a long and difficult opus discussing the subtleties of Zen practice and philosophy, Dogen's is an exceedingly strange answer because it seems to convey nothing regarding any of these topics. For Ozeki, a novelist, the placement of this statement at the end of her short memoir is perhaps even more strange: is that really all she has to say?

Dogen scholarship once again helps to unravel what is going on here. One reading of Dogen's words is that he is not making an absolute statement.[93] Rather, the statement acts as an antidote to those who would make Zen only a literary or philosophical matter, and for Dogen, of course, it is not: his aim is to teach liberation, not to indulge in intellectual gymnastics. The statement is a tool to counter a certain interpretation of Zen but should not be taken at face (yes!) value. Language here is performative, not descriptive, and perhaps Ozeki implies something similar about her own oeuvre: we read her books, and in doing so, we see the world in a new way. We learn to take ourselves more lightly and not obsess so much about being present and being ourselves. Like Huineng, Ozeki points to the moon.

We tend to think of the present as "a fleeting yet substantive time-unit which is severed from existence and endures while the future approaches and forever recedes into the past."[94] In response to this, we posit something enduring, an eternal Presence, whether it be God, or Truth, or Love, a Soul, an Atman, or even Buddha-nature, that would stand outside of the vicissitudes of time. In such a view, time is our jailor, and we are its prisoners, and our quest should be to escape time altogether, to reach that eternal Presence and stay there for an eternal Present.

For Dogen, as we have seen, this commonly held view did not accord with reality: if the Buddha was right to see reality as constant change, then there cannot be a self that is imprisoned by time, because to imprison something, there needs to be a something to imprison. For Dogen, we are time, and there is not the minutest separation between time and us. Present, past, and future are constantly here, interpenetrating, and yet they never change into each other (because to do so would be to suppose there is *something* that moves from past to present to future). Instead, we have countless moments, and endless connections between these countless moments, and these countless moments include us, our time being. To focus on the present at the expense of the future or the past is a mistake, just as focusing only on the future or past would be a mistake. Likewise, it is also a mistake to focus only on our own presence and not on the presence of everything else. As I have argued, this is also one of the core messages of both *A Tale for the Time Being* and *The Face*. In these novels, everything inter-is, both existentially and temporally.

What I get from Ozeki's books is that it is good to have stories to tell about ourselves. As the scholar Steven Heine points out, this is another implication of Dogen's time being: "the simultaneous interrelatedness of past and present experiences of enlightenment demands that the Dharma be perpetually reexplored and renewed by the True Man through creative divulgences of the innumerable and inexhaustible dimensions and meanings of the Way."[95] Even though there is no self, stories about the self matter. It matters that we write down the stories we tell about ourselves and about individuals who have mattered to us. This is what Nao wants to do with Jiko, and this is also no doubt what many Zen students in the past did with their teachers. To write down autobiographical and biographical narratives is also to open up the possibility of playing with them, of having some fun in the absence of the teacher or the author.

For Plato, a looming presence in this whole chapter, it was exactly this aspect of writing that bothered him the most. As one of my professors once said in a literary theory seminar, "Plato doesn't want us to fuck!" Or, in my words, Plato doesn't want us to play. Plato didn't want things to be misinterpreted:

when we write something down, it leaves us behind, can be read by others and misunderstood because we are not present to control the reception of our writing. People can make fun of what we said, even if we were dead serious. By extension, then, people who take themselves too seriously shouldn't write autobiographies of themselves.

In this way, then, writing a Zen autobiography becomes a way to destabilize who we think we are: here's my story, Ozeki says, do with it as you wish. I'm not in it, not really.[96] Don't take it too seriously. Have some fun. Koan help her create that fun but also help her structure the books: Dogen's essay on the time being allows characters to interact with each other across time and space. His "Genjo" koan and "Mountains and Waters Sutra" help Ozeki think about memory, forgetting, and selfhood. And Joshu's "what is your original face?" allows her to see her face as containing all of the universe. Koan for Ozeki are not an escape from language, as they weren't for Dogen. Instead, they allow us to "enter more deeply into the universal and non-anthropocentric language of mountains and rivers, bushes and trees."[97]

But fun is something that is best enjoyed with others. Because if we can't really be present, then our time being needs another. Nao in the now is lonely and sad. Remember her, on her own at the train station, her father about to commit suicide. This is where her diary would have ended were it not for Ruth, who leaps across time and space into Nao's narrative and fixes everything. She convinces Nao's father not to end his life, and he appears on the train platform to help his daughter. Ruth reached out to Nao's time being and saved her. As time beings we help each other out.

One of my favorite quotations is Zen master Joan Sutherland on the most important contribution of the Zen school to humankind: the understanding that enlightenment takes place in "relationship, in encounters and conversations."[98] Ozeki's books, always written from a double perspective, and often using the "you" form, engage the reader in a dialogue, telling us we're not and will never be alone. For her, this is ultimately the way we can read and write books: "Literature works because we complete each other," she said once.[99] If we were completely pressent, it would be impossible to relate to someone else because we'd be too full of ourselves. It is exactly because we are empty of this full presence, because we are interdependent, that we can understand each other's stories. And in reading them, we change those stories as well, because stories are, as Nao incessantly reminds us, time beings. *A Tale*, *The Face*, Ozeki says elsewhere, are not her work anymore, "It's our book."[100]

CONCLUSION

I started this book with Peter Matthiessen, who finds koan to be deeply meaningful. I'll begin its conclusion with Mario Poceski, who argues they don't mean anything at all. For this prominent Zen scholar, koan are "nonessential ramblings, a peculiar type of religious gibberish. Basically, we are confronted with countless examples of mass-produced textual materials that tend to be highly formulaic, numbingly repetitive, and ostensibly pointless. One of the things that keeps amazing me is how otherwise intelligent or sincere people can take this sort of stuff seriously, although the history of religion is filled with blind spots of that sort."[1]

This book was partly conceived as a response to Poceski's provocative assessment. I can now summarize that response as follows: it is because they mean so little that koan can be used to do so much. Americans read these tiny riddles and imagine the Zen temple as a utopian space and the teacher as a detached holy man. They imagine a way of living where people live in harmony despite their differences, or one where every day is a carnival. They imagine themselves as the characters in koan, as student and/or master. They can see any event in today's America as a koan in and of itself, promising insight when properly understood, an insight that then is expressed using koan again. Some even see writing and reading itself as Zen practice. Koan as autobiography, autobiography as koan, nonsense as essence, essence as nonsense. Endless mirrors that reflect, refract, warp, curve, and distort.

The authors I have been using as case studies in this book represent a mix of very famous Buddhist teachers (Kapleau and Suzuki), equally famous authors (Matthiessen, Van de Wetering, Ozeki), and less well-known students and teachers. Though these case studies were drawn from different periods, I have tended toward including more recently written books because the diversity of Zen autobiographical writing has increased significantly after the 1990s. I did not include any books written by practitioners outside of Japanese convert lineages, nor did I include accounts from "cradle" Zen Buddhists: individuals who were born into Zen families.[2]

In choosing this set of authors, I did not intend to reinforce the idea that convert American Zen Buddhists are somehow more authentic, genuine, serious (more *anything*, really) than cradle Buddhists or any other type of American Buddhists. Indeed, much has been done to contest earlier scholarly categories of American Buddhism as racist constructs tied up with colonialism and orientalism.[3] One example is the "Two Buddhisms" idea, which distinguishes between convert Buddhism and "ethnic" Buddhism, a division that assumes the first category is composed entirely of Caucasian Americans and the second of minority Americans.[4] Prioritizing convert American Buddhists as somehow more authentic can play into the idea that it is white men who recover original Buddhism through the investigation of its most sacred texts.[5] Often, "American Buddhism" is seen as synonymous with "pure, authentic" Buddhism but also with "democratic, progressive, philosophical" Buddhism. In other words, convert Buddhism is portrayed as good, ethnic Buddhism as bad.

As a white convert male Buddhist of sorts myself, I've gradually come to see the fault lines within this discourse of privilege, and it occurred to me that I was better placed to take it apart rather than to recover the many other histories, literary and otherwise, of American Buddhism.[6] I sought to sketch one potentially dangerous version of that ideology in chapter 1. In chapter 2, I showed how failure is one way of taking apart ideas of Zen that subtly value only some people, only some experiences. In chapter 3, I looked at how the two truths discourse can function in a manner similar to failure, and how it can be used to reinforce privilege but also to undermine it from within. And in chapters 4 and 5, I focused on more radical literary experiments, captured in terms such as fictionalization and interdependence, to show how nothing exists apart from anything else, and how becoming attached to any identity, including that of "Being a Zen Buddhist," is a big mistake.

Now, at the end of the book, I am in a position to outline its larger contributions. First, I will discuss my response to Poceski in more detail. If koan are gibberish, they nevertheless fascinate because, as meaning-making animals, we make sense of them. This is what happens when we solve a riddle. Studying koan as riddles allows us to compare them to other genres and undo the idea that koan are unique in world literature. It also explains Zen awakening as a confusion of metaphorical ordering, a boundary-crossing that allows us to see reality as it really is, chaotic and unstructured. Then, I discuss a theme that has come up several times in this book, namely that writing and reading autobiography can be a form of Zen practice, a means of awakening. Finally, I put these two elements together to examine what happens when koan are used in autobiography. When these two genres enter into dialogue with each other, they transform each other. Koan in autobiography become an American type of literature. But autobiographers who use koan to narrate their lives become living Buddhas.

KOAN AS RIDDLES

In this book, I've shown how koan can mean a great variety of things. Like a Rorschach inkblot, people read them with their own concerns in mind, and for them koan come to mean things relevant to these concerns. For Goldberg, Katagiri has to be like Deshan's teacher Longtan because that turns a very dark episode in her life into a stepping-stone to insight. Schireson reads Miaozong as a protofeminist, and this justifies her standing up to the Japanese monastic establishment. Van de Wetering sees Deshan being berated for being early for lunch and takes this as a lesson to put his ego aside. How can we account for this variety of meanings? Or, to use Poceski's wording, how do people make sense out of nonsense?

I have come to believe that interpreting a koan is very much like unriddling a riddle. In this section, I will first discuss some general properties of riddles that are relevant to examining koan. Then, I will show how only some of the properties of the classic, or "true," riddle apply to koan. This led me to think of koan as a specific subcategory of riddles, namely the "neck riddle." I conclude this section by showing what examining koan as neck riddles does for scholarship in Zen studies and comparative literature.

What is a riddle? Like so often with questions of genre, the best answer is to look at an example. Here is one: "A kettle is boiling out on the heath, without wood, without fuel."[7] Sounds epic, doesn't it? Do you know what it is? I certainly didn't when I first read it (the answer is in the endnote).[8] This riddle is an example of what scholars call a "true" riddle. Did you notice that this riddle immediately establishes a hierarchy? When you see the question by itself, you want to know the answer. The answer is known by someone, namely by the person who poses the riddle. In this case, that's me. In case you can't figure out the riddle on your own, this means that you know less than the person who riddled you. And it could then be that you want to ask them for the answer. If they won't tell you, maybe you'll buy them a beer if they tell you. See what's happening? A structure of desire and authority emerges when one person puts a riddle to another. It is at the very least "a game of knowing and not-knowing."[9]

Riddles are designed to confuse. A normal kettle cannot burn without firewood, and definitely not on the heath, because it would set the heath on fire. More specifically, riddles confuse the metaphors we live by. Let me explain. Scholars of riddles have posited that at heart, riddles are like metaphors.[10] Metaphors, which always imply a "like," such as "life is like a roller-coaster," make sense of the world and order it. This is a key insight of cognitive science, popularized in books such as *Metaphors We Live By*. That book is one of those where the title contains the argument, which is that human beings are incapable of understanding the world literally but always approach reality figuratively (and these figures of speech are rooted in the body).[11]

Here's an example. Life is this ephemeral, unfathomable thing. But once I tell you that it's like a roller-coaster, you can attribute meaning to it after thinking about it for a second. Have you ever ridden a roller-coaster? If you have, do you feel butterflies in your belly when you think of one? Do you perhaps see the faces of the friends and family who were there with you? Perhaps you taste the sugary aftertaste of the popcorn you ate beforehand? All these remembered sensations allow us to solve the mini-riddle that is posed implicitly by the metaphor. How is life like a roller-coaster? Well, it's fun and exhilarating.

That was an easy game. But riddles make up a much harder game. Instead of metaphors we live by, riddles are metaphors that kill. Anthropologists and folklorists have associated the riddle with carnival-like rituals because they upset our mind's ability to make sense of things. Imagine a kettle boiling on the heath without fuel. If you're like me, this scene quickly becomes surreal, because it is. And yet, the solution ties this imagery together. The riddle opens up the creative ability of the human mind to create meaning out of everything, and that is a vista that is as exhilarating as it is frightening: "Riddles in this sense are playfully displaced items of language, testing our competence to interpret the world around us by selectively confusing the very domains which we usually use as means of asserting order."[12]

The kettle is no longer just a household item, nor is the anthill just an annoying heap of vermin. The riddle makes both things into something extraordinary. We see things whose nature and use-value we might consider self-evident ("Ants must die! Pot for eating!") in a new way. As one scholar puts it: "Whereas stories make the strange familiar, riddles make the familiar strange; stories permit one narrator to keep charge of the situation and force the others to inactivity, whereas riddles draw all participants into highly active roles."[13] Because that's another aspect of the game: you need to think about a riddle. If you don't attempt to solve it, the riddler might never tell you the answer. You might never know!

Another thing about riddles is that they are tiny. They don't take up much space. Here's another one: "A house full, a yard full. Couldn't catch a bowl full.—Smoke."[14] Riddles are what Mikhail Bakhtin describes as a "primary genre."[15] According to Bakhtin, primary genres constitute a type of oral communication that occurs in daily life. These genres can be incorporated into larger wholes like novels, dramatic plays, epic poems, and so on, which then constitute secondary genres.

That's simple enough, and it explains how riddles are always part of larger narratives or riddle collections. But, when two genres interact, things can get really complicated. We saw an example of that in chapter 1, where koan, as a primary genre, took over the larger secondary genre, a book introducing Zen Buddhism, that they were integrated within. When koan integrate with autobiographies, however, something marvelous happens that I only came to realize quite late in writing this book. Koan transform autobiographies, but autobiographies also transform koan. I mentioned this insight at the very beginning of the book, but only now, at the end of it, will I be able to substantiate it. So stay with me for a little longer.

Riddles are time beings, but time in these texts is different from time in autobiographical narratives. Time in autobiography is largely linear (OK, Ozeki contests this, but she can contest it because it's such a commonsensical idea): though an autobiographical narrative might jump back and forth in time (flashbacks and flashforwards, something very elaborate in *The Great*

Failure), within a single time slot (say, Van de Wetering seeking admission to Daitokuji), time progresses the way it does in our world. This is a very basic narratological understanding of how stories work, namely that they put events next to each other and proceed to narrate these events in sequential order.[16]

Riddles, however, are different. Time does not progress in a riddle: a question is posed, and that question waits for an answer. It could wait eternally; it does not matter. The question is always just being posed to the reader or is already solved by the reader. Although the perspective through which we approach the riddle can be different, the riddle itself knows no conventional progression in time.[17] That is not to say that reading or speaking the riddle doesn't take time; it does. But unlike narrative, where there's gradual progression and development, in a riddle there is only a before and after: before it is solved and after it is solved.

Now how are koan riddles? Let's do the easy bits first: like riddles, koan integrate easily into larger texts. They establish a hierarchy between a student and a master. They make those who don't know work for a solution. And now for the harder part: like riddles, koan confuse our metaphorical categories in ways that allow us to rethink Zen enlightenment, at least those enlightenment experiences that are the result of koan practice. When Linji compares the True Man without rank to a shitstick, he upsets categories that were ingrained in his audience. He kills the metaphors they live by because he compares the most sacred goal to what you do in the toilet. And from exactly that confusion, we can glimpse the true nature of the world, which is a complete inchoate void without any meaning whatsoever, a ruthlessness. Seeing that makes everything we believe in seem only for the time being. We are released into a world that no longer is all-important, because, like Neo in the science fiction film *The Matrix*, we now see that it's a made-up world.

That vision of the world does not just encompass all of space, but it also encompasses all of time. When we stand face-to-face with Joshu, we are no longer in a realm of linear temporality but have entered a place that, enclosed within itself, lasts forever. Joshu can repeat "Mu" endlessly, and this is exactly what people meditating on the koan do. People like Matthiessen, Kapleau, Chadwick, Van de Wetering, and so many others throughout Zen's long history.

There are some problems with this account of koan though. I just compared koan to the "true form" of the riddle. A true riddle typically contains its answer, and its answer is, as can be seen in the kettle and smoke examples, a banal object that is made extraordinary in the riddling description. This answer can usually be guessed by a participant.[18] But koan are not like this. They are the inverse: they often use the banal (for example, a shitstick, a dog, a cat, a tree) to point to the extraordinary. Moreover, koan never contain their answer, and they do not typically allow us to derive the answer using any kind of reasoning.

Koan, then, are not true riddles. Instead, I propose that they are neck riddles. Again, an example of the neck riddle is good to start with:

> There was a man convicted of having stolen a sheep; he was sentenced to death, but the magistrates said he could go free if he could ask a riddle they could not answer, and he was liberated for three days so that he might invent one. As he went out of prison he saw a horse's skull by the roadside. Returning to prison on the third day in despair he noticed that in it was a bird's nest with six young ones, and he thought of the following riddle:
>
> As I walked out,
> As I walked out,
> From the dead I saw the living spring.
> Blessed may Christ Jesu be
> For the six have set the seventh free.[19]

The "seventh" here is of course the man convicted. What is typical of the neck riddle here is that there is no way to logically solve it: the only way the magistrates in the story could have solved the riddle would be to see exactly the same thing as the man did. You need information that is not given; you need to enter the mind of the person who created the neck riddle to solve it.

Neck riddles are quite old and have several striking features. As their name implies, they describe a life-or-death scenario. One scholar has proposed that this is indeed where they originate, in the premodern judicial scenario of a test of wits, some traces of which can be found in indigenous societies today.[20] But death is not just a feature of the story within which the riddle appears; it is also deeply embedded in the content of the riddle itself. Look again at the riddle above: it encodes a kind of life from death in the horse's skull that becomes a nest for small birds. No wonder Jesus, who rose from the dead as well, is mentioned! The life-from-death scenario is thus present on several levels of this deceivingly simple text.

Neck riddles do not just violate the boundary between life and death. They also often portray other types of transgressive actions, such as incestuous sexuality and humans turning into animals. In the example above, the phrase "For the six have set the seventh free" implicitly equates the prisoner with the young birds and thus temporarily abolishes the boundary between the human and the animal.

But where's the incest, you might wonder? Well, that theme is quite prominent in the frame story of the most famous of all neck riddles, Oedipus's encounter with the Sphinx in Sophocles's *Oedipus Rex*.[21] The story is as follows: the Sphinx, a monster that plagues the city of Thebes, asks everyone it meets the following question: "What kind of animal is it that stands on four legs in the morning, two in the day, and three in the evening?" When people give the wrong answer, it eats them. Only Oedipus answers correctly, that the animal in question is the human being, which crawls in infancy, then walks, and then requires a walking stick. This answer makes the Sphinx kill itself. As you probably know, the story doesn't end happily for Oedipus either: he will later discover that he killed his father and married his mother. He then gouges out his eyeballs.

In addition to the themes of incest and death, which are fairly clear, note that the Sphinx asks about an "animal," thereby again questioning the anthropocentric distinction between humans and animals. Questioning the distinction is the Sphinx, which is itself a human-animal mix.[22]

Finally, note the structure of the neck riddle. It consists of two parts, namely the riddle itself, and its solution, in the form of an oral or folk tale. The neck riddle is thus a hybrid of two (primary) genres. This has significant consequences for the contents of neck riddles. As we saw earlier, riddles are in principle atemporal: time does not progress. But in the framing story, time of course does progress: the criminal is arrested, the magistrates determine his punishment, and he gains his freedom by making up an unsolvable riddle. One scholar has seen this confrontation of two types of temporalities as essential to the neck riddle. It's because these two—fundamentally incompatible—time frames clash, that the neck riddle thematizes randomness (remember the horse skull coincidentally encountered by the prisoner) and contingency.[23]

CONCLUSION · 169

Koan are a type of neck riddle. It was Van de Wetering who gave me a clue in this direction. In *Afterzen*, he defined koan as "riddles that are deliberately phrased obscurely. There are pieces missing."[24] This is a perfect description of how neck riddles usually work: you can't figure the riddle out on your own, and you're not meant to.

Like neck riddles, koan were born from an environment of testing and examination. Etymologically, the Chinese means "[cases on the] table of the [legal] magistrate" (*gongan*).[25] It is well attested that in koan Zen masters saw themselves sitting in judgment of the achievement of students, much like a Chinese magistrate was authorized to judge the merits of a particular individual in a legal case.

But there's more. Analyzing koan as neck riddles also explains why koan can be so shocking, why there's all this stuff about killing cats and murdering Buddhas and perfect people being like shitsticks. Koan differ from neck riddles in that they do not necessarily involve incestuous sex, transformation into animals, or violent death (although there are famous examples to be found of the latter two instances),[26] but koan are similar in that they articulate something usually called "unspeakable," which is exactly what a taboo is. Koan cross boundaries, they confuse us, and thus force us to face this unspeakable. And, by solving the riddle, we might turn death into life. Remember the koan that *Afterzen*'s Bobbie tried to solve, the koan where you're hanging by your teeth from a tree, a tiger is growling below, and some oaf comes along and asks you about the meaning of Buddhism? That's a neck riddle. The stakes are high. A koan promises to set us free.

You might object that koan are unlike the neck riddle in that they do not require us to enter someone else's mind. But this seems to be what Mumon, the compiler of the *Mumonkan*, thought.[27] Numerous comments in that koan collection attest to the idea that to understand a koan is to meet the patriarchs face-to-face, to breathe the same air, and to become one with them. The Zen Buddhists I study in this book do exactly that, but they do it by exploring their own mind. Ultimately, what they are looking for is the mind of the patriarchs within themselves, and when they find that mind, they solve the koan. That mind, of course, never was someone else's. It was always ours. The Zen masters just borrowed it for a while.

I've thus far mainly focused on the "riddle" part of koan. But, like the neck riddle, koan, as they appear in autobiographies, have two parts. One is the riddle itself ("Mu"), the other is the frame story: "A student asked

Joshu..." The Zen tradition itself was well aware of this, separating between the so-called *huatou* of a koan (which is what Rinzai adherents focused upon in meditation) and the remainder of the narrative.[28] However, unlike the neck riddle, the frame story does not provide a solution. So, what *does* it do?

In the autobiographies I've surveyed, the narrative (which, like the neck riddle, is indeed sometimes a folk narrative; think of the tragic story of the woman Qian as cited by Manuel) leading up to the koan is at least as important as the riddle itself. Whereas focusing on the riddle leads to people having transformative experiences, focusing on the background story allows these authors to humanize the patriarchs: these guys are just like us. I've argued elsewhere that koan can do this because their background stories contain so few details, making them easily adaptable to any time and place. In imagining the characters of koan, we fill in our personal details as if we were modifying a template.[29] This is what happens when Schireson sees Miaozong as a feminist in a patriarchal environment, or when Goldberg sees herself in a similar situation as Deshan. Though koan therefore are different from the neck riddle in that the function of the frame story is different (it doesn't give away the solution), like the neck riddle they consist of two parts that can be characterized as a story and the riddle itself.

So, to conclude this section: koan are riddles. They are riddles in that they establish a hierarchy between the riddler and the riddled. They are riddles in that they kill the metaphors we live by and awaken us to the truth that our perception of the world is constructed. They are riddles in that they require our active participation. They are riddles in that they are a primary genre that integrates with larger texts. They are riddles in that they portray a different time, an eternal time where Joshu is always waiting for us to answer his question, or where we always have known the answer.

Koan are neck riddles. They consist of a framing story and an unsolvable riddle. They originate within a legal context. They portray a matter of (spiritual) life and death. They are transgressive, discussing how humans change into animals and how we should kill the Buddha when we meet him. They require us to get into the head of the riddler.

Why does this matter? By examining koan as "neck riddles," scholars of religious literature gain a valuable tool for comparing koan to other texts. This is significant because it challenges the common assumption among riddle scholars that koan are incomparable in nature.[30] Some of these scholars argue that koan are not riddles because they are about enlightenment, others that koan are not riddles because their answers are memorized in advance.³¹ Both these viewpoints are based on partial understandings of koan. First, to maintain "enlightenment" as an impenetrable category is to also maintain the Suzuki-like mystique of Zen as incomprehensible to analysis. It is to uncritically accept claims that Zen is completely unique among world religions. Second, though there exist koan manuals allowing memorization, it's not clear to me how that disqualifies us from discussing them as riddles, which often originate in oral traditions that rely deeply on memorization. In short, the exclusion of koan in discussions of riddles as world literature is unjustified and holds back our understanding of these texts. By showing how koan operate in one specific set of contemporary texts, I have hoped to demonstrate the promising directions for future comparative scholarship.

In arguing that koan are neck riddles, I also aimed to answer Poceski's provocative idea that koan are nonsense. They are nonsense, but a special kind of nonsense, a nonsense that bears in it the promise of meaning, a deep meaning that will change the way we see ourselves and the world. This promise is conveyed through generic conventions that cast koan as containers of wisdom. If we were unfamiliar with these conventions, koan would indeed be nonsense, but when we're familiar with the genre—as all authors discussed in this book are—we try to solve them. There are two ways Zen autobiographers solve a koan: either they focus on solving the riddle part of the neck riddle ("Mu"), or they identify with one or more of the characters within the background story (Joshu, the anonymous student, the old lady selling sweets, and so on). These two ways of interfacing with koan are, of course, not exclusive. Matthiessen claims satori through Mu, but he also imagines Soen as Bodhidharma.

A little more on the force of genre, since that will be important in the next section as well. Genre is "a form of symbolic action: the generic organization of language, images, gestures, and sound makes things happen by actively shaping the way we understand the world.... [F]ar from being merely 'stylistic' devices, genres create effects of reality and truth, authority and plausibility, which are central to the different ways the world is understood in the writing of history or of philosophy or of science, or in painting, or in everyday talk."³² According to this definition, genre is a force that shapes its own interpretations. We read something, such as "Make America Great Again," and almost without thinking we attribute meaning to it: this is the campaign slogan for Donald Trump; the "again" refers to the assumption that the Obama administration put the United States in bad shape; "make" presupposes the president has some kind of power that trumps larger historical factors, etc. In the interpretation of this slogan, genre has acted; the text has determined its own interpretative framework. That does not mean misreading is impossible: someone unfamiliar with contemporary American politics might take the slogan to be bad poetry, or a socialist call for the working classes of the American continent to unite. Likewise, someone completely unfamiliar with koan can look at any sample and declare that it doesn't make any sense. Someone who doesn't buy into the generic framing that promises insight might come to the same conclusion.

REWRITING AND REREADING THE SELF

In the previous section of this conclusion, I've given a fresh answer to what koan are. In this section, I want to return to the matter of what autobiography is. As mentioned in the introduction, autobiography is usually conceived of either as writing down a self that preexists it (recording a preexisting self) or as calling that self into existence (the more progressive and theoretically advanced viewpoint). But as I will now show, autobiography can also be the destruction of a self. This discussion of autobiography as an unwriting will set the stage for my analysis of what happens when autobiography and koan are put in dialogue with each other. I will ultimately show that koan and autobiography mutually transform each other, with koan becoming a modern American genre, and American autobiographers becoming like the patriarchs of koan.

As I mentioned in the introduction, John Barbour has described how Buddhist travel narratives unmake a self. At the end of his book, he claims that autobiography can do this to both writer and reader.[33] I, too, have come to see literature as having that power. I see the potential of writing and reading to rewire our thinking in the way Jeffrey Kripal does, namely as a means of becoming free of cultural scripts. Trying to explain why so many of his readers write to him saying his books caused them to have strange experiences, Kripal says that sometimes

> writing and reading become, in effect, paranormal powers capable of freeing us from our deeply inscripted beliefs and assumptions, be these

cultural, religious, or intellectual. We rely on these cultural scripts and languages to become human, self-reflexive, and social. But some of us also grow weary or suspicious of this scripting. We see its dark and dangerous sides. We sometimes write and read, then, to not be so completely written and read. We write to balk against our script, as Philip K. Dick came to understand his writing practice after his own experience of Valis, his name for the cosmic mind at the back of the movie theater.[34]

Kripal suspects that this is the case because his whole work as a scholar has been to expand the range of what we consider reality. He does this, for example, by taking seriously accounts of UFO abductions, often dismissed by scholars as delusional fantasies. In other works he has seen near-death experiences as disclosing one aspect of reality, and so on. Whatever you think of the value of these claims, Kripal's prose expands the realm of the possible, and so readers begin to see the world in a—sometimes startlingly—different way.

In surveying the autobiographical production of convert Zen, there's a growing awareness of the strange effects that writing and reading have, effects that can involve a rewiring of who we are. Here is one story. A Zen student experiences an awakening during an intensive practice period. So far so good. But he still isn't sure of some stuff, doesn't understand reincarnation. His teacher won't answer his questions, and he is told instead to read the letters on the topic in *The Three Pillars of Zen*: "And one day I was reading one of these letters in a car going to work—I was in a car pool, and my office was about an hour from the Zen Center—and a powerful opening occurred right in the car, much more powerful than the first. One phrase triggered it, and all my questions were resolved."[35] This is the account of Zen master Bernie Glassman, one of Matthiessen's teachers. His second awakening takes place while reading Kapleau's book, during a car ride to work.

What this means is that outside of any ritual context, literature can still produce extraordinary experiences. Kapleau himself, incidentally, was aware of the effects reading could produce. Unlike Robert Aitken, who refused to conduct *sanzen* in his personal correspondence, Kapleau's correspondence contains multiple letters attesting to such interactions.[36] In them, Kapleau both approves answers to koan and denies them, sometimes adding the sound of the *sanzen* bell: "ding-a-ling, ding-a-ling! Sorry but you've missed it!"[37]

Some Zen practitioners are extremely clear that writing and reading autobiography are pathways to insight. Ozeki saw *A Tale* as a commentary on

Dogen, as "performed philosophy," and as conveying the idea that our identity is just another narrative. She brings this idea to life by inserting someone like herself (but not exactly herself) in *A Tale*, and by disseminating elements from her own life story across the novel's characters. Nao's insistence in addressing the reader of *A Tale* in the second person ("you") makes her speak directly to us. In the process, we can wonder how different we really are from Nao. Are we fictions as well? Is Nao real? *The Face* similarly recasts readers and writers as putting on masks. In the end, we are invited to dissolve our everyday identity in these books, to play with the ideas we hold about ourselves. As Nao tells us from the beginning, "You wonder about me. I wonder about you."[38] Ozeki's books make us wonder about ourselves.

Likewise, in *Afterzen* Van de Wetering saw himself reflected in all characters of his autobiography. He undermines the idea that autobiography should be about a "real" person, and he does so by freely changing facts into fiction, and koan into his own stories. By carnivalizing Zen masters, he is out to shock his readers so they won't take themselves so seriously.

But the first example of approaching life writing as a form of Zen practice was Goldberg, who saw *The Great Failure* as a way of hitting rock bottom, a way of abandoning previously held notions about herself, her teacher, and her community. What frames this dark night of the soul is a series of koan that show how darkness can lead to great insight. Like Goldberg, Haubner saw narrating his story as a way to turn himself into both the protagonist and the antagonist of his narrative, to see himself split again and again until he burst open the shell of his phallic being and solved the koan that is his male body.

AMERICAN KOAN

In arguing that koan are riddles without a solution, and in showing that autobiography can deconstruct as well as construct a self, I arrive at the final point I want to make in this book, which is that when koan appear in American autobiographies, these East Asian riddles become a type of American literature. Conversely, their American authors are transformed into living Buddhas. Koan and autobiography change each other.

The first point of this proposition, how koan become American, is perhaps the most straightforward. We've seen throughout this book how

American Zen Buddhists treat koan as mirrors for their own lives. That does not mean that these mirrors reflect in a clear, straightforward manner. They can also distort, twist, and invert the image of what is in front of them. But always these authors bring their ideas and concerns and teachers to their readings of koan, asking the mirror on the wall who or what they are.

This questioning of the self through koan is given literary form by extracting koan from classical texts and inserting them into that most modern of genres, the life narrative, whether it takes the form of a Zen manual, novel, or memoir. That extraction focuses not on the elaborate commentaries and verses that accompanied koan in those texts but on the "encounter dialogues," the interactions between masters and teachers. All this is something new. No premodern Zen authors that I can think of bring their own lives into dialogue with koan to the extent that the people discussed in this book do. For them, koan both symbolize and hold the answers to any problem they encounter, however mundane it may be. This is everyday Zen.

The completion of this process is when American Buddhists start writing their own koan, like Janwillem and Jim, like Nao and Jiko, like Haubner and Sasaki, like Manuel and Mustafa. This has led to a new type of koan collection that is "made in America." An example is Sean Murphy's edited volume *One Bird, One Stone: 108 Contemporary Zen Stories*. The volume contains koan featuring Kapleau, Fischer, Goldberg, and many others we have met. In his foreword to the book, Zen master John Daido Loori cites Joshu's Mu, and how this koan was incorporated in Mumen's *Mumonkan*. He sees Murphy, his student, as continuing this tradition of collecting stories that are characterized by "timelessness" and "immense potential," hoping that they will once function the same way Joshu's words do, guiding practitioners to insight.[39] In many ways, Murphy is indeed repeating a well-known koan origin myth: he is a student collecting and writing down anecdotes from masters who, because they're floating too far beyond "words and letters," can't or won't do it themselves. For example, when he meets Nowick on his nationwide travels, the latter gruffly interrogates him: "Now, what's all this book business you want to talk to me about? . . . As you may have heard, I'm not very big on books."[40]

Yet while Murphy's quest resembles how anonymous students supposedly gathered the feats of their awesome teachers, he is also doing much of what the authors discussed in the present volume do: he frames these koan within thematic (and roughly chronologically organized) chapters that are sprinkled with details from his own Zen journey. If Daido Loori is right then, future generations of practitioners will be working with koan that feature

American teachers and that are contained within the larger story of a personal journey. In short, they will be practicing with American koan.

But what about the other part of this mutual transformation, the part about authors and readers becoming living Buddhas? Sure, Zen masters like Kapleau lay claim to this title, but what about all the other people discussed here? Did Van de Wetering really think he was a living Buddha? Does David Chadwick?

Let's start with the observation that, in commenting on koan, every one of these authors assumes a role that is traditionally reserved for a Zen master. They thus effectively act as living Buddhas. Remember the legal context of koan: Zen masters were deemed to sit in judgment of a "case," and in East Asian koan collections, this meant that their comments were a demonstration of their mastery. Often, these classic commentaries are so incomprehensible that they are riddles in themselves, which of course demonstrates how much these masters are not attached to words and letters.

Certainly, none of the writers I discussed in this book (except for Suzuki) revel in purposely enigmatic comments. They use a familiar language, that of personal experience, to express what they have seen. Yet, as we first saw with Matthiessen, what they say remains hard to access for those of us who have not had these experiences. The language of experience is stretched to give voice to that which they claim lies beyond language, and in doing so, they speak like Zen masters do.

Narratives of Zen that do not feature enlightenment, like *The Empty Mirror* or *Thank You and OK!*, are easier to access. But this does not prevent Van de Wetering and Chadwick from commenting on koan. They can do so because koan, as they appear in these narratives, have two parts: the riddle and the background story. This is how Greenwood can claim enlightenment is a male fantasy and still imagine herself as a tea lady by the side of the road hitting monks over the head. In commenting on koan, all these autobiographers, however humble they are, implicitly assume the role of Zen master, of living Buddha. No wonder Janwillem is called "Jan-Buddha" by Roshi.

Now let's talk again about time. When koan are incorporated into autobiographical narratives, their "riddle" component encodes a notion of time that is different from narrative time. Narrative time happily progresses linearly: in Haubner's and Goldberg's books, the scandals are gradually revealed. In Kapleau's diary, he moves from ignorance to enlightenment. Time within the riddle component, however, does not progress at all: it only has two modes, namely "not solved" or "already solved." When a Zen autobiographer claims to understand a koan, they enter this eternal time frame. They are no longer just Philip Kapleau or Grace Schireson. Instead, they are iterations of eternal Buddhahood.

The riddle waits, and waits forever. Some pass through its doors and are gone. Some wait their entire lives, but in waiting, they imagine themselves as the patriarchs. They put on their mask and see the world through their eyes. They can do this because the background story of koan gives them Buddhahood anyway. Their sparse details allow them to project their own lives onto those of the patriarchs, becoming of one mind with them. Through the gate of riddle or the gate of story, there is no barrier to American autobiographers imagining themselves as Buddhas, and all of them do.

And so can we: as readers of these books, we can enter eternity and claim Buddhahood as well. As Ozeki describes at the end of *The Face*, what happens when we read is that we put on a mask, we explore the world from a new perspective. When I read *The Empty Mirror* for the first time, Janwillem's struggles with the pain of meditation were very vivid to me as someone who struggled with sitting in lotus position all his life. But Nao's struggles were equally real to me, even though what happens in her narrative should be impossible. We are in this with the author, and in these books it is we who are being unwritten as well, who are being transformed into the beings that appear within koan, who are wondering why the hell Nansen killed the cat, and who are tearing the animal apart while waiting for Joshu to arrive.

CODA

In medieval China, Buddhist writers wrought monumental changes to their religion. They made certain obscure teachers with a relatively small following into living Buddhas directly connected to Shakyamuni. These living Buddhas embodied complete freedom, a liberation from the chains of thought and language. Dead in fact (and in some cases never having existed in the first place), these Buddhas live on in koan, in the minds of readers eager to explore who they are.

Many things separate modern-day Americans from the patriarchs of old and the authors who invented them. But today Zen Buddhists still turn to these teachers for insight. In doing so, they bring concerns specific to their place and time to these age-old riddles, and in doing so, they transform these riddles as much as these riddles transform them. When they write down the stories of their lives, they—sometimes unconsciously but nevertheless inevitably—transform themselves into living Buddhas as well. Their stories teach the teaching without words and letters with every sentence they write. And in reading them, we become living Buddhas as well. In this writing and reading, koan become American.

Back in 1967, when Kapleau introduced his collection of eight autobiographies, he thought it was no coincidence that most of the samples described the lives of Americans: "In Zen's emphasis on self-reliance, in its clear awareness of the dangers of intellectualism, in its empirical appeal to personal experience and not philosophic speculation as the means of verifying ultimate truth, in its pragmatic concern with mind and suffering, and in its direct, practical methods for body-mind emancipation, Americans find much that is congenial to their native temperament, their historical conditioning, and their particular *Weltanschauung*."[41] In the "updated and revised" thirty-fifth anniversary edition, this passage is absent. I can only speculate that Kapleau thought that this statement, which could be taken as an expression of American exceptionalism, would alienate his by-then global audiences. Surely, there is much here we can disagree with. But Kapleau was right about one thing: Zen would thrive in America, and Americans would make its literature their own.

Kapleau followed his assertion of the compatibility of the American worldview with Zen with a short but dire picture of the challenges ahead. He firmly believed that Zen would give hope in the face of global unrest, of the endless suffering that went on in his day as it continues in ours. Enlightenment allows us to discover who we are but also to see how we are connected with everything else. In the end, I find it impossible to be cynical about this vision of a world where we can sit down and meet Bodhidharma face-to-face. And in that face, we see everything all at once.

NOTES

PREFACE

1. Sekida, *Two Zen Classics*, 58.
2. Sekida, *Two Zen Classics*, 58–59.

INTRODUCTION

1. Matthiessen, *Nine-Headed Dragon River*, 3–4.
2. Matthiessen, *Nine-Headed Dragon River*, 10.
3. To be entirely accurate, koan are used in the curriculum of the Rinzai sect of the Zen school. Whereas the other main sect of Zen, Soto, has historically refrained from using koan as a focus for meditation, koan nevertheless appear quite often in the writings of Dogen, the most famous Japanese Soto master. In the twentieth century, as Zen became more syncretic, koan appear even more often in Soto training. The famous Soto teacher Shunryu Suzuki uses koan quite often in his recorded speeches, and the Soto students discussed in this book often draw upon koan in their writing.
4. McRae, "The Antecedents of Encounter Dialogue," 46; Buswell, *The Zen Monastic Experience*, 5.
5. For the debate on what to call Zen (a school, sect, etc.), see Weinstein, "Buddhism, Schools of: Chinese Buddhism"; Welter, "The Problem with Orthodoxy"; Foulk, "The Ch'an Tsung in Medieval China"; McRae, "Buddhism, Schools of: Chinese Buddhism"; and Yu, "Revisiting the Notion of Zong."
6. Poceski, *The Records of Mazu*, 25.

7. Cole, *Patriarchs on Paper*, 284. A similar proposal is to see Chan as an "imaginary construct" based on biographical literature (Foulk, "'Authentic,'" 466).
8. Hori, *Zen Sand*.
9. Schlütter, *How Zen Became Zen*.
10. Welter, *The Linji Lu*, 109–30.
11. Poceski, *The Records of Mazu*.
12. Faure, "Bodhidharma as Textual and Religious Paradigm."
13. McRae, *Seeing through Zen*, xix.
14. McRae, *Seeing through Zen*.
15. Heine, *Zen Skin, Zen Marrow*.
16. Bocking, "Mysticism: No Experience Necessary?"; Sharf, "The Zen of Japanese Nationalism"; Sharf, "Buddhism Modernism"; Sharf, "The Rhetoric of Experience."
17. Sharf, "Sanbōkyōdan"; Sharf, "Ritual."
18. Sharf, "Buddhism Modernism," 268.
19. Matthiessen, *Nine-Headed Dragon River*, 21.
20. The scholarship is too massive to survey here. For an overview of the debate, see Martin and McCutcheon, *Religious Experience*.
21. Kripal, *Secret Body*, 122–23.
22. Nicholls, *John Cage*; Larson, *Where the Heart Beats*; Haskins, "Aspects of Zen Buddhism."
23. Quli, "Western Self, Asian Other," 3.
24. Quli, "Western Self, Asian Other," 15.
25. Braun, *The Birth of Insight*; Sharf, "Is Mindfulness Buddhist?"; McMahan and Braun, *Meditation, Buddhism, and Science*.
26. McMahan, *The Making of Buddhist Modernism*.
27. McMahan, *The Making of Buddhist Modernism*, 18–20.
28. Wilson, *Mindful America*.
29. Gleig, *American Dharma*, 278.
30. Stalling, *Poetics of Emptiness*.
31. Garton-Gundling, *Enlightened Individualism*.
32. Whalen-Bridge and Storhoff, *The Emergence of Buddhist American Literature*, 3.
33. Eakin, *How Our Lives Become Stories*, 98.
34. Smith and Watson, *Reading Autobiography*, 47.
35. Eakin, *How Our Lives Become Stories*, 101.
36. Butler, *Giving an Account of Oneself*; Eakin, *How Our Lives Become Stories*; Lionnet, *Postcolonial Representations*.
37. Jacoby, *Love and Liberation*.
38. Baroni, *Love, Rōshi*.

39. Baroni, *Love, Rōshi*, 15.
40. Schedneck, "Buddhist Life Stories"; Schedneck, "Constructions of Buddhism"; Schedneck, "Transcending Gender"; Schedneck, "The Promise of the Universal."
41. Barbour, *Journeys of Transformation*, 2.
42. Barbour, *Journeys of Transformation*, 307.
43. Jonathan Z. Smith, "Interview with J. Z. Smith," interview by Sinhababu.
44. Ferns, *Narrating Utopia*.
45. Ferns, *Narrating Utopia*, 31–66.
46. Iwamura, *Virtual Orientalism: Asian Religions and American Popular Culture*, 6.
47. Matthiessen, *Nine-Headed Dragon River*, 135.
48. Oppenheimer, "The Zen Predator."
49. Matthiessen, *Nine-Headed Dragon River*, 61.
50. Matthiessen, *Nine-Headed Dragon River*, 63–64.
51. App, *The Birth of Orientalism*, xvi.
52. McNicholl, "Being Buddha, Staying Woke," 886.
53. I don't want to make fargoing historical claims about the validity of this observation except to note that a recent book has made a similar claim for early Zen in China, that it was all about visualization (and even dream interpretation) (see Greene, *Chan before Chan*). I myself have claimed that Song dynasty usage of koan was aimed at visualizing lineage ancestors (see Van Overmeire, "Reading Chan Encounter Dialogue"). There seems to be an increasing interest in this topic, as a recent NEH seminar titled "Buddhism and the Imagination" demonstrates. The Zen priest Norman Fischer recently published a book about the imagination and utopian thinking connected with the bodhisattva vows (see Fischer, *The World Could Be Otherwise*).
54. Mitchell, *Buddhism in America*, 63–65.
55. Gleig, *American Dharma*, 34–49.
56. Smith and Watson, *Reading Autobiography*, 3.
57. Smith and Watson, *Reading Autobiography*, 225n4.2.
58. Smith and Watson, *Reading Autobiography*, 3.
59. Good starting points are McRae, "The Antecedents of Encounter Dialogue"; Foulk, "The Form and Function"; Broughton, "Chan Literature"; and Schlütter, "Rhetoric in the Platform Sūtra," 66–70.
60. Kripal, *Secret Body*, 4.

1. ENLIGHTENMENT

1. Fields, *How the Swans Came to the Lake*, 195.
2. De Martino, "On My First Coming," 71.
3. Kapleau, *Zen: Dawn in the West*, 263.
4. Kapleau, *Zen: Dawn in the West*, 263.
5. De Martino, "On My First Coming," 72.
6. Suzuki, Fromm, and De Martino, *Zen Buddhism & Psychoanalysis*; Harrington, "Zen, Suzuki, and the Art of Psychotherapy."
7. Kraft, *Zen Teaching, Zen Practice*.
8. Kapleau, *The Three Pillars of Zen* (2000), 382–83.
9. Kapleau, *The Three Pillars of Zen* (2000), 388.
10. Currently, the best place to start an exploration of Suzuki and his heritage is in Richard Jaffe's introductions to recent republications of Suzuki's work: Suzuki, *Zen and Japanese Culture*; and Suzuki, *Selected Works*. Additionally, a recent edited volume, to which I also contributed, contains a representative diversity of opinions: Breen, Sueki, and Yamada, *Beyond Zen*.
11. Fields, *How the Swans Came to the Lake*, 128.
12. Suzuki, "Early Memories," 208–10.
13. Snodgrass, "Publishing Eastern Buddhism," 59–61.
14. This focus on texts and the past continues to determine scholarship on Buddhism today (see Schopen, "Archaeology and Protestant Presuppositions"; and Quli, "Western Self, Asian Other"). Moreover, as we have seen in the introduction, the persistent operation of orientalism prevents scholars of Buddhism from taking American Buddhism seriously.
15. Snodgrass, "Publishing Eastern Buddhism," 49–52.
16. Snodgrass, "Publishing Eastern Buddhism," 62–63.
17. Suzuki, *An Introduction to Zen Buddhism*, 2.
18. Suzuki, *An Introduction to Zen Buddhism*, 6.
19. Sharf, "Buddhism Modernism."
20. Suzuki, Fromm, and De Martino, *Zen Buddhism & Psychoanalysis*, 11.
21. Snodgrass, "Publishing Eastern Buddhism," 63.
22. Sharf, "The Zen of Japanese Nationalism."
23. Schlütter, *How Zen Became Zen*.
24. Suzuki, *An Introduction to Zen Buddhism*, 81.
25. Suzuki, *An Introduction to Zen Buddhism*, 7.
26. Suzuki, *An Introduction to Zen Buddhism*, 72.
27. Suzuki, *An Introduction to Zen Buddhism*, 73–74.

28. Suzuki, *An Introduction to Zen Buddhism*, 78.
29. Suzuki, *An Introduction to Zen Buddhism*, 75.
30. Suzuki, *An Introduction to Zen Buddhism*, 19.
31. Suzuki, *An Introduction to Zen Buddhism*, 21.
32. Corey, *Leviathan Wakes*, 311.
33. Dällenbach, *Mirror in the Text*, 43.
34. Suzuki, *An Introduction to Zen Buddhism*, 59–60.
35. Suzuki, *An Introduction to Zen Buddhism*, 58.
36. Suzuki, *An Introduction to Zen Buddhism*, 62.
37. Suzuki, *An Introduction to Zen Buddhism*, 88. Though Suzuki is talking about a monastery, it is clear that his audience also took him to be speaking about temples that had practitioners connected to them. For example, Kapleau will call Engakuji "Engaku monastery" in the next section, whereas the "ji" character indicates that it is a temple.
38. Suzuki, *An Introduction to Zen Buddhism*, 94.
39. Suzuki, *An Introduction to Zen Buddhism*, 100–101.
40. Suzuki, *An Introduction to Zen Buddhism*, 90.
41. Suzuki, *An Introduction to Zen Buddhism*, 88, 93.
42. Foulk, "Myth, Ritual, and Monastic Practice," 156–57; Poceski, "Monastic Innovator, Iconoclast, and Teacher," 15–20.
43. Suzuki, *An Introduction to Zen Buddhism*, 97–99.
44. Suzuki, *An Introduction to Zen Buddhism*, 91, 93.
45. Suzuki, *An Introduction to Zen Buddhism*, 93.
46. Suzuki, *An Introduction to Zen Buddhism*, 93.
47. Suzuki, *An Introduction to Zen Buddhism*, 93.
48. Suzuki, *An Introduction to Zen Buddhism*, 102.
49. Kapleau, *The Three Pillars of Zen* (1967), 189.
50. Kapleau, *The Three Pillars of Zen* (1967), 189.
51. Kapleau, *The Three Pillars of Zen* (1967), 191. Kapleau here quotes the biblical book of Isaiah, demonstrating that, like Suzuki, he believes that Zen experience is accessible to seekers from any religious affiliation.
52. Kapleau, *The Three Pillars of Zen* (1967), 208. Kapleau frequently uses ellipses in his diary. When I have added ellipses to quotations in his book, I indicate this using square brackets.
53. Kapleau, *The Three Pillars of Zen* (1967), 208.
54. Kapleau, *The Three Pillars of Zen* (1967), 209.
55. Kapleau, *The Three Pillars of Zen* (1967), 210. Suzuki's statement disparaging real monasteries in Japan shows how the monastic life portrayed in *An Introduction* was meant to depict what Zen ideally would be like, not what it

was like in reality. But this was consistently misunderstood by his readers, who departed to Japan in search of the experience and space portrayed in Suzuki's work.

56. Kapleau, *The Three Pillars of Zen* (1967), 210.
57. Kapleau, *The Three Pillars of Zen* (1967), 211–12.
58. Kapleau, *The Three Pillars of Zen* (1967), 212.
59. Kapleau, *The Three Pillars of Zen* (1967), 212.
60. Kapleau, *The Three Pillars of Zen* (1967), 65.
61. Kapleau, *The Three Pillars of Zen* (1967), 219.
62. Kapleau, *The Three Pillars of Zen* (1967), 222.
63. Kapleau, *The Three Pillars of Zen* (1967), 224.
64. Kapleau, *The Three Pillars of Zen* (1967), 222.
65. Sharf, "Sanbōkyōdan."
66. Kapleau, *The Three Pillars of Zen* (1967), 224–25.
67. Yasutani, "Letter to Jean Kapleau," November 9, 1957.
68. Kapleau, *The Three Pillars of Zen* (1967), 227–28.
69. Kapleau, *The Three Pillars of Zen* (1967), 228.
70. Kapleau, *Zen: Dawn in the West*, 267.
71. Kapleau, "Letter to Ann Kahl," February 11, 1992.
72. Kapleau, "Letter to Jim Kupecz," September 28, 1994.
73. Kapleau, "Letter to Jim Kupecz," September 28, 1994.
74. Brooke Schedneck has made a similar point for individuals traveling to Thailand to practice: their autobiographical narratives also demonstrate how much idealized presuppositions about Buddhism determine individual experiences (Schedneck, "Constructions of Buddhism").
75. Sharf, "Sanbōkyōdan."
76. Faure, *Chan Insights and Oversights*; Sharf, "The Zen of Japanese Nationalism"; Sharf, "Buddhism Modernism"; Snodgrass, "Publishing Eastern Buddhism"; Victoria, *Zen at War*; Van Overmeire, "Inventing the Zen Buddhist Samurai"; Van Overmeire, "Portraying Zen Buddhism."
77. Suzuki, *Zen and Japanese Culture*; Suzuki, *Selected Works*. As mentioned in the introduction, Steven Heine has called these two very different approaches to Zen Traditional Zen Narrative (TZN) and Historical and Cultural Criticism (HCC) and, like Jaffe, has demonstrated that they can indeed be reconciled (Heine, *Zen Skin, Zen Marrow*).
78. For Suzuki's influence on the Beat Generation, see Falk, "The Beat Avant-Garde," 92–135; for his influence on the music composer John Cage, see Nicholls, *John Cage*, 46–48. For the most important examination of his influence on Buddhist studies, see Sharf, "The Zen of Japanese Nationalism."

2. FAILURE

79. Jane Iwamura uses Suzuki as one case study of the stereotype of the "oriental monk" discussed in the introduction to this book (Iwamura, *Virtual Orientalism: Asian Religions and American Popular Culture*).

1. Van de Wetering, introduction to *The Zen Koan as a Means of Attaining Enlightenment*, by Daisetz Teitaro Suzuki.
2. Van de Wetering, introduction to *The Zen Koan as a Means of Attaining Enlightenment*, by Daisetz Teitaro Suzuki.
3. Van de Wetering, *The Empty Mirror*, 143.
4. In his 1975 review of Van de Wetering's memoir, the famous Japanese Zen scholar Hisao Inagaki described the book as "another addition to the long list of books produced in the current worldwide boom of Zen" but "probably unique in not pretending to know what satori is" (Inagaki, "Experiences in a Japanese Zen Monastery," 87).
5. An important inspiration for Van de Wetering was likely the English Buddhist John Blofeld's *The Wheel of Life*. Blofeld had spent significant time in Republican China studying Buddhism, and one chapter of his autobiography is devoted to a stay in a Zen monastery. Like Van de Wetering, Blofeld left that monastery after a short time without having achieved enlightenment (although he "made some progress" toward understanding Buddhist truths) (Blofeld, *Wheel of Life*, 170).
6. Sandage, *Born Losers*.
7. See Howlett, "A Fateful Rite of Passage," for how the Chinese national college entrance exam functions to create a "myth of meritocracy" in China; and Blum, "I Love Learning; I Hate School," for how grading negatively affects student attitudes toward education. Blum has also edited a volume proposing alternative approaches, known collectively as "ungrading" (Blum, *Ungrading: Why Rating Students Undermines Learning [and What to Do Instead]*).
8. Pei, Wang, and Li, "30 Million Canvas Grading Records Reveal Widespread Sequential Bias and System-Induced Surname Initial Disparity."
9. Ball, *False Starts*, 7.
10. Ahmed, *The Promise of Happiness*, 50–87; Halberstam, *The Queer Art of Failure*, 129.
11. Ahmed, *The Promise of Happiness*, 219. I am not the first to use Ahmed's critical examination of happiness to examine contemporary Buddhism (see Edelglass, "Buddhism, Happiness, and the Science of Meditation").

12. Rak, *Boom!*
13. Anderson, *Autobiography*, 115; Marcus, *Autobiography*, 73–74.
14. Rak, *Boom!*
15. Fass, "The Memoir Problem"; Miller, "But Enough about Me."
16. Zwerdling, *The Rise of the Memoir*, 5.
17. As mentioned in the introduction, I sometimes choose to clearly distinguish between the protagonist of an autobiographical narrative and its real-life author. The autobiographical work of Van de Wetering is one corpus where it is worthwhile to do so because, as we will see in chapter 4, he often fictionalizes his own life story.
18. Van de Wetering, *The Empty Mirror*, 3.
19. The most comprehensive resource on Van de Wetering's life and work is Beijering, *Op zoek naar het ongerijmde*. For English-language approaches, see Barbour, *Journeys of Transformation*, 63–70; Van Overmeire, "Portraying Zen Buddhism"; Van Overmeire, "Hard-Boiled Zen"; and Van Overmeire, "DT Suzuki's Literary Influence."
20. Van de Wetering, *The Empty Mirror*, 5.
21. Van de Wetering, *The Empty Mirror*, 6.
22. Though Van de Wetering never identifies this master, it is clear from the contents that Daito Kokushi (National Teacher Daito), the founder of Daitokuji, is meant here. For a discussion of Daitō including this story, see Dumoulin, *Japan*, 185–90.
23. Van de Wetering, *The Empty Mirror*, 6.
24. Van de Wetering, *The Empty Mirror*, 6.
25. This Zen master, whom Van de Wetering will later identify as Oda Sesso (1901–1966), remains unnamed throughout the entire book.
26. Van de Wetering, *The Empty Mirror*, 6.
27. Van de Wetering, *The Empty Mirror*, 7.
28. Van de Wetering, *The Empty Mirror*, 7.
29. Van de Wetering, *The Empty Mirror*, 8.
30. Van de Wetering, *The Empty Mirror*, 8.
31. Van de Wetering, *Afterzen*, 65.
32. Van de Wetering, *The Empty Mirror*, 14.
33. Van de Wetering, *The Empty Mirror*, 23.
34. Van de Wetering, *The Empty Mirror*, 20.
35. Van de Wetering, *The Empty Mirror*, 20–21.
36. Van de Wetering, *The Empty Mirror*, 35.
37. Van de Wetering, *The Empty Mirror*, 89–90.
38. Van de Wetering, *The Empty Mirror*, 39.

39. Van de Wetering, *The Empty Mirror*, 54–55.
40. Van de Wetering, *The Empty Mirror*, 38.
41. Van de Wetering, *The Empty Mirror*, 136.
42. Note that the very ordinariness of the master does conform to the ideals of the Zen biographical tradition, but not the elements Janwillem is familiar with. Van de Wetering might be contrasting the orientalist tradition of portraying Zen teachers with the trope of the ordinary master.
43. Gerald is the book's representation of the famous Beat poet Gary Snyder, who was in Daitokuji at the same time as Van de Wetering (Snyder and McLean, *The Real Work*, 178).
44. Van de Wetering, *The Empty Mirror*, 134.
45. Van de Wetering, *The Empty Mirror*, 120.
46. Van de Wetering, *The Empty Mirror*, 145.
47. Chadwick, *Thank You and OK!*, 434.
48. Chadwick, *Crooked Cucumber*.
49. Downing, *Shoes outside the Door*.
50. Chadwick, *Thank You and OK!*, 322.
51. P'ang, *A Man of Zen*, trans. Sasaki and Iriya, 49. On the Zen-influenced Buddhist modernist stress on the everyday, see McMahan, *The Making of Buddhist Modernism*, 215–40.
52. Chadwick, *Thank You and OK!*, 322–23.
53. Chadwick, *Thank You and OK!*, 435.
54. Chadwick, *Thank You and OK!*, 176.
55. Chadwick, *Thank You and OK!*, 179, 364.
56. Sharf, "Whose Zen? Zen Nationalism Revisited," 47–48.
57. Chadwick, *Thank You and OK!*, 231.
58. Chadwick, *Thank You and OK!*, 290.
59. In a further touch of irony, this type of exchange mirrors how koan exchanges are usually executed in traditional Japanese Zen monasteries (see Sharf, "Ritual"). That this understanding of what is called Dharma combat, namely as a predominantly ritual demonstration of the master's Buddha-nature, where questions and answers are decided in advance, continues in Japan today is attested to by many, including Claire Gesshin Greenwood, whose work will be discussed in chapter 3.
60. Chadwick, *Thank You and OK!*, 248–49.
61. Chadwick, *Thank You and OK!*, 248.
62. Chadwick, *Thank You and OK!*, 446–47.
63. Chadwick, *Thank You and OK!*, 447.
64. Chadwick, *Thank You and OK!*, 364.

65. Goldberg, *Writing down the Bones*, 10.
66. Kerouac, "Belief and Technique for Modern Prose."
67. Hori, *Zen Sand*.
68. Goldberg, *The Great Failure*, 9–10.
69. Goldberg, *The Great Failure*, 2.
70. Goldberg, *The Great Failure*, 3.
71. Goldberg, *The Great Failure*, 29–32.
72. Goldberg, *The Great Failure*, 110.
73. Goldberg, *The Great Failure*, 94.
74. Goldberg, *The Great Failure*, 94.
75. Goldberg, *The Great Failure*, 102.
76. As psychoanalysis has been a "shaping force on 20th-century autobiography" as well as on Zen modernity, the usage of a psychoanalytical framework in these life narratives should hardly be surprising (Marcus, *Autobiography*, 61). Already in the 1990s, in the wake of sex scandals in Buddhist communities, Insight meditation teacher Jack Kornfield proposed a model of projection very similar to the one we find in Goldberg and Haubner's books (Kornfield, *A Path with Heart*, 262–71; I wish to thank Hsiao-Lan Hu for this reference).
77. Goldberg, *The Great Failure*, 90–91.
78. Goldberg, *The Great Failure*, 91.
79. Goldberg, *The Great Failure*, 144.
80. Goldberg, *The Great Failure*, 3.
81. This account is similar to Grace Schireson's analysis of the sex scandals, as described by Gleig (Gleig, *American Dharma*, 89–91). Schireson's solution to this problem includes organizing teacher training, like the one we will see Manuel participate in, and co-teaching, to prevent an idealization of the teacher. So for Schireson, idealizing the teacher is bad. But Goldberg is a bit more ambiguous: under the right circumstances idealizing the teacher can also lead to liberation. Projection is a tool, and it's possible that reducing the teachers to "ordinary human beings" will prevent this mechanism from operating.
82. Goldberg, *The Great Failure*, 75.
83. Goldberg, *The Great Failure*, 145.
84. In his book on Buddhist attitudes toward sexuality, Bernard Faure calls this "the logic of transcendence," where transgression becomes pedagogy (Faure, *The Red Thread*).
85. Goldberg, *The Great Failure*, 92.
86. Goldberg, *The Great Failure*, 103–4.
87. Goldberg, *Long Quiet Highway*, 158.
88. Goldberg, *The Great Failure*, 115.

89. Goldberg, *The Great Failure*, 100.
90. Goldberg, *The Great Failure*, 20–21.
91. Goldberg, *The Great Failure*, 49.
92. Goldberg, *The Great Failure*, 165.
93. Goldberg, *The Great Failure*, 147–48.
94. Goldberg, *The Great Failure*, 191.
95. Goldberg, *The Great Failure*, 133.
96. Goldberg, *The Great Spring*; Rivera, "Natalie Goldberg on the Zen of Writing."
97. Zigmund, "Writing through the Heart."
98. Haubner, *Zen Confidential*, 8.
99. Haubner, *Zen Confidential*, 3.
100. Haubner, *Single White Monk*, 6.
101. Haubner, *Single White Monk*, 8.
102. Haubner, *Single White Monk*, 7.
103. Wilson, *Charming Cadavers*.
104. Haubner, *Zen Confidential*, 99.
105. Haubner, *Zen Confidential*, 100.
106. Haubner, *Zen Confidential*, 102.
107. Haubner, *Zen Confidential*, 100.
108. Haubner, *Single White Monk*, 63.
109. Haubner, *Single White Monk*, 167.
110. Haubner, *Single White Monk*, 168.
111. Linji, *The Record of Linji*, trans. Sasaki, 130.
112. Linji, *The Record of Linji*, trans. Sasaki, 129–31.
113. Faure, *The Power of Denial*; Gyatso, "One Plus One Makes Three"; Gyatso, "Sex."
114. Haubner, *Single White Monk*, 157–58.
115. Haubner, *Single White Monk*, 162.
116. Haubner, *Single White Monk*, 162.
117. Haubner, *Single White Monk*, 164.
118. Haubner, *Single White Monk*, 81.
119. Haubner, *Single White Monk*, 90.
120. Haubner, *Single White Monk*, 167.
121. Levering, "Lin-Chi (Rinzai) Ch'an and Gender," 144–45. For more on this term and its relation to gender, see Grant, "Da Zhangfu: The Gendered Rhetoric of Heroism and Equality in Seventeenth-Century Chan Buddhist Discourse Records."
122. Elsewhere, I have explored this way of reading koan in more depth and have also examined how American woman practitioners have resisted this rhetoric (Van Overmeire, "'Mountains, Rivers, and the Whole Earth'").

123. Haubner, *Single White Monk*, 178.
124. Haubner, *Single White Monk*, 130.
125. Haubner, *Single White Monk*, 161.
126. Haubner, *Single White Monk*, 162.
127. Haubner, *Single White Monk*, 165.
128. Haubner, *Single White Monk*, 179.
129. Haubner, *Single White Monk*, 170.
130. Haubner, *Single White Monk*, 137; The Osho Council of Rinzai-ji, "An Open Letter."
131. Haubner, *Single White Monk*, 200, 136.
132. Haubner, *Single White Monk*, 203.
133. Haubner, *Single White Monk*, 205.
134. Haubner, *Single White Monk*, 208.
135. Haubner, "Re: Single White Monk," July 31, 2018.

3. THE TWO TRUTHS

1. Huineng, *The Platform Sutra*, trans. McRae, 18.
2. McRae, who translated *The Platform Sutra*, explains that the term "hunter" here was "a generic reference for non-Chinese people in general, with stereotypical implications of such people as being lazy, engaging in hunting (which was looked down upon by the agrarian Chinese), and exhibiting a barbarian lack of culture" (Huineng, *The Platform Sutra*, trans. McRae, 114).
3. Huineng, *The Platform Sutra*, trans. McRae, 18.
4. The scholarly consensus is that it is impossible to consider *The Platform Sutra* as anything but an inventive fiction. It in no way represents the views of the historical Huineng (McRae, *Seeing through Zen*, 67).
5. Huineng, *The Platform Sutra*, trans. McRae, 20.
6. Huineng, *The Platform Sutra*, trans. McRae, 22.
7. For the Chinese of the poems, see *Liuzu tanjing T* no. 2007, 48: 0337c01–02 and *T* no. 2007, 48: 0338a07–08. Earlier editions of *The Platform Sutra* feature another verse that goes as follows: "The mind is the Bodhi tree,/The body is the mirror stand./The mirror is originally clean and pure;/Where can it be stained by dust?" (Huineng, *The Platform Sutra*, trans. Yampolsky, 132; *T* no. 2007, 48: 0338a10–11). Though the body does make a reappearance in this second verse, note that Huineng again dismisses individual differences in favor of an ultimate reality where everything is the same. McRae has seen Huineng's verse as inseparable from Shenxiu's, as expressing one

single message and not, as is often supposed, competing views (McRae, *Seeing through Zen*, 63–65).
8. Gleig, *American Dharma*, 88–94.
9. Schireson, *Zen Women*.
10. Schireson, *Naked in the Zendo*, xii.
11. Schireson, *Naked in the Zendo*, 3.
12. Schireson, *Naked in the Zendo*, 16.
13. Levering, "Miao-Tao," 188–89.
14. Caplow and Moon, *The Hidden Lamp*, 107.
15. Schireson, *Naked in the Zendo*, 62.
16. Schireson, *Naked in the Zendo*, 62.
17. Schireson, *Naked in the Zendo*, 48.
18. Schireson, *Naked in the Zendo*, 49.
19. Schireson, *Naked in the Zendo*, 65.
20. Schireson, *Naked in the Zendo*, 65.
21. Schireson, *Naked in the Zendo*, 71.
22. Schireson, *Naked in the Zendo*, 71.
23. Schireson, *Naked in the Zendo*, 72; her parentheses.
24. Schireson, *Naked in the Zendo*, 72.
25. Schireson, *Naked in the Zendo*, 77.
26. Schireson, *Naked in the Zendo*, 80.
27. Schireson, *Naked in the Zendo*, 79.
28. Schireson, *Naked in the Zendo*, xi.
29. https://www.shin-ibs.edu/academics/faculty/greenwood/. For the postmodern blurring of categories between practitioners and scholars, see Gleig, *American Dharma*.
30. Greenwood and Adler, *Just Enough*.
31. Greenwood, *Bow First, Ask Questions Later*, 2.
32. Hsieh, "Images of Women," 166, 170, 175–76.
33. Greenwood, *Bow First, Ask Questions Later*, 25.
34. Greenwood, *Bow First, Ask Questions Later*, 26.
35. Greenwood, *Bow First, Ask Questions Later*, 77.
36. Greenwood, *Bow First, Ask Questions Later*, 75.
37. Greenwood, *Bow First, Ask Questions Later*, 75.
38. Greenwood, *Bow First, Ask Questions Later*, 93.
39. Greenwood, *Bow First, Ask Questions Later*, 89.
40. Greenwood, *Bow First, Ask Questions Later*, 87.
41. Greenwood, *Bow First, Ask Questions Later*, 87.
42. Greenwood, *Bow First, Ask Questions Later*, 89.

43. Greenwood, *Bow First, Ask Questions Later*, 89.
44. Greenwood, *Bow First, Ask Questions Later*, 93.
45. Greenwood, *Bow First, Ask Questions Later*, 148.
46. Greenwood, *Bow First, Ask Questions Later*, 148.
47. Sharf, "Ritual."
48. Linji, *The Record of Linji*, trans. Sasaki.
49. Greenwood, *Bow First, Ask Questions Later*, 102–3.
50. Greenwood, *Bow First, Ask Questions Later*, 181.
51. Greenwood, *Bow First, Ask Questions Later*, 38.
52. Greenwood, *Bow First, Ask Questions Later*, 116.
53. Greenwood, *Bow First, Ask Questions Later*, 199.
54. Greenwood, *Bow First, Ask Questions Later*, 200.
55. Seligman et al., *Ritual and Its Consequences*, 180.
56. Seligman et al., *Ritual and Its Consequences*, 181.
57. I owe this insight to Ann Gleig, from whose work I also draw the distinction between modernist and postmodernist Zen (Gleig, *American Dharma*).
58. Crenshaw, "Mapping the Margins."
59. Gleig, "Undoing Whiteness."
60. Manuel, *The Way of Tenderness*, 17.
61. Manuel, *The Way of Tenderness*, 70.
62. Manuel, *The Way of Tenderness*, 58.
63. Gleig, "Buddhists and Racial Justice."
64. Manuel, *The Way of Tenderness*, 56.
65. McNicholl, "Being Buddha, Staying Woke," 894.
66. angel Kyodo williams qtd. in McNicholl, "Being Buddha, Staying Woke," 894.
67. angel Kyodo williams, *Being Black*.
68. Manuel, *The Way of Tenderness*, 37.
69. Garton-Gundling, *Enlightened Individualism*, 119–20.
70. Manuel, *The Way of Tenderness*, 91.
71. Noland, "Embodiment."
72. Fanon, "The Fact of Blackness"; Noland, "Embodiment."
73. Manuel, *The Way of Tenderness*, 44.
74. Manuel, *The Way of Tenderness*, 91.
75. Schireson, *Naked in the Zendo*, 76.
76. Schireson, *Naked in the Zendo*, 79.
77. Faure, *The Rhetoric of Immediacy*.
78. Manuel, *The Way of Tenderness*, 27.
79. Manuel, *The Way of Tenderness*, 27.
80. Manuel, *The Way of Tenderness*, 46.

NOTES TO PAGES 98–110 • 193

81. Gleig, "Undoing Whiteness," 37–38.
82. Manuel, *Sanctuary*, 11.
83. Sekida, *Two Zen Classics*, 106.
84. Manuel, *Sanctuary*, 12–13.
85. Manuel, *Sanctuary*, 13–14.
86. Manuel, *Sanctuary*, 47–49.
87. Cutts et al., "SFZC Leadership Statement"; "Troubling Experience at Green Gulch," August 2, 2018.
88. Chadwick, "Edward Brown." For a framing of Brown's dismissal within the right-wing American Buddhist backlash, see Gleig and Artinger, "#BuddhistCultureWars."
89. Warner, "Inclusivity in Zen."
90. Warner, "Challenging Cherished Beliefs."
91. Warner, "Inclusivity in Zen."
92. Warner, "Zentertainment Weakly."
93. Greenwood, *Bow First, Ask Questions Later*, vii.
94. Greenwood, *Bow First, Ask Questions Later*, vii.

4. DETACHMENT IN VAN DE WETERING'S *AFTERZEN*

1. *Janwillem van de Wetering—To Infinity and Beyond*, 29:57–31:33.
2. Bakhtin, *Rabelais and His World*, 89ff.
3. Bakhtin, *Rabelais and His World*, 165–66.
4. Lejeune, *On Autobiography*.
5. The initial questioning of the narrative happened here: The Smoking Gun, "A Million Little Lies."
6. In seeing Van de Wetering as a trickster figure, I am following the lead of Sabine Vanacker, who has studied Van de Wetering's detective novels in this manner. She argues that Van de Wetering satirizes political correctness and racism. He does so to correct the global image of Amsterdam as an open, multicultural, and tolerant city (Vanacker, "Imagining a Global Village").
7. Van de Wetering, *A Glimpse of Nothingness*, 30.
8. Van de Wetering, *A Glimpse of Nothingness*, preface.
9. Van de Wetering, *A Glimpse of Nothingness*, 30.
10. Van de Wetering, *Afterzen*, 117.
11. Van de Wetering, *A Glimpse of Nothingness*, 52.
12. Van de Wetering, *A Glimpse of Nothingness*, 54.

13. Van de Wetering, "Interview with J. Van de W," by Walker, 7.
14. The satori experience of *Glimpse*, incidentally, is never mentioned in *Afterzen*, which revisits many events described in both *Glimpse* and *The Empty Mirror*, but not this one. As with Kapleau, this likely has more than a little to do with Van de Wetering's changed relationship with his Zen teacher. As we will see, in *Afterzen* "Peter" has become the representative of everything that is bad about institutional Zen Buddhism.
15. Translations from both *Het dagende niets* en *Zuivere leegte*, the Dutch versions of *Glimpse* and *Afterzen* respectively, are all mine. I quote from the Dutch when there are significant differences between Dutch and English versions of the books. Instead of having someone translate them, Van de Wetering rewrote all his books in English himself. This is also true of his detective fiction (Vanacker, "Imagining a Global Village," 172).
16. Van de Wetering, *Het dagende niets*.
17. Van de Wetering, *Afterzen*, 10.
18. Beijering, *Op zoek naar het ongerijmde*, 106–7.
19. Van de Wetering, *Afterzen*, 1.
20. Van de Wetering, *Afterzen*, 1.
21. Van de Wetering, *The Empty Mirror*, 1; Van de Wetering, *A Glimpse of Nothingness*, i.
22. Van de Wetering, *Afterzen*, 6.
23. Van de Wetering, *Afterzen*, 7.
24. Van de Wetering, *Zuivere leegte*, 140.
25. Van de Wetering, *Afterzen*, 78.
26. Van de Wetering, *Afterzen*, 184.
27. Van de Wetering, *Afterzen*, 33.
28. Van de Wetering, *Afterzen*, 33.
29. Note that this striking aspect of Janwillem's first meeting with the abbot was not mentioned in *The Empty Mirror*, nor was Roshi described as suffering from Parkinson's in that book. This attests to the continuous way in which Van de Wetering engineered his own autobiography and revised his past.
30. Van de Wetering, *Afterzen*, 35.
31. Beijering, *Op zoek naar het ongerijmde*, 124–25. Trungpa also wrote a cover blurb for more recent editions of *The Empty Mirror*.
32. Van de Wetering, *Afterzen*, 129.
33. Van de Wetering, *Afterzen*, 132.
34. Van de Wetering, *Afterzen*, 145.
35. Van de Wetering, *Afterzen*, 138.

36. Van de Wetering, *Afterzen*, 140.
37. Van de Wetering, *Afterzen*, 145.
38. Van de Wetering, *Zuivere leegte*, 177.
39. Van de Wetering, *Afterzen*, 2.
40. Van de Wetering, *Afterzen*, 3.
41. Van de Wetering, *Afterzen*, 85–86.
42. Van de Wetering, *Afterzen*, 21–25.
43. Van de Wetering, *Afterzen*, 23.
44. Van de Wetering, *Afterzen*, 112.
45. Van de Wetering, *Afterzen*, 112.
46. For an authoritative study of the idea of the decline of the Dharma, see Nattier, *Once upon a Future Time*.
47. *Afterzen*'s description does not match Thera van de Wetering's description of her father's break with Nowick. She says that, when she needed surgery, Nowick pushed her father not to go and instead to focus on his Zen study. Van de Wetering got so angry at this that he promptly left the community and sold his house there (Thera van de Wetering, interview by Van Overmeire about Janwillem van de Wetering). That the description of the break with Nowick is possibly entirely fictional makes paying particular attention to it all the more important, following the first of John McRae's "Rules of Zen Studies," which is "It's not true, and therefore it's more important" (McRae, *Seeing through Zen*, xix). Of course, McRae was talking about the vast number of Zen Buddhists reimagining their tradition over time, and his point was that their mythology deserved much more attention than a quest for what is "true" could ever bear to give. I would argue, though, that this is true for modern Zen writing as well: when an author chooses not to give the facts, we should pay attention.
48. Van de Wetering, *Afterzen*, 116–17.
49. Van de Wetering, *Afterzen*, 7.
50. Van de Wetering, *Afterzen*, 81.
51. Van de Wetering, *Afterzen*, 20, 92.
52. Jansma, "De vrijheid."
53. Van de Wetering, *Afterzen*, 40.
54. Van de Wetering, *Afterzen*, 41.
55. Van de Wetering, *Afterzen*, 153.
56. Van de Wetering, *Afterzen*, 154.
57. Van de Wetering, *Afterzen*, 156.
58. Van de Wetering, *Afterzen*, 152.
59. Van de Wetering, *Afterzen*, 41.
60. Van de Wetering, *Afterzen*, 45.

61. Van de Wetering, *Afterzen*, 156–57.
62. Van de Wetering, *Afterzen*, 159.
63. Van de Wetering, *Afterzen*, 164.
64. Van de Wetering, *Afterzen*, 184.
65. Van de Wetering, *Afterzen*, 58.
66. Van de Wetering, *Afterzen*, 13–14.
67. For your reference, here is how the younger Van de Wetering described koan in *The Empty Mirror*: "In Zen training concentration is on the *koan*, a subject which the master presents to the disciple. One tries to become one with the *koan*, to close the distance between oneself and the *koan*, to lose oneself in the *koan*, till everything drops or breaks away and nothing is left but the *koan* which fills the universe. And if that point is reached enlightenment, the revelation, follows" (Van de Wetering, *The Empty Mirror*, 15; his italics). The description is clearly inspired by Suzuki's definition of the genre, who saw koan as tools to undo dualist ways of thinking.
68. Van de Wetering, *Afterzen*, 27.
69. Van de Wetering, *Afterzen*, 28.
70. Van de Wetering, *Afterzen*, 29.
71. Van de Wetering, *Afterzen*, 13.
72. The koan refers to case 38 of the *Gateless Barrier*. The patriarch in question is Goso Hōen (C. Wuzu Fayan; 1024–104).
73. He is talking about this book, the translation of which was first published in 1975: Hoffman and Burstein, *The Sound of the One Hand*.
74. Van de Wetering, *Afterzen*, 17.
75. Van de Wetering, *Afterzen*, 52.
76. Van de Wetering, *Afterzen*, 56.
77. Blyth, *Zen and Zen Classics*; Sekida, *Two Zen Classics*. For the original Chinese, see *Wumenguan T* no. 2005, 48: 0297a13.
78. Van de Wetering lists the sources he used for the translations in the Dutch version of the book (Van de Wetering, *Zuivere leegte*, 6).
79. This is not the only alteration: in the original koan, the monk asks for the way to Mount Taishan, not Sumeru. The addition of Mount Sumeru seems a streamlining of koan on the part of Van de Wetering, as he mentions this mountain several times in *Afterzen*. Sumeru is the symbolic mountain at the center of the world in Indian Buddhist cosmology, and Taishan is an important pilgrimage mountain in Chinese tradition, so it makes sense that Van de Wetering would think of replacing one with the other.
80. Van de Wetering, *Afterzen*, 175.
81. Van de Wetering, *Afterzen*, 175.

82. Incidentally, the medieval Japanese master Dogen already got annoyed at this rhetorical deployment of silence based on the Vimalakirti sutra (see Wright, "Silence and Eloquence").
83. Van de Wetering, *Afterzen*, 183–84.
84. Van de Wetering, *Afterzen*, 185.
85. Van de Wetering, *Afterzen*, 164.
86. Van de Wetering, *Afterzen*, 186.
87. Van de Wetering, *Afterzen*, 187.
88. *Janwillem van de Wetering—To Infinity and Beyond*, 55:00–57:50.
89. *Janwillem van de Wetering—To Infinity and Beyond*, 57:05–50.
90. Van de Wetering, "Interview with J. Van de W," 6.

5. INTERDEPENDENCE IN THE WORK OF RUTH OZEKI

1. For more on Fischer, see Sigalow, *American Jewbu*.
2. A discussion of *The Book of Form and Emptiness* is beyond the scope of this book. In many ways, it is an even more radical novel than *A Tale*. In it, Ozeki moves beyond the autobiographical (although she is clearly present in the book) to express the idea that even seemingly insentient things can speak. One narrator of that novel is "The Book," which is literally a book that speaks to (or writes to?) the reader.
3. Ozeki, "Ruth Ozeki on Catastrophe," interview by Hall.
4. Ozeki, "Ruth Ozeki, 'The Contemplative "I."'"
5. Torres, "Longtermism"; Lewis-Kraus, "The Reluctant Prophet."
6. Tolle, *The Power of Now*, chap. 3.
7. Tolle, *The Power of Now*, chap. 3.
8. My suspicion is that Tolle is referring to this passage: "*ěr jīn yòngchù 、qiànshǎo shímó wù 、xiūbǔ héchù?*" (T no. 1985, 47: 0499c03). "What is lacking in your present activity? What still needs to be patched up?" (Linji, *The Record of Linji*, trans. Sasaki, 217). The phrase "activity" (*yòngchù*) appears a number of times in Rinzai's Record of Sayings and appears to denote something that you are doing, which seems different from Tolle's idea that Rinzai is simply commenting on the now as something lacking in and of itself. A "present activity" could be, for example, ruminating on the past, exactly what Tolle does not think the "now" should be about.
9. I am drawing here on Derrida's famous essay on Plato, "Plato's Pharmacy."

10. Davis, "Fictional Transits," 93. Like Davis, I will use "Ozeki" to refer to the author Ruth Ozeki, and "Ruth" to refer to the character.
11. Ozeki, "Confessions of a Zen Novelist."
12. Ozeki, "Ruth Ozeki on Catastrophe," interview by Hall.
13. Ozeki, "Ruth Ozeki, 'The Contemplative "I."'"
14. Ozeki, "A Universe of Many Worlds," interview by Ty, 162–63.
15. Ozeki, *A Tale for the Time Being*, 59.
16. Ozeki, *A Tale for the Time Being*, 392.
17. Ozeki, "A Universe of Many Worlds," interview by Ty, 163–64.
18. Ozeki, *A Tale for the Time Being*, 77.
19. Ozeki, *A Tale for the Time Being*, 46.
20. Davis, "Fictional Transits," 95.
21. This latter fact is only disclosed in Ozeki's *The Face*, which I will turn to in the second part of this chapter.
22. Ozeki, *A Tale for the Time Being*, 1, n2.
23. Ty, *Unfastened*, xxvi.
24. Ozeki, *A Tale for the Time Being*, 373.
25. Most scholarship on *A Tale* has, in fact, focused on the question of gender and the posthuman and often also on what resources Buddhism offers to advance this discussion. For Sue Lovell, "Buddhism is aligned well with the project of decentering the anthropocentric self. It places human life, the experience of self, in relation to the overall web of life" (Lovell, "Toward a Poetics of Posthumanist Narrative Using Ruth Ozeki's *A Tale for the Time Being*," 65). This is similar to Leslie Fernandez, who sees the novel's engagement with Zen as a useful means to focus on our connections with others, making a posthumanist ethic possible (Fernandez, "Extrospection"). Another in-depth exploration of how Buddhism is thought in relation to gender in *A Tale* is Starr, "Beyond Machine Dreams." Starr argues that ultimately Buddhist ideas of no-self and nonduality as well as meditation practices are insufficient for Nao, as they do not release her from the gendered violence she is subjected to. For her, Ozeki's novel criticizes both the move of privileging ultimate reality (there are no women, yet Nao is a girl) and of privileging provisional reality (there are women, but Nao is not really one of them), settling ultimately in an in-between position that emphasizes the relationship between Ruth and Nao as a form of nonhierarchical feminism. These ideas might remind the reader of the mechanisms discussed in chapter 3, which can be applied to an analysis of *A Tale* as well. I agree with Starr that the novel's position on Buddhist feminism is ultimately ambiguous: Ozeki certainly does not present Buddhism as strongly advocating for gender equality, but as we will see it also offers, in the figure of Jiko, ways of affirming women in positions of power.

26. Ozeki, *A Tale for the Time Being*, 299.
27. For a detailed examination of the novel's nuanced portrayal of kamikaze pilots, see McKay, "The Right Stuff."
28. Like so much in *A Tale*, that encounter might have autobiographical roots. Visiting Japan as a young child, Ozeki recalls meeting a lot of war veterans, but her mother later claimed that these soldiers were never there (Ozeki, "A Vacation with Ghosts").
29. Ozeki, *A Tale for the Time Being*, 409.
30. Ozeki, *A Tale for the Time Being*, 413.
31. Ozeki, *A Tale for the Time Being*, 414; her emphasis.
32. Ozeki, *A Tale for the Time Being*, 415.
33. Ozeki, *A Tale for the Time Being*, 136.
34. McMahan, *The Making of Buddhist Modernism*, 149–82.
35. Qtd. in Ozeki, *A Tale for the Time Being*, 259.
36. Raud, "'Place' and 'Being-Time.'"
37. Heine, *Existential and Ontological Dimensions*, 106.
38. Heine, *Existential and Ontological Dimensions*, 25–26.
39. Heine, *Existential and Ontological Dimensions*, 27–28.
40. Ozeki, *A Tale for the Time Being*, 4.
41. Heine, *Existential and Ontological Dimensions*, 57–58.
42. Ozeki, *A Tale for the Time Being*, 98.
43. Ozeki, *A Tale for the Time Being*, 87.
44. Ozeki, *A Tale for the Time Being*, 341.
45. Ozeki, *A Tale for the Time Being*, 238.
46. Nao's beating the drum as an image of the now, as an image of emptiness, works particularly well when you think about the fact that the Sanskrit word for emptiness, *shunyata*, implies something blown up but empty inside, like a balloon or a drum.
47. Ozeki, *A Tale for the Time Being*, 122.
48. Ozeki, *A Tale for the Time Being*, 122.
49. Ozeki, *A Tale for the Time Being*, 123.
50. Smith, "Chapter 5—Empirical Metaphysics."
51. Ozeki, *A Tale for the Time Being*, 176.
52. Starr, "Beyond Machine Dreams," 111–12.
53. Ozeki, *A Tale for the Time Being*, 287–88.
54. Cleary and Cleary, *The Blue Cliff Record*, 619.
55. The history of comparing Derrida's idea with Zen ideas, including Dogen, is long and complicated. For a recent contribution that also focuses on the concern with representation, see Olson, "Playing in the Non-Representational Mode." My own position is that Derrida has been cast too often as needing

"mending," as an early substantial contribution to the debate announces (Magliola, *Derrida on the Mend*). I think this ignores the extent to which Derrida himself would criticize the idea that something needs repair as another function of some transcendent idea, which is to say another effect of the very logocentrism he sets out to demonstrate.

56. Derrida, "Plato's Pharmacy."
57. Ozeki said the character of Jiko was inspired by Masako, Ozeki's own mother, and by a recently deceased Japanese Zen nun named Setouchi Jakucho (Ozeki, "Ruth Ozeki, 'The Contemplative "I"'").
58. Ozeki, *A Tale for the Time Being*, 194.
59. Ozeki, *A Tale for the Time Being*, 194.
60. Ozeki, *A Tale for the Time Being*, 362.
61. Ozeki, *A Tale for the Time Being*, 362.
62. Ozeki, *A Tale for the Time Being*, 364.
63. For more on the concept of the "great man," or masculine hero (*dazhangfu*), in Zen, see the discussion of Haubner's work in chapter 2.
64. Ozeki, *A Tale for the Time Being*, 192.
65. Kotler and Tanahashi, "Mountains and Waters Sutra (Sansui-Kyō)," 163. I've modified one word of the translation here: "green" in English represents the character *qing* in Chinese, which in fact means a color between blue and green. Interesting traces of this remain in contemporary Japanese, where the character is commonly used in the name of the color blue *ao*, but it also is used to indicate that a traffic light has turned green. (Incidentally, this drives me crazy.)
66. Ozeki, *A Tale for the Time Being*, 4.
67. Kotler and Tanahashi, "Mountains and Waters Sutra (Sansui-Kyō)," 167.
68. Ozeki, "A Universe of Many Worlds," interview by Ty, 163.
69. Ozeki, *A Tale for the Time Being*, 114.
70. Lee, "Sharing Worlds through Words," 48.
71. Ozeki, *A Tale for the Time Being*, 222.
72. Ozeki, *A Tale for the Time Being*, 295.
73. Ozeki, *A Tale for the Time Being*, 323.
74. Stambaugh, *Impermanence Is Buddha-Nature*, 11–14.
75. Ozeki, *A Tale for the Time Being*, 222.
76. Ozeki, *A Tale for the Time Being*, 382.
77. Ozeki, *The Face*, 6–7.
78. Ozeki, *The Face*, 8.
79. Ozeki, *The Face*, 30.
80. Ozeki, "Ruth Ozeki, 'The Contemplative "I."'"
81. Ozeki, *The Face*, 70.

82. Ozeki, *The Face*, 132.
83. Ozeki, *The Face*, 132.
84. Filgate, "Writing the Body."
85. Ozeki, *The Face*, 56.
86. Ozeki, "Ruth Ozeki, 'The Contemplative "I."'"
87. Ozeki, *The Face*, 19.
88. Ozeki, *The Face*, 106–10.
89. Ozeki, *The Face*, 109.
90. Ozeki, *The Face*, 47.
91. Later editions of the book have the changed title *Timecode of a Face*
92. Ozeki, *The Face*, 126.
93. Stambaugh, *Impermanence Is Buddha-Nature*, 18–20.
94. Heine, *Existential and Ontological Dimensions*, 106.
95. Heine, *Existential and Ontological Dimensions*, 57.
96. Accordingly, in interviews Ozeki has given about her work, she continuously stresses that she is no longer the author who wrote these books!
97. Van der Braak, "Dōgen on Language and Experience," 9.
98. Caplow and Moon, *The Hidden Lamp*, 293.
99. Ozeki, "Ruth Ozeki, 'The Contemplative "I."'"
100. Luchette, "Ruth Ozeki on *A Tale for the Time Being*."

CONCLUSION

1. Poceski, *The Records of Mazu*, 170–71.
2. I adopt the self-explanatory category of "cradle" Buddhists from Tweed, "Night-Stand Buddhists and Other Creatures: Sympathizers, Adherents, and the Study of Religion." Ozeki is a borderline case because her grandparents were Zen Buddhists (one scene in *The Face* narrates how she, as a young girl, discovered them deep in meditation). Yet she only started engaging with Buddhism much later in her life.
3. Hickey, "Two Buddhisms, Three Buddhisms, and Racism."
4. The category of cradle Buddhism avoids this problem because one can be white and born into a Buddhist family. It doesn't assume any of the stereotypes that the category of "ethnic" Buddhism does, although we still need to be careful not to essentialize the category.
5. Cheah, "Buddhism, Race, and Ethnicity."
6. Indeed, that recovery is ongoing. For good examinations of Americans of Chinese, Japanese, Korean, and Vietnamese backgrounds in America, see

Chandler, "Chinese Buddhism in America"; Williams and Moriya, *Issei Buddhism in the Americas*; Ama, *Immigrants to the Pure Land*; D. R. Williams, *American Sutra*; Han, *Be the Refuge*; and Masatsugu, *Reorienting the Pure Land*. Scott Mitchell's new book, just published at the time I write this, argues that Japanese American Buddhists made possible American Buddhist modernism as a whole (Mitchell, *The Making of American Buddhism*).

7. Kaivola-Bregenhøj, *Riddles*, 9.
8. It's an anthill!
9. Frow, *Genre*, 39.
10. Abrahams, *Between the Living and the Dead*, 13–17.
11. Lakoff and Johnson, *Metaphors We Live By*.
12. Abrahams, *Between the Living and the Dead*, 17.
13. McDowell, *Children's Riddling*, 133.
14. Kaivola-Bregenhøj, *Riddles*, 10.
15. Bakhtin, *Speech Genres and Other Late Essays*, 60–102.
16. Dorst, "Neck-Riddle as a Dialogue of Genres," 423.
17. Dorst, "Neck-Riddle as a Dialogue of Genres," 423–24.
18. Frow, *Genre*, 34; Kaivola-Bregenhøj, *Riddles*, 9.
19. Abrahams, *Between the Living and the Dead*, 8.
20. Abrahams, *Between the Living and the Dead*, 11.
21. Kaivola-Bregenhøj, *Riddles*, 12.
22. Abrahams, *Between the Living and the Dead*, 20. Incidentally, I first encountered the Oedipus riddle through a role-playing video game, which demonstrates to me how widely known it is. Not getting it right got you lightning-bolted, so they also got the life-or-death context right. Thankfully, the game did not involve gouging out my character's eyeballs.
23. Dorst, "Neck-Riddle as a Dialogue of Genres," 424.
24. Van de Wetering, *Afterzen*, 13–14.
25. Foulk, "The Form and Function," 18.
26. For a violent death, think of Gento's shout that could be heard for miles around, a shout Nao imitated. Before he actually died, Gento offered his neck to another monk who says he brought a sword, and lets out another shout. This is documented in case 66 of the *Blue Cliff Record*. For transformation into animals, a famous instance is the second case of the *Mumonkan*, which features a Zen master who was turned into a fox as a punishment for denying the workings of karma.
27. Van Overmeire, "Reading Chan Encounter Dialogue," 218–19.
28. Most definitions of koan would include commentary on koan as an essential part of the koan (Foulk, "The Form and Function," 27). However, the authors

I have surveyed almost never cite the commentary on a koan. Instead, they themselves comment on koan, implicitly assuming the identity of a Zen master even when on the surface they refuse this identification. I return to this in the last section of this conclusion.

29. Van Overmeire, "Reading Chan Encounter Dialogue."
30. As for scholars of Zen, though the term "riddle" is sometimes used for koan, in-depth discussions are rare. The most substantial I've found is Faure, *Chan Insights and Oversights*, 226–27. For Faure, calling koan riddles is a way to place them in the oral world, but he eventually rejects the term "riddle" because koan are engineered to sound like oral literature but are in fact not so. From my understanding, though, the designation "riddle" is not dependent on there being an oral tradition in place (although often there is). What matters to me is the structure and themes of the riddle, and this is where I see the strongest resemblances between koan and (neck) riddles.
31. Frow, *Genre*; Pepicello and Green, *The Language of Riddles*.
32. Frow, *Genre*, 3.
33. Barbour, *Journeys of Transformation*, 301–13.
34. Kripal, *Secret Body*, 15.
35. Matthiessen, *Nine-Headed Dragon River*, 125.
36. On Aitken's silent refusal to conduct *sanzen* through written correspondence, see Baroni, *Love, Rōshi*, 166.
37. Kapleau, "Letter to Charlotte and Lee Kramer," September 16, 1992.
38. Ozeki, *A Tale for the Time Being*, 3.
39. Murphy, *One Bird, One Stone*, xix.
40. Murphy, *One Bird, One Stone*, 140.
41. Kapleau, *The Three Pillars of Zen* (1967), 204.

BIBLIOGRAPHY

Abrahams, Roger D. *Between the Living and the Dead*. Helsinki: Suomalainen Tiedeakatemia, 1980.

Ahmed, Sara. *The Promise of Happiness*. Durham, NC: Duke University Press, 2010.

Ama, Michihiro. *Immigrants to the Pure Land: The Modernization, Acculturation, and Globalization of Shin Buddhism, 1898–1941*. Pure Land Buddhist Studies. Honolulu: University of Hawai'i Press, 2011.

Anderson, Linda. *Autobiography*. 2nd ed. New York: Routledge, 2011.

App, Urs. *The Birth of Orientalism*. Encounters with Asia. Philadelphia: University of Pennsylvania Press, 2010.

Bakhtin, Mikhail. *Rabelais and His World*. Translated by Helene Iswolsky. Midland Book ed. Bloomington: Indiana University Press, 1984.

———. *Speech Genres and Other Late Essays*. Edited by Michael Holquist and Caryl Emerson. Translated by Vern W. McGee. University of Texas Press Slavic Series 8. Austin: University of Texas Press, 1986.

Ball, David M. *False Starts: The Rhetoric of Failure and the Making of American Modernism*. Evanston, IL: Northwestern University Press, 2015.

Barbour, John D. *Journeys of Transformation: Searching for No-Self in Western Buddhist Travel Narratives*. New York: Cambridge University Press, 2022. https://doi.org/10.1017/9781009106337.

Baroni, Helen J. *Love, Rōshi: Robert Baker Aitken and His Distant Correspondents*. Albany: State University of New York Press, 2012.

Beijering, Marjan. *Op zoek naar het ongerijmde: Leven en werk van Janwillem van de Wetering (1931–2008)*. Waarbeke, Belgium: Asoka, 2021.

Blofeld, John. *Wheel of Life: The Autobiography of a Western Buddhist*. 3rd ed. Boston: Shambhala, 1988.

Blum, Susan D. *"I Love Learning; I Hate School": An Anthropology of College.* Ithaca, NY: Cornell University Press, 2016.

———, ed. *Ungrading: Why Rating Students Undermines Learning (and What to Do Instead).* Morgantown: West Virginia University Press, 2020.

Blyth, R. H. *Zen and Zen Classics.* Vol. 4. 5 vols. Tokyo: Hokuseido, 1966.

Bocking, Brian. "Mysticism: No Experience Necessary?" *Diskus* 7 (2006): 1–13.

Braak, André van der. "Dōgen on Language and Experience." *Religions* 12, no. 3 (March 10, 2021): 181. https://doi.org/10.3390/rel12030181.

Braun, Erik. *The Birth of Insight: Meditation, Modern Buddhism, and the Burmese Monk Ledi Sayadaw.* Buddhism and Modernity. Chicago: University of Chicago Press, 2013.

Breen, John, Fumihiko Sueki, and Shōji Yamada, eds. *Beyond Zen: D. T. Suzuki and the Modern Transformation of Buddhism.* Honolulu: University of Hawai'i Press, 2022.

Broughton, Jeffrey L. "Chan Literature." In *Oxford Research Encyclopedia of Religion*, edited by Georgios T. Halkias and Richard K. Payne. New York: Oxford University Press, 2017. https://doi.org/10.1093/acrefore/9780199340378.013.214.

Buswell, Robert E. *The Zen Monastic Experience: Buddhist Practice in Contemporary Korea.* Princeton, NJ: Princeton University Press, 1992.

Butler, Judith P. *Giving an Account of Oneself.* New York: Fordham University Press, 2009.

Caplow, Zenshin Florence, and Reigetsu Susan Moon, eds. *The Hidden Lamp: Stories from Twenty-Five Centuries of Awakened Women.* Somerville, MA: Wisdom, 2013.

Chadwick, David. *Crooked Cucumber: The Life and Teaching of Shunryu Suzuki.* Reprint. Chatsworth, CA: Harmony, 2011.

———. "Edward Brown Barred from Teaching at SFZC." *Cuke.com* (blog). October 5, 2018. http://www.cuke.com/Cucumber%20Project/brown-edward/barred-from-sfzc.htm#abbots&gsc.tab=0.

———. *Thank You and OK! An American Zen Failure in Japan.* Boston: Shambhala, 1994.

Chandler, Stuart. "Chinese Buddhism in America: Identity and Practice." In *The Faces of Buddhism in America,* 13–30. Oakland: University of California Press, 1998.

Cheah, Joseph. "Buddhism, Race, and Ethnicity." In *The Oxford Handbook of Contemporary Buddhism,* by Michael Jerryson, vol. 1. New York: Oxford University Press, 2016. https://doi.org/10.1093/oxfordhb/9780199362387.013.16.

Cleary, Thomas F., and J. C. Cleary, trans. *The Blue Cliff Record.* Boston: Shambhala, 1977.

Cole, Alan. *Patriarchs on Paper: A Critical History of Medieval Chan Literature.* Oakland: University of California Press, 2016.

Corey, James S. A. *Leviathan Wakes*. Book 1 of *The Expanse* series. New York: Orbit, 2011.

Crenshaw, Kimberle. "Mapping the Margins: Intersectionality, Identity Politics, and Violence Against Women of Color." *Stanford Law Review* 43, no. 6 (1991): 1241–99. https://doi.org/10.2307/1229039.

Cutts, Eijiun Linda Ruth, Rinso Ed Sattizahn, Fu Schroeder, Brian McCaffrey, and Shinchi Linda Galijan. "SFZC Leadership Statement on Edward Brown Matter." October 11, 2018. http://www.cuke.com/Cucumber%20Project/brown-edward/leadership-statement-sangha-news.htm#gsc.tab=0.

Dällenbach, Lucien. *The Mirror in the Text*. Translated by Jeremy Whiteley and Emma Hughes. Cambridge, UK: Polity, 1989.

Davis, Rocío G. "Fictional Transits and Ruth Ozeki's *A Tale for the Time Being*." *Biography* 38, no. 1 (2015): 87–103. https://doi.org/10.1353/bio.2015.0007.

De Martino, Richard J. "On My First Coming to Meet Dr. D. T. Suzuki." *Eastern Buddhist* 2, no. 1 (August 1967): 69–74.

Derrida, Jacques. "Plato's Pharmacy." In *Dissemination*, translated by Barbara Johnson, 61–119. Chicago: University of Chicago Press, 1981.

Dorst, John D. "Neck-Riddle as a Dialogue of Genres: Applying Bakhtin's Genre Theory." *Journal of American Folklore* 96, no. 382 (October 1983): 413. https://doi.org/10.2307/540982.

Downing, Michael. *Shoes outside the Door: Desire, Devotion, and Excess at San Francisco Zen Center*. Washington, DC: Counterpoint, 2001.

Dumoulin, Heinrich. *Japan*. Vol. 2 of *Zen Buddhism: A History*. New York: Macmillan, 1990.

Eakin, Paul John. *How Our Lives Become Stories: Making Selves*. Cornell Paperbacks. Ithaca, NY: Cornell University Press, 1999.

Edelglass, William. "Buddhism, Happiness, and the Science of Meditation." In *Meditation, Buddhism, and Science*, edited by David L. McMahan and Erik Braun, 62–83. New York: Oxford University Press, 2017.

Falk, Jane E. "The Beat Avant-Garde, the 1950's, and the Popularizing of Zen Buddhism in the United States." PhD diss., Ohio State University, 2002.

Fanon, Frantz. "The Fact of Blackness." In *Black Skin, White Masks*, translated by Charles Lam Markmann. New York: Grove, 1967.

Fass, Paula S. "The Memoir Problem." *Reviews in American History* 34, no. 1 (2006): 107–23. https://doi.org/10.1353/rah.2006.0004.

Faure, Bernard. "Bodhidharma as Textual and Religious Paradigm." *History of Religions* 25, no. 3 (1986): 187–98. http://www.jstor.org/stable/1062511.

———. *Chan Insights and Oversights: An Epistemological Critique of the Chan Tradition*. Princeton, NJ: Princeton University Press, 1993.

———. *The Power of Denial: Buddhism, Purity, and Gender*. Buddhisms. Princeton, NJ: Princeton University Press, 2003.

———. *The Red Thread: Buddhist Approaches to Sexuality*. Princeton, NJ: Princeton University Press, 1998.

———. *The Rhetoric of Immediacy: A Cultural Critique of Chan/Zen Buddhism*. Princeton, NJ: Princeton University Press, 1991.

Fernandez, Leslie J. "Extrospection: Zen and the Art of Being Posthuman in Ruth Ozeki's *A Tale for the Time Being*." *Textual Practice* 36, no. 10 (October 3, 2022): 1645–64. https://doi.org/10.1080/0950236X.2021.1971747.

Ferns, C. S. *Narrating Utopia: Ideology, Gender, Form in Utopian Literature*. Liverpool Science Fiction Texts and Studies 19. Liverpool, UK: Liverpool University Press, 1999.

Fields, Rick. *How the Swans Came to the Lake: A Narrative History of Buddhism in America*. 3rd ed. Boston: Shambhala, 1992.

Filgate, Michele. "Writing the Body: Trauma, Illness, Sexuality, and Beyond: Eileen Myles, Ruth Ozeki, Porochista Khakpour, Anna March & Alexandra Kleeman." *Literary Hub* (blog). December 6, 2016. https://lithub.com/writing-the-body-trauma-illness-sexuality-and-beyond/.

Fischer, Norman. *The World Could Be Otherwise: Imagination and the Bodhisattva Path*. Boulder, CO: Shambhala, 2019.

Foulk, T. Griffith. "'Authentic': Rehabilitating Two Chan Buddhist Masters Neglected in Zen Studies." *Harvard Journal of Asiatic Studies* 77, no. 2 (2017): 465–86. https://doi.org/10.1353/jas.2017.0034.

———. "The Ch'an Tsung in Medieval China: School, Lineage, or What?" *Pacific World* 8 (1992): 18–31.

———. "The Form and Function of Kōan Literature: A Historical Overview." In *The Kōan: Text and Contexts in Zen Buddhism*, edited by Steven Heine and Dale S. Wright. Oxford: Oxford University Press, 2000.

———. "Myth, Ritual, and Monastic Practice in Sung Ch'an Buddhism." In *Religion and Society in T'ang and Sung China*, edited by Patricia Buckley Ebrey and Peter N. Gregory, 147–208. Honolulu: University of Hawai'i Press, 1993.

Frow, John. *Genre*. 2nd ed. The New Critical Idiom. New York: Routledge, 2015.

Garton-Gundling, Kyle. *Enlightened Individualism: Buddhism and Hinduism in American Literature from the Beats to the Present*. Literature, Religion, and Postsecular Studies. Columbus: Ohio State University Press, 2019.

Gleig, Ann. *American Dharma: Buddhism beyond Modernity*. New Haven, CT: Yale University Press, 2019.

———. "Buddhists and Racial Justice: A History." *Tricycle: The Buddhist Review*, July 24, 2020. https://tricycle.org/trikedaily/buddhists-racial-justice/.

———. "Undoing Whiteness in American Buddhist Modernism: Critical, Collective, and Contextual Turns." In *Buddhism and Whiteness: Critical Reflections*, edited by Emily McRae and George Yancy. Philosophy of Race. Lanham, MD: Lexington, 2019.

Gleig, Ann, and Brenna Artinger. "#BuddhistCultureWars: BuddhaBros, Alt-Right Dharma, and Snowflake Sanghas." *Journal of Global Buddhism* 22, no. 1 (2021): 19–48. https://doi.org/10.5281/ZENODO.4727561.

Goldberg, Natalie. *The Great Failure: A Bartender, a Monk, and My Unlikely Path to Truth*. San Francisco: Harper, 2004.

———. *The Great Spring: Writing, Zen, and This Zigzag Life*. Boulder, CO: Shambhala, 2016.

———. *Long Quiet Highway: Waking up in America*. New York: Bantam, 1993.

———. *Writing down the Bones: Freeing the Writer Within*. Boston: Shambhala, 1986.

Grant, Beata. "Da Zhangfu: The Gendered Rhetoric of Heroism and Equality in Seventeenth-Century Chan Buddhist Discourse Records." *Nan Nü* 10, no. 2 (2008): 177–211.

Greene, Eric M. *Chan before Chan: Meditation, Repentance, and Visionary Experience in Chinese Buddhism*. Honolulu: University of Hawai'i Press, 2021.

Greenwood, Gesshin Claire. *Bow First, Ask Questions Later: Ordination, Love, and Monastic Zen in Japan*. Somerville, MA: Wisdom, 2018.

Greenwood, Gesshin Claire, and Tamar Adler. *Just Enough: Vegan Recipes and Stories from Japan's Buddhist Temples*. Novato, CA: New World Library, 2019.

Gyatso, Janet. "One Plus One Makes Three: Buddhist Gender, Monasticism, and the Law of the Non-Excluded Middle." *History of Religions* 43, no. 2 (November 2003): 89–115. http://www.jstor.org/stable/10.1086/423006.

———. "Sex." In *Critical Terms for the Study of Buddhism*, edited by Donald S. Lopez, 271–90. Buddhism and Modernity. Chicago: Chicago University Press, 2005.

Halberstam, Judith. *The Queer Art of Failure*. Durham, NC: Duke University Press, 2011.

Han, Chenxing. *Be the Refuge: Raising the Voices of Asian American Buddhists*. Berkeley, CA: North Atlantic, 2021.

Harrington, Anne. "Zen, Suzuki, and the Art of Psychotherapy." In *Science and Religion, East and West*, edited by Yiftach Fehige, 48–69. New York: Routledge, 2016.

Haskins, Rob. "Aspects of Zen Buddhism as an Analytical Context for John Cage's Chance Music." *Contemporary Music Review* 33, no. 5–6 (November 2, 2014): 616–29. https://doi.org/10.1080/07494467.2014.998426.

Haubner, Shozan Jack. "Re: Single White Monk," July 31, 2018.

———. *Single White Monk: Tales of Death, Failure, and Bad Sex (Although Not Necessarily in That Order)*. Boulder, CO: Shambhala, 2017.

———. *Zen Confidential: Confessions of a Wayward Monk*. Boston: Shambhala, 2013.

Heine, Steven. *Existential and Ontological Dimensions of Time in Heidegger and Dōgen*. SUNY Series in Buddhist Studies. Albany: State University of New York Press, 1985.

———. *Zen Skin, Zen Marrow: Will the Real Zen Buddhism Please Stand Up?* New York: Oxford University Press, 2008. https://doi.org/10.1093/acprof:oso/9780195326772.001.0001.

Hickey, Wakoh Shannon. "Two Buddhisms, Three Buddhisms, and Racism." *Global Buddhism* 11 (2010). https://doi.org/http://dx.doi.org/10.5281/zenodo.1306702.

Hoffman, Yoel, and Dror Burstein. *The Sound of the One Hand: 281 Zen Koans with Answers*. Translated by Yoel Hoffmann. New York: NYRB Classics, 2016.

Hori, Victor Sōgen. *Zen Sand: The Book of Capping Phrases for Kōan Practice*. Honolulu: University of Hawai'i, 2003.

Howlett, Zachary M. "A Fateful Rite of Passage: The Gaokao and the Myth of Meritocracy." In *Meritocracy and Its Discontents: Anxiety and the National College Entrance Exam in China*, edited by Howlett, 1–40. Ithaca, NY: Cornell University Press, 2021. https://doi.org/10.7591/cornell/9781501754432.003.0001.

Hsieh, Ding-hwa. "Images of Women in Ch'an Buddhist Literature." In *Buddhism in the Sung*, edited by Daniel A. Getz and Peter N. Gregory. Honolulu: Hawai'i University Press, 1999.

Huineng. *The Platform Sutra of the Sixth Patriarch*. Translated by John R. McRae. BDK English Tripiṭaka, 73-II. Berkeley, CA: Numata Center for Buddhist Translation and Research, 2000.

———. *The Platform Sutra of the Sixth Patriarch; the Text of the Tun-Huang Manuscript with Translation, Introduction, and Notes*. Translated by Philip B. Yampolsky. Records of Civilization: Sources and Studies 76. New York: Columbia University Press, 1967.

Inagaki, Hisao. "Experiences in a Japanese Zen Monastery." Review of *The Empty Mirror*. *Journal of the Royal Asiatic Society*, n.s., vol. 107, no. 1 (January 1975): 87. http://journals.cambridge.org/article_S0035869X0013268X.

Iwamura, Jane Naomi. *Virtual Orientalism: Asian Religions and American Popular Culture*. New York: Oxford University Press, 2011.

Jacoby, Sarah H. *Love and Liberation: Autobiographical Writings of the Tibetan Buddhist Visionary Sera Khandro*. New York: Columbia University Press, 2014.

Jansma, Bert. "De vrijheid van Janwillem van de Wetering." *Finale-Het Binnenhof*. May 21, 1983. Howard Gotlieb Archival Research Center.

Janwillem van de Wetering—To Infinity and Beyond. Boeddhistische Omroep Stichting, August 29, 2004. https://www.uitzendinggemist.net/aflevering/22656/Janwillem_Van_De_Wetering_To_Infinity_And_Beyond.html.

Kaivola-Bregenhøj, Annikki. *Riddles: Perspectives on the Use, Function and Change in a Folklore Genre.* Studia Fennica 10. Helsinki: Finnish Literature Society, 2001.

Kapleau, Philip. "Letter to Ann Kahl." February 11, 1992. David M. Rubenstein Rare Book & Manuscript Library, Duke University.

———. "Letter to Charlotte and Lee Kramer." September 16, 1992. David M. Rubenstein Rare Book & Manuscript Library, Duke University.

———. "Letter to Jim Kupecz." September 28, 1994. David M. Rubenstein Rare Book & Manuscript Library, Duke University.

———. *The Three Pillars of Zen: Teaching, Practice, and Enlightenment.* Boston: Beacon, 1967.

———. *The Three Pillars of Zen: Teaching, Practice, and Enlightenment.* 35th anniversary ed. New York: Anchor, 2000.

———. *Zen: Dawn in the West.* Garden City, NY: Anchor, 1979.

Kerouac, Jack. "Belief and Technique for Modern Prose." *Evergreen Review* 2, no. 8 (1959).

Kornfield, Jack. *A Path with Heart: A Guide through the Perils and Promises of Spiritual Life.* New York: Bantam, 1993.

Kotler, Arnold, and Kazuo Tanahashi. "Mountains and Waters Sutra (Sansui-Kyō)." In *Zen Sourcebook: Traditional Documents from China, Korea, and Japan,* edited by Stephen Addiss, Stanley Lombardo, and Judith Roitman, 162–72. Indianapolis, IN: Hackett, 2008.

Kraft, Kenneth, ed. *Zen Teaching, Zen Practice: Philip Kapleau and "The Three Pillars of Zen."* Trumbull, CT: Weatherhill, 2000.

Kripal, Jeffrey J. *Secret Body: Erotic and Esoteric Currents in the History of Religions.* Chicago: University of Chicago Press, 2017. https://doi.org/10.7208/chicago/9780226491486.001.0001.

Lakoff, George, and Mark Johnson. *Metaphors We Live By.* Chicago: University of Chicago Press, 2003.

Larson, Kay. *Where the Heart Beats: John Cage, Zen Buddhism, and the Inner Life of Artists.* New York: Penguin, 2012.

Lee, Hsiu-chuan. "Sharing Worlds through Words: Minor Cosmopolitics in Ruth Ozeki's *A Tale for the Time Being.*" *Ariel: A Review of International English Literature* 49, no. 1 (2018): 27–52. https://doi.org/10.1353/ari.2018.0001.

Lejeune, Philippe. *On Autobiography.* Edited by Paul John Eakin. Translated by Katherine M. Leary. Theory and History of Literature 52. Minneapolis: University of Minnesota Press, 1989.

Levering, Miriam L. "Lin-Chi (Rinzai) Ch'an and Gender: The Rhetoric of Equality and the Rhetoric of Heroism." In *Buddhism, Sexuality, and Gender,* by José Ignacio Cabezón, 137–56. Albany: State University of New York Press, 1992.

———. "Miao-Tao and Her Teacher Ta-Hui." In *Buddhism in the Sung*, edited by Peter N. Gregory and Daniel A. Getz. Kuroda Studies in East Asian Buddhism 13. Honolulu: University of Hawai'i Press, 1999.

Lewis-Kraus, Gideon. "The Reluctant Prophet of Effective Altruism." *New Yorker*, August 8, 2022. https://www.newyorker.com/magazine/2022/08/15/the-reluctant-prophet-of-effective-altruism.

Linji. *The Record of Linji*. Edited by Thomas Yūhō Kirchner. Translated by Ruth Fuller Sasaki. Honolulu: University of Hawai'i Press, 2009.

Lionnet, Françoise. *Postcolonial Representations: Women, Literature, Identity*. Ithaca, NY: Cornell University Press, 1995.

Lovell, Sue. "Toward a Poetics of Posthumanist Narrative Using Ruth Ozeki's *A Tale for the Time Being*." *Critique: Studies in Contemporary Fiction* 59, no. 1 (January 2018): 57–74. https://doi.org/10.1080/00111619.2017.1360834.

Luchette, Claire. "Ruth Ozeki on *A Tale for the Time Being*: We All Have a Buddhist Nun inside Us." *Bustle*, January 14, 2014. https://www.bustle.com/articles/12387-ruth-ozeki-on-a-tale-for-the-time-being-we-all-have-a-buddhist-nun-inside.

Magliola, Robert R. *Derrida on the Mend*. West Lafayette, IN: Purdue University Press, 1984.

Manuel, Zenju Earthlyn. *Sanctuary: A Meditation on Home, Homelessness, and Belonging*. Kindle. Somerville, MA: Wisdom, 2018.

———. *The Way of Tenderness: Awakening through Race, Sexuality, and Gender*. Kindle. Somerville, MA: Wisdom, 2015.

Marcus, Laura. *Autobiography: A Very Short Introduction*. Illustrated ed. New York: Oxford University Press, 2018.

Martin, Craig, and Russell T. McCutcheon, eds. *Religious Experience: A Reader*. New York: Routledge, 2014.

Masatsugu, Michael K. *Reorienting the Pure Land: Nisei Buddhism in the Transwar Years, 1943–1965*. Intersections: Asian and Pacific American Transcultural Studies. Honolulu: University of Hawai'i Press, 2023.

Matthiessen, Peter. *Nine-Headed Dragon River: Zen Journals, 1969–1982*. Boston: Shambhala, 1985.

McDowell, John Holmes. *Children's Riddling*. Bloomington: Indiana University Press, 1979.

McKay, Daniel. "The Right Stuff: The Kamikaze Pilot in Kerri Sakamoto's *One Hundred Million Hearts* and Ruth Ozeki's *A Tale for the Time Being*." *MELUS: Multi-Ethnic Literature of the United States* 41, no. 1 (March 2016): 6–26. https://doi.org/10.1093/melus/mlv081.

McMahan, David L. *The Making of Buddhist Modernism*. New York: Oxford University Press, 2008.

McMahan, David L., and Erik Braun, eds. *Meditation, Buddhism, and Science*. New York: Oxford University Press, 2017.

McNicholl, Adeana. "Being Buddha, Staying Woke: Racial Formation in Black Buddhist Writing." *Journal of the American Academy of Religion*, July 13, 2018. https://doi.org/10.1093/jaarel/lfy019.

McRae, John R. "The Antecedents of Encounter Dialogue in Chinese Ch'an Buddhism." In *The Kōan: Text and Contexts in Zen Buddhism*, edited by Steven Heine and Dale S. Wright. Oxford: Oxford University Press, 2000.

———. "Buddhism, Schools of: Chinese Buddhism." In *Encyclopedia of Religion*, edited by Lindsay Jones, 2nd ed., 1235–41. Detroit, MI: Macmillan, 2005.

———. *Seeing through Zen: Encounter, Transformation, and Genealogy in Chinese Chan Buddhism*. Berkeley: University of California Press, 2003.

Miller, Nancy K. "But Enough about Me, What Do You Think of My Memoir?" *Yale Journal of Criticism* 13, no. 2 (2000): 421–36.

Mitchell, Scott A. *Buddhism in America: Global Religion, Local Contexts*. London: Bloomsbury Academic, 2016.

———. *The Making of American Buddhism*. Oxford: Oxford University Press, 2023.

Murphy, Sean. *One Bird, One Stone: 108 Contemporary Zen Stories*. Charlottesville, VA: Hampton Roads, 2013.

Nattier, Jan. *Once upon a Future Time: Studies in a Buddhist Prophecy of Decline*. Berkeley, CA: Asian Humanities Press, 1991.

Nicholls, David. *John Cage*. American Composers. Urbana: University of Illinois Press, 2007.

Noland, Carrie. "Embodiment." In *Encyclopedia of Aesthetics*, by Michael Kelly, 2nd ed. New York: Oxford University Press, 2014.

Olson, Carl. "Playing in the Non-Representational Mode of Thinking: A Comparison of Derrida, Dōgen, and Zhuangzi." *Comparative and Continental Philosophy* 12, no. 1 (January 2, 2020): 30–43. https://doi.org/10.1080/17570638.2020.1709684.

Oppenheimer, Mark. "The Zen Predator of the Upper East Side." *The Atlantic*, December 18, 2014. https://www.theatlantic.com/national/archive/2014/12/the-zen-predator-of-the-upper-east-side/383831/.

The Osho Council of Rinzai-ji. "An Open Letter to the Buddhist Community from the Osho Council of Rinzai-Ji." *Tricycle: The Buddhist Review*, January 11, 2013. https://tricycle.org/trikedaily/open-letter-buddhist-community-osho-council-rinzai-ji/.

Ozeki, Ruth. "Confessions of a Zen Novelist." *Lion's Roar*, February 15, 2013. https://www.lionsroar.com/confessions-of-a-zen-novelist/.

———. *The Face: A Time Code*. New York: Restless, 2015.

———. "Ruth Ozeki, 'The Contemplative "I": Zen and the Art of Autobiographical Fiction' (November 12, 2018)." Smith College, November 16, 2018. https://www.youtube.com/watch?v=60ZoSNYZPgc.

———. "Ruth Ozeki on Catastrophe, Thought Experiments and Writing as Performed Philosophy." Interview by Leanne Hall. September 14, 2013. https://www.youtube.com/watch?v=I0--yah7K7U.

———. *A Tale for the Time Being*. New York: Penguin, 2013.

———. "'A Universe of Many Worlds': An Interview with Ruth Ozeki." By Eleanor Ty. *MELUS: Multi-Ethnic Literature of the United States* 38, no. 3 (September 1, 2013): 160–71. https://doi.org/10.1093/melus/mlt028.

———. "A Vacation with Ghosts." *New York Times*, August 11, 2004, Opinion. https://www.nytimes.com/2004/08/11/opinion/a-vacation-with-ghosts.html.

P'ang, Yun. *A Man of Zen: The Recorded Sayings of Layman P'ang*. Translated by Ruth Fuller Sasaki and Yoshitaka Iriya. New York: Weatherhill, 1972.

Pei, Jiaxin, Zhihan (Helen) Wang, and Jun Li. "30 Million Canvas Grading Records Reveal Widespread Sequential Bias and System-Induced Surname Initial Disparity." SSRN scholarly paper. Rochester, NY, October 16, 2023. https://papers.ssrn.com/abstract=4603146.

Pepicello, W. J., and Thomas A. Green. *The Language of Riddles: New Perspectives*. Columbus: Ohio State University Press, 1984.

Poceski, Mario. "Monastic Innovator, Iconoclast, and Teacher of Doctrine: The Varied Images of Chan Master Baizhang." In *Zen Masters*, edited by Steven Heine and Dale S. Wright, 3–32. New York: Oxford University Press, 2010.

———. *The Records of Mazu and the Making of Classical Chan Literature*. New York: Oxford University Press, 2015.

Quli, Natalie E. "Western Self, Asian Other: Modernity, Authenticity, and Nostalgia for 'Tradition' in Buddhist Studies." *Journal of Buddhist Ethics* 16 (2009): 1–38.

Rak, Julie. *Boom! Manufacturing Memoir for the Popular Market*. Illustrated ed. Waterloo, ON: Wilfrid Laurier University Press, 2013.

Raud, Rein. "'Place' and 'Being-Time': Spatiotemporal Concepts in the Thought of Nishida Kitaro and Dogen Kigen." *Philosophy East and West* 54, no. 1 (January 2004): 29+.

Rivera, Erica. "Natalie Goldberg on the Zen of Writing, Minnesota Haunts, and Cookie Meditations." *City Pages*, June 14, 2016. http://www.citypages.com/arts/natalie-goldberg-on-the-zen-of-writing-minnesota-haunts-and-cookie-meditations-8301150.

Sandage, Scott A. *Born Losers: A History of Failure in America*. Cambridge, MA: Harvard University Press, 2006.

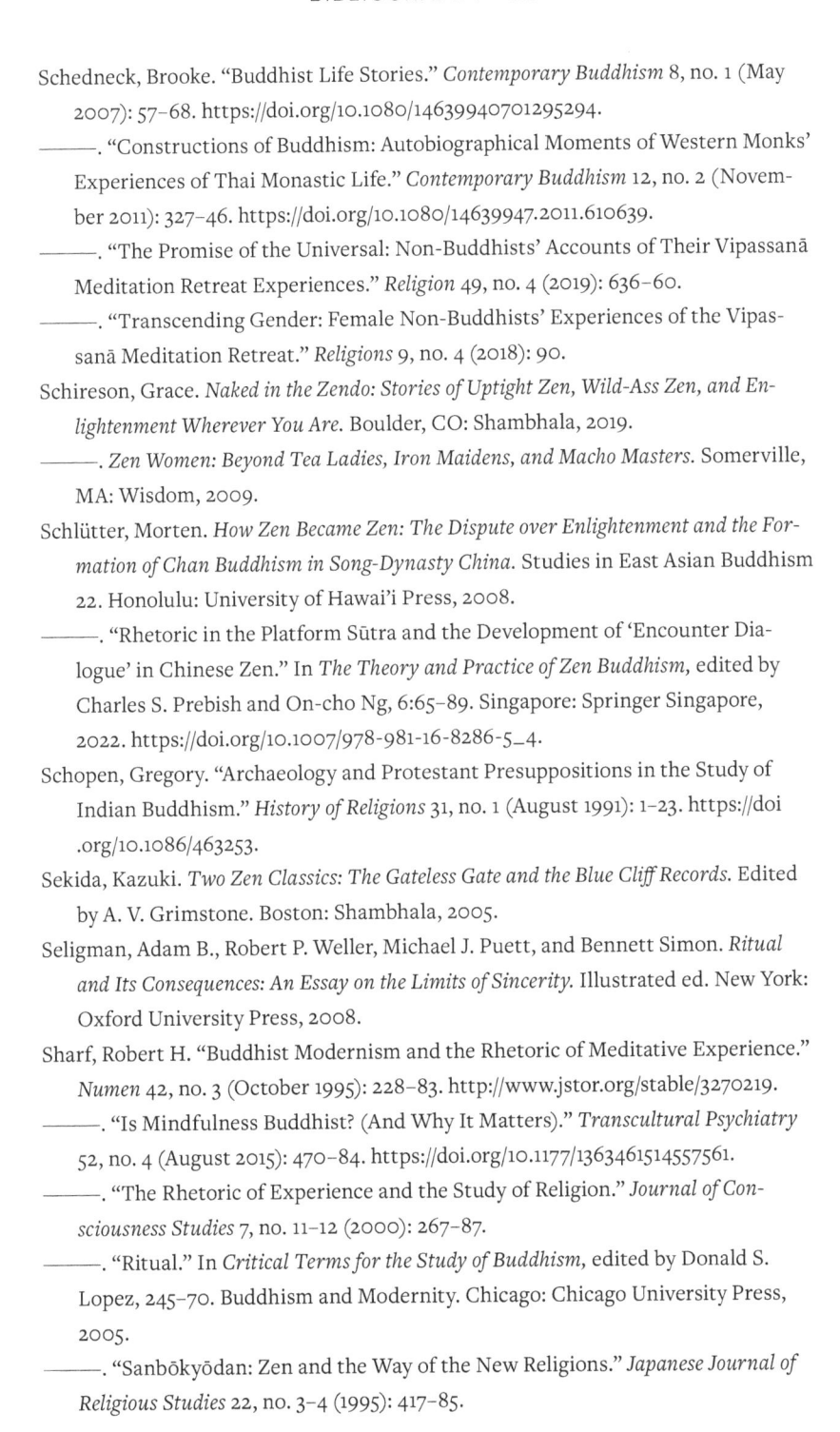

Schedneck, Brooke. "Buddhist Life Stories." *Contemporary Buddhism* 8, no. 1 (May 2007): 57–68. https://doi.org/10.1080/14639940701295294.

———. "Constructions of Buddhism: Autobiographical Moments of Western Monks' Experiences of Thai Monastic Life." *Contemporary Buddhism* 12, no. 2 (November 2011): 327–46. https://doi.org/10.1080/14639947.2011.610639.

———. "The Promise of the Universal: Non-Buddhists' Accounts of Their Vipassanā Meditation Retreat Experiences." *Religion* 49, no. 4 (2019): 636–60.

———. "Transcending Gender: Female Non-Buddhists' Experiences of the Vipassanā Meditation Retreat." *Religions* 9, no. 4 (2018): 90.

Schireson, Grace. *Naked in the Zendo: Stories of Uptight Zen, Wild-Ass Zen, and Enlightenment Wherever You Are*. Boulder, CO: Shambhala, 2019.

———. *Zen Women: Beyond Tea Ladies, Iron Maidens, and Macho Masters*. Somerville, MA: Wisdom, 2009.

Schlütter, Morten. *How Zen Became Zen: The Dispute over Enlightenment and the Formation of Chan Buddhism in Song-Dynasty China*. Studies in East Asian Buddhism 22. Honolulu: University of Hawai'i Press, 2008.

———. "Rhetoric in the Platform Sūtra and the Development of 'Encounter Dialogue' in Chinese Zen." In *The Theory and Practice of Zen Buddhism*, edited by Charles S. Prebish and On-cho Ng, 6:65–89. Singapore: Springer Singapore, 2022. https://doi.org/10.1007/978-981-16-8286-5_4.

Schopen, Gregory. "Archaeology and Protestant Presuppositions in the Study of Indian Buddhism." *History of Religions* 31, no. 1 (August 1991): 1–23. https://doi.org/10.1086/463253.

Sekida, Kazuki. *Two Zen Classics: The Gateless Gate and the Blue Cliff Records*. Edited by A. V. Grimstone. Boston: Shambhala, 2005.

Seligman, Adam B., Robert P. Weller, Michael J. Puett, and Bennett Simon. *Ritual and Its Consequences: An Essay on the Limits of Sincerity*. Illustrated ed. New York: Oxford University Press, 2008.

Sharf, Robert H. "Buddhist Modernism and the Rhetoric of Meditative Experience." *Numen* 42, no. 3 (October 1995): 228–83. http://www.jstor.org/stable/3270219.

———. "Is Mindfulness Buddhist? (And Why It Matters)." *Transcultural Psychiatry* 52, no. 4 (August 2015): 470–84. https://doi.org/10.1177/1363461514557561.

———. "The Rhetoric of Experience and the Study of Religion." *Journal of Consciousness Studies* 7, no. 11–12 (2000): 267–87.

———. "Ritual." In *Critical Terms for the Study of Buddhism*, edited by Donald S. Lopez, 245–70. Buddhism and Modernity. Chicago: Chicago University Press, 2005.

———. "Sanbōkyōdan: Zen and the Way of the New Religions." *Japanese Journal of Religious Studies* 22, no. 3–4 (1995): 417–85.

———. "Whose Zen? Zen Nationalism Revisited." In *Rude Awakenings: Zen, the Kyoto School, and the Question of Nationalism,* by James W. Heisig and John C. Maraldo, 40–51. Nanzan Studies in Religion and Culture. Honolulu: University of Hawai'i Press, 1995.

———. "The Zen of Japanese Nationalism." *History of Religions* 33, no. 1 (August 1993): 1–43. http://www.jstor.org/stable/1062782.

Sigalow, Emily. *American Jewbu: Jews, Buddhists, and Religious Change.* Princeton, NJ: Princeton University Press, 2019.

Smith, Huston. "Chapter 5—Empirical Metaphysics." In *The Ecstatic Adventure,* edited by Ralph Metzner. New York: Macmillan, 1968.

Smith, Jonathan Z. "Interview with J. Z. Smith." By Supriya Sinhababu. *Chicago Maroon,* June 2, 2008. https://www.chicagomaroon.com/2008/06/02/interview-with-j-z-smith/.

Smith, Sidonie, and Julia Watson. *Reading Autobiography: A Guide for Interpreting Life Narratives.* Minneapolis: University of Minnesota Press, 2001.

The Smoking Gun. "A Million Little Lies." July 23, 2010. http://www.thesmokinggun.com/documents/celebrity/million-little-lies.

Snodgrass, Judith. "Publishing Eastern Buddhism: D. T. Suzuki's Journey to the West." In *Casting Faiths: Imperialism and the Transformation of Religion in East and Southeast Asia,* edited by Thomas David DuBois, 46–72. Basingstoke, UK: Palgrave Macmillan, 2009.

Snyder, Gary, and William Scott McLean. *The Real Work: Interviews & Talks, 1964–1979.* New York: New Directions, 1980.

Stalling, Jonathan. *Poetics of Emptiness: Transformations of Asian Thought in American Poetry.* New York: Fordham University Press, 2011. https://doi.org/10.1515/9780823244355.

Stambaugh, Joan. *Impermanence Is Buddha-Nature: Dōgen's Understanding of Temporality.* Honolulu: University of Hawai'i Press, 1990.

Starr, Marlo. "Beyond Machine Dreams: Zen, Cyber-, and Transnational Feminisms in Ruth Ozeki's *A Tale for the Time Being.*" *Meridians* 13, no. 2 (March 1, 2016): 99–122. https://doi.org/10.2979/meridians.13.2.06.

Suzuki, Daisetz Teitaro. "Early Memories." In *Selected Works of D. T. Suzuki,* vol 1: *Zen,* edited by Richard M. Jaffe, 202–10. Berkeley: University of California Press, 2014.

———. *An Introduction to Zen Buddhism.* New York: Grove, 2004.

———. *Selected Works of D. T. Suzuki.* Vol. 1: *Zen.* Edited by Richard M. Jaffe. 3 vols. Berkeley: University of California Press, 2015.

———. *Zen and Japanese Culture.* Edited by Richard M. Jaffe. Bollingen Series 64. Princeton, NJ: Princeton University Press, 2010.

Suzuki, Daisetz Teitaro, Erich Fromm, and Richard J. De Martino. *Zen Buddhism & Psychoanalysis*. New York: Harper, 1960.

Tolle, Eckhart. *The Power of Now: A Guide to Spiritual Enlightenment*. Kindle. Novato, CA: New World Library, 2010.

Torres, Émile P. "Why Longtermism Is the World's Most Dangerous Secular Credo." *Aeon*, October 19, 2021. https://aeon.co/essays/why-longtermism-is-the-worlds-most-dangerous-secular-credo.

"Troubling Experience at Green Gulch," August 2, 2018. http://www.cuke.com/pdf-2015/troubling-experience-at-green-gulch.pdf.

Tweed, Thomas A. "Night-Stand Buddhists and Other Creatures: Sympathizers, Adherents, and the Study of Religion." In *American Buddhism: Methods and Findings in Recent Scholarship*, edited by Duncan Ryūken Williams and Christopher S. Queen, 71–90. Richmond, Surrey, UK: Curzon, 1999.

Ty, Eleanor. *Unfastened: Globality and Asian North American Narratives*. Minneapolis: University of Minnesota Press, 2010.

Van de Wetering, Janwillem. *Afterzen: Experiences of a Zen Student Out on His Ear*. New York: St. Martin's, 1999.

———. *The Empty Mirror: Experiences in a Japanese Zen Monastery*. 1st American ed. Boston: Houghton Mifflin, 1973.

———. *A Glimpse of Nothingness: Experiences in an American Zen Community*. Boston: Houghton-Mifflin, 1975.

———. *Het dagende niets: Beschrijving van een eerste bewustwording in zen*. Amsterdam: De Driehoek, 1974.

———. "Interview with J. Van de W." By David R. Walker. *Preview*, July 8–14, 1985. Howard Gotlieb Archival Research Center, Boston University.

———. Introduction to *The Zen Koan as a Means of Attaining Enlightenment*, by Daisetz Teitaro Suzuki. Boston: C. E. Tuttle, 1994.

———. *Zuivere leegte: Ervaringen van een respectloze zenleerling*. Rotterdam: Asoka, 2000.

Van de Wetering, Thera. Interview by Ben Van Overmeire about Janwillem van de Wetering. Facebook Messenger, June 5, 2020.

Van Overmeire, Ben. "DT Suzuki's Literary Influence: Utopian Narrative in American and European Memoirs of Zen Life." In *Beyond Zen: D. T. Suzuki and the Modern Transformation of Buddhism*, edited by John Breen, Sueki Fumihiko, and Yamada Shōji, 247–67. Honolulu: University of Hawai'i Press, 2022.

———. "Hard-Boiled Zen: Janwillem van de Wetering's *The Japanese Corpse* as Buddhist Literature." *Contemporary Buddhism* 19, no. 2 (July 3, 2018): 382–97. https://doi.org/10.1080/14639947.2018.1480890.

———. "Inventing the Zen Buddhist Samurai: Yoshikawa Eiji's Musashi and Japanese Modernity." *Journal of Popular Culture* 49, no. 5 (2016): 1125–45. https://doi.org/10.1111/jpcu.12461.

———. "'Mountains, Rivers, and the Whole Earth': Koan Interpretations of Female Zen Practitioners." *Religions* 9, no. 4 (April 2018): 125. https://doi.org/10.3390/rel9040125.

———. "Portraying Zen Buddhism in the Twentieth Century: Encounter Dialogues as Frame-Stories in Daisetz Suzuki's *An Introduction to Zen Buddhism* and Janwillem van de Wetering's *The Empty Mirror*." *Japan Studies Review* 21 (2017): 3–24.

———. "Reading Chan Encounter Dialogue during the Song Dynasty: *The Record of Linji*, the Lotus Sutra, and the Sinification of Buddhism." *Buddhist-Christian Studies* 37 (October 28, 2017): 209–21. https://doi.org/10.1353/bcs.2017.0015.

Vanacker, Sabine. "Imagining a Global Village: Amsterdam in Janwillem van de Wetering's Detective Fiction." In *Imagining Global Amsterdam: History, Culture, and Geography in a World City*, edited by Marco de Waard, 169–86. Amsterdam: Amsterdam University Press, 2012.

Victoria, Brian. *Zen at War*. 2nd ed. Lanham, MD: Rowman & Littlefield, 2006.

Warner, Brad. "Challenging Cherished Beliefs." *Hardcore Zen* (blog). October 12, 2018. https://web.archive.org/web/20181012101548/http://hardcorezen.info/challenging-cherished-beliefs/6016.

———. "Inclusivity in Zen." *Hardcore Zen* (blog). October 13, 2018. https://web.archive.org/web/20181013092749/http://hardcorezen.info/inclusivity-in-zen/6012.

———. "Zentertainment Weakly." *Hardcore Zen* (blog). December 18, 2018. https://web.archive.org/web/20181218004613/http://hardcorezen.info/zentertainment-weakly/6037.

Weinstein, Stanley. "Buddhism, Schools of: Chinese Buddhism." In *The Encyclopedia of Religion*, edited by Mircea Eliade, 2:482–87. New York: Macmillan, 1987.

Welter, Albert. *The Linji Lu and the Creation of Chan Orthodoxy: The Development of Chan's Records of Sayings Literature*. New York: Oxford University Press, 2008.

———. "The Problem with Orthodoxy in Zen Buddhism: Yongming Yanshou's Notion of Zong in the Zongjin Lu (Records of the Source Mirror)." *Studies in Religion/Sciences Religieuses* 31, no. 1 (2002): 3–18.

Whalen-Bridge, John, and Gary Storhoff. *The Emergence of Buddhist American Literature*. Albany: State University of New York Press, 2009.

williams, angel Kyodo. *Being Black: Zen and the Art of Living with Fearlessness and Grace*. Harmondsworth, UK: Penguin, 2002.

Williams, Duncan Ryūken. *American Sutra: A Story of Faith and Freedom in the Second World War*. Cambridge, MA: Harvard University Press, 2019.

Williams, Duncan Ryūken, and Tomoe Moriya, eds. *Issei Buddhism in the Americas*. The Asian American Experience. Urbana: University of Illinois Press, 2010.

Wilson, Jeff. *Mindful America: The Mutual Transformation of Buddhist Meditation and American Culture*. New York: Oxford University Press, 2014.

Wilson, Liz. *Charming Cadavers: Horrific Figurations of the Feminine in Indian Buddhist Hagiographic Literature*. Chicago: University of Chicago Press, 1996.

Wright, Dale S. "Silence and Eloquence: How Dōgen's Dharma Match with Vimalakīrti Might Have Turned Out." In *The Theory and Practice of Zen Buddhism: A Festschrift in Honor of Steven Heine*, edited by Charles S. Prebish and On-cho Ng, 91–101. Singapore: Springer Singapore, 2022.

Yasutani, Hakuun. "Letter to Jean Kapleau," November 9, 1957. David M. Rubenstein Rare Book & Manuscript Library, Duke University.

Yu, Jimmy. "Revisiting the Notion of Zong: Contextualizing the Dharma Drum Lineage of Modern Chan Buddhism." *Chung-Hwa Buddhist Journal* 26 (2013): 113–51.

Zigmund, Dan. "Writing through the Heart." *Tricycle: The Buddhist Review*, February 7, 2016. https://tricycle.org/magazine/writing-through-heart/.

Zwerdling, Alex. *The Rise of the Memoir*. Oxford: Oxford University Press, 2016.

INDEX

ableism, 94, 96, 102

absence/presence, 136–40, 156

African American literature, 95–96. *See also* Black Buddhists

Ahmed, Sarah, 47

Aichi Senmon Nisodo, 87

Aitken, Robert, 6, 14, 173

American Buddhism, 11, 19, 162, 174–78, 182n14; and Kapleau, 36–37; literature of, 10–15; Manuel on, 101; and orientalism, 11, 182n14; and Ozeki, 132. *See also specific sects*

Aoyama, Shundo, 87

App, Urs, 17–18

artificial intelligence (AI), 134–35

autobiography, 13–15, 48, 160, 174–75; definitions of, 19–20; Kapleau on, 41, 42, 127–28; as life narrative, 14, 19–20, 175; Ozeki on, 132–34, 156–58, 160, 165; and psychoanalysis, 188n76; Van de Wetering on, 45, 107, 120–21, 128, 186n17

awakening. *See* enlightenment

ayahuasca, 75

Baker, Richard, 46, 55

Bakhtin, Mikhail, 106, 114, 126

Ball, David, 47

Barbour, John, 14–15, 172

Baroni, Helen, 14

Baso Doitsu (Ma-tsu Tao-yi; Mazu Daoyi), 33–34

Beat Generation, 12, 24, 59, 155

Black Buddhists, 17, 19, 93–96, 99

Blofeld, John, 185n5

Blum, Susan D., 185n7

Bodhidharma (Zen patriarch), 2–3, 6–8, 109, 116–17, 125

Bodhisattvas, 27

Brown, Ed, 102

Buddha-nature, 145, 152, 154, 159

Buddhism: Eightfold Path of, 52; "ethnic," 79, 162, 201n2, 201n4; Mahayana, 4, 26–27, 149; Pure Land, 30; Tantric, 18; Theravada, 14, 27. *See also specific sects*

Butler, Judith, 136

Cage, John, 11, 24

Caodong. *See* Soto Zen

Caoshan Benji, 5
capitalism, 43; meritocratic rhetoric of, 47; Suzuki on, 35, 38; utopian critiques of, 16, 25, 34, 35
carnivalesque, 105–8, 124, 126
Carus, Paul, 26
Chadwick, David, 54–59, 76–77, 102; *Thank You and OK!*, xi–xii, 45, 46, 54–60, 176
Chan (or Ch'an) Buddhism, 4–5, 23, 180n7; Faure on, 203n30; Levering on, 83; McRae on, 7. See also Zen Buddhism
Christian churches, 26–27, 52, 57, 100, 117, 135, 143
Churchill, Winston, 48
civil rights activists, 17–18, 19, 95, 98
climate change, 134–35
Corey, James S. A., 32
"cradle" Buddhists, 162, 201n2, 201n4

dadaists, 77
Dahui Zonggao (Daie Soko), 5, 29, 83
Daikan Eno (Huineng), 79–80, 98, 102, 142
Daito Kokushi, 186n22
Daitokuji monastery, 49–53, 186n22; founder of, 186n22; Snyder at, 187n43; Van de Wetering at, 108; Zen master of, 50–53, 108, 186n25
Dällenbach, Lucien, 32–33
Danxia Tianran (Tanka Tennen), 39
Daoism, 26, 70, 94, 100
Dazi-Kawa, 115
De Martino, Richard, 24
Derrida, Jacques, 136–37, 149–50, 197n9, 199n55
Descartes, René, 145

Deshan Xuanjian. *See* Tokusan Senkan
detective fiction, 32
Dharma combat, 91, 187n59
Dharmapala, Anagarika, 26
Diamond Sutra, 60
Dick, Philip K., 173
Dogen, Eihei, 5, 61, 88, 92, 159; on enlightenment, 144; Genjo koan of, 133, 153, 160; on interdependence, 144–45; "Mountains and Waters Sutra" of, 152, 160; and Ozeki, 133, 149, 158, 173–74; on "time being," 144–46, 159, 160
domestic violence, 82, 85, 86. *See also* sexual abuse
Dongshan Liangjie, 5

Eightfold Path, 52
emptiness, 126–28, 143–44, 147–48; "pure," 128; and *shunyata*, 199n46; "vast," 3
Engakuji monastery, 23, 38
enlightenment, 23–25, 54, 170–71; Dogen on, 144; Goldberg on, 65–66; Greenwood on, 89, 91, 176; Haubner on, 72; Huineng on, 80; inexpressibility of, 34; Kapleau on, 38–40, 42; Manuel on, 98, 100; Ozeki on, 157–58; Sutherland on, 160; Van de Wetering on, 43, 49–54, 109–11
entanglement, 141–42
"ethnic" Buddhism, 79, 162, 201n2, 201n4

failure, 45–48, 77, 162; Chadwick on, 46, 55–59; Goldberg on, 46, 48, 58–66; Haubner on, 46, 48, 66,

69–72, 75–76; Van de Wetering on, 44–45, 52
Fanon, Frantz, 96–97
Faure, Bernard, 7, 8, 98, 188n84, 203n30
feminism, 19; Ahmed on, 47; Butler on, 136; fourth-wave, 93; Schireson on, 82, 85–87. *See also* gender issues
Fernandez, Leslie, 198n25
Fischer, Norman, 132, 138, 181n53
Foulk, Griffith, 35
Frey, James, 107
Fukushima, Keido, 85
Fukushima nuclear accident (2011), 141, 145, 153

Garton-Gundling, Kyle, 12
Gautama, Siddhartha, 2
gender issues, 19, 47, 72, 102; Butler on, 136; and Greenwood, 89–90; and intersectionality, 81, 93, 96–98, 102; and Miaozong, 83–84; and Ozeki, 140; and Schireson, 82, 85–87
Ginsberg, Allen, 12, 24
Glassman, Bernie, 173
Gleig, Ann, 12, 19, 188n81, 192n57; on Manuel, 94, 95
Goldberg, Natalie, 46, 58–66, 88–89; on enlightenment, 65–66; *The Great Failure*, xii, 45, 48, 58–66, 77–78, 88, 174; and Haubner, 67–68; *Long Quiet Highway*, 64; on sexual abuse, 61–65, 163; *Writing down the Bones*, 59
Greenwood, Gesshin Claire, 87–93, 101–2; *Bow First, Ask Questions Later*, 81, 87–93; on Dharma combat, 91, 187n59; on enlightenment, 89, 91, 176; and Goldberg, 88; and Manuel, 94; on ritual, 81, 90–93; and Schireson, 87–88, 92–93, 101, 103; Warner on, 103

haiku poetry, 12
Hakuin Ekaku, 5, 36
Hakuun Yasutani, 1–2
Halberstam, Judith, 47
Hanh, Thich Nhat, 144
Haubner, Jack, 46, 66–78; and Goldberg, 67–68; and Schireson, 82; *Single White Monk*, xii, 45, 48, 66–68, 73–77, 82, 174; *Zen Confidential*, 67–69, 71
Heine, Steven, 7, 159
Historical Cultural Criticism (HCC), 7–8
Hongren (Fifth Patriarch), 79–80, 99–100
Huineng (Daikan Eno), 79–80, 98, 102, 142
Huxley, Aldous, 41
Hyakujo Ekai (Baizhang Huaihai), 33–36

Inagaki, Hisao, 185n4
indifference, 126–27
inset stories, 32
interdependence: Dogen on, 144–45; Ozeki on, 132, 133, 142–44, 152–53
intersectionality, 81, 93, 96–98, 102
Isaiah, book of, 183n51
Iwamura, Jane, 16, 185n79

Jaffe, Richard, 42, 180n10
James, William, 28

jazz music, 20, 121, 127
Joshu Jushin (Zhaozhou Congshen), ix–x, 41, 124–25, 132, 166, 170–71
Joshu's Mu koan, 39, 170–71, 175; Chadwick on, 57–58; Kapleau on, 40, 58; Matthiessen on, 8–9; Ozeki on, 154; Schireson on, 84; Van de Wetering on, 104, 112, 126, 129. *See also* koan

Kahl, Ann, 41
kanhua (koan) meditation, 5, 8
Kapleau, Philip, 6, 23–25, 36–43, 178; on autobiography, 41, 42, 127–28; enlightenment of, 38–40, 42; on Joshu's Mu koan, 40, 58; on satori, 38; suicidal thoughts of, 38; on Suzuki, 36–42; *The Three Pillars of Zen*, xi, 24–25, 37–43, 173; and Yasutani, 39–42, 150; *Zen: Dawn in the West*, 40–42
karuna (compassion), 38
Katagiri, Dainin, 54–59, 60–66, 163
Kerouac, Jack, 12, 24, 59
ki (*qi*), 82–83
Kjolhede, Bodhin, 25
koan: definitions of, 20, 30, 39, 161, 169, 202n28; functions of, 15, 121–22; Genjo, 133, 153, 160; Greenwood on, 81, 89, 101; Manuel on, 81, 94, 99–101, 102; as mirrors, 32–33; misunderstandings of, 45; Ozeki on, 152–55, 160; Poceski on, 161–63, 171; of quantum physics, 142; as riddles, 101, 163–72, 174–77, 203n30; Schireson on, 81, 84, 85–86; Suzuki on, 25, 30–36, 39, 42, 176, 196n67; Van de Wetering on, 53, 105–7, 117, 120–27, 169, 196n67

koan interviews, 85, 88, 91, 104, 120
Kornfield, Jack, 188n76
Kripal, Jeffrey, 10, 20–21, 172–73
Kyger, Joanne, 6

Levering, Miriam, 83
Leviathan Wakes (Corey), 32
life narrative, 14, 19–20, 175. *See also* autobiography
liminality, 72, 88
Linji school: and Caodong, 5; *kanhua* meditation of, 5; *Record of Sayings of Linji*, 197n8
Linji Yixuan (Rinzai Gigen), 5–6, 39, 70–71, 166; on Dharma combat, 91; on slaying the Buddha, 85–86, 101; Tolle on, 135–36
Longtan Chongxin (Ryotan Sushin), 62–63, 64
"longtermism," 134–35
Loori, John Daido, 175

Madagascar, 101
magical realism, 141
Magliola, Robert R., 200n55
Mahayana Buddhism, 4, 26–27, 149
Manuel, Zenju Earthlyn, xii, 19, 81, 93–101; Gleig on, 94, 95; on intersectionality, 81, 93, 96–98, 102; on koan, 81, 94, 99–101, 102; *A Meditation on Home, Homelessness, and Belonging*, 100, 103; on multiplicity in oneness, 97; *Sanctuary*, 81, 99; on "sanctuary sanghas," 94; and Schireson, 94, 98; *The Way of Tenderness*, 81, 93–99, 101; "When Crocodiles Die," 100–101

masks, 41, 94; Ozeki on, 129–30, 133–34, 155–58, 174, 177; Van de Wetering on, 105, 107, 109, 112–20, 126, 128–29
Ma-tsu Tao-yi. *See* Baso Doitsu
Matthiessen, Peter, 6, 161; on "Joshu's Mu," 8–9; *Nine-Headed Dragon River*, xi, 2–3, 16; orientalism of, 16–18
Mazu Daoyi. *See* Baso Doitsu
McMahan, David, 11–12, 144
McNicholl, Adeana, 17–18
McRae, John, 7, 195n47
memory, 150–54, 160
meritocracy, 185n7
Merleau-Ponty, Maurice, 96
metaphor, 164–65
methodology, 18–21
Miaozong. *See* Wuzhuo Miaozong
mirrors, 15, 32–33, 54, 175
mise en abyme, 32
More, Thomas, 15–16
Mu koan. *See* Joshu's Mu koan
Murphy, Sean, 175

Nagasena (Indian Buddhist), 143
Nakagawa Soen, 2, 16, 38, 39
Nansen Fugan (Nanquan Puyuan), ix, 34, 142
Native Americans, 95, 167
nihilism, 31
Nirvana, 144
Noh theater, 155–56
Nowick, Walter, 24, 108–9, 116, 175, 195n47

Oda Sesso (Zen master), 114–15, 186n25
Oedipus Rex (Sophocles), 168

okesa (robe), 92
oneness, 80, 95, 97
orientalism, 94; and American Buddhism, 11, 182n14; Chadwick on, 56–57; De Martino on, 24; Manuel on, 98–99; Matthiessen on, 2; and utopianism, 15–18; Van de Wetering on, 51–52, 113, 187n42
"oriental monks," 18
Ozeki, Ruth: on autobiography, 132–34, 156–58, 160, 165; *The Book of Form and Emptiness*, 132, 197n2; and Dogen, 133, 149, 158, 173–74; *The Face*, 132, 133, 154–58, 174; on interdependence, 132, 133, 142–44, 152–53; on masks, 129–30, 133–34, 155–58, 174, 177; on memory, 150–54, 160; *A Tale for the Time Being*, 131–56, 159–60, 173–74, 198n25; and Tolle, 146, 147; and Van de Wetering, 129–30

Pali Canon, 27
Pawa of Nao, 144–50
perennialism, 9–10
Platform Sutra, The (Huineng), 79–80, 190n7
Plato, 136, 149–50, 159–60, 197n9
Poceski, Mario, 161–63, 171
Pound, Ezra, 12
prajna (wisdom), 38
presence/absence, 136–40, 156
"pressence," 136
projection, 61–62, 68, 188n81
Proust, Marcel, 140
psychoanalysis, 61–62; and Zen, 24, 188n76
Pure Land Buddhism, 30

qi (*ki*), 82–83
Qiannü (Seijo), 99–100, 102
quantum physics, 133, 141–44
Quli, Natalie, 11

race, 86, 95–97, 99; intersectionality of, 81, 93, 96–98, 102
relationality, 13–14
religion, 152–53; and science, 26, 28
religious experience, 8–10; Suzuki on, 42; "unselfing" as, 14
rewriting the self, 172–74
riddles, 101, 163–72, 174–77, 203n30
Rimbaud, Arthur, 155
Rimpoche, 115–16, 127
Rinzai Gigen. *See* Linji Yixuan
Rinzai Zen, 40, 135–36; Haubner on, 67, 70; Kapleau on, 38–39; koan study in, 28–29, 170, 179n3; and Soto Zen, 5–6, 29; Suzuki on, 28–30; Tolle on, 197n8
ritual, 19, 106, 155–56; Dharma combat as, 91, 187n59; Greenwood on, 81, 87, 91–93, 103; Kapleau on, 38–39; Ozeki on, 157; Schireson on, 85–87, 92, 93
Rochester Zen Center, 25, 42
Rousseau, Jean-Jacques, 48
Ryotan Sushin (Longtan Chongxin), 62–63, 64
Ryutakuji temple, 38–39

Sanbokyodan school, 39–40
"sanctuary sanghas," 94–95
Sandage, Scott, 46
San Francisco Zen Center, 102–3
Sasaki, Joshu, 67, 72–76

satori. *See* enlightenment
Schedneck, Brooke, 14, 184n74
Schireson, Grace, xii, 81–87, 163, 188n81; and Greenwood, 87–88, 92–93, 101, 103; and Haubner, 82; and Manuel, 94, 98; *Naked in the Zendo*, 81–87
Schloegl, Irmgard, 6
Schrödinger's cat, 141–42
science, 31; and religion, 26, 28
science fiction, 32
Seijo (Qiannü), 99–100, 102
seiza, 86–87, 98
self-reliance, 37, 178
Seppo Gizon (Xuefeng Yicun), 122–23, 149
Sera Khandro (saint), 14
sexual abuse, 46, 77, 82, 89, 102; by Baker, 55; by Katagiri, 60–66; by Sasaki, 72, 74–75; by Shimano, 17, 18. *See also* domestic violence
sexuality, 72, 107; intersectionality of, 81, 93, 96–98
"shadow archive," 47, 66
Shakyamuni Buddha, 2, 4, 177; McNicholl on, 17–18; Suzuki on, 35
Shambhala Press, 13
Sharf, Robert, 8, 9
Shenxiu, 80
Shimano Eido (Tai-san), 2, 16, 17, 18
Shogaku Zen Institute, 82
siddhi (supernatural powers), 56
silence, 125–26; Goldberg on, 66; "thunderous," 126
Smith, Huston, 148
Smith, Jonathan Z., 15
Smith Sidonie, 19–20
Snyder, Gary, 6, 12, 24, 187n43
social justice. *See* civil rights activists

Soen, Shaku, 3, 26; Matthiessen on, 16; and Suzuki, 25
Song dynasty, 7, 30, 83
Sophocles, 168
Soto Zen (Caodong), 29, 40; and Dogen, 5, 179n3; and D. T. Suzuki, 29, 30; and Shunryu Suzuki, 6, 179n3
Spivak, Gayatri, 136
Stalling, Jonathan, 12
Starr, Marlo, 198n25
suicidal thoughts: and Greenwood, 90, 93; and Kapleau, 38; and Ozeki, 131, 137, 140, 141, 147, 151
Sung. *See* Song dynasty
superposition, 141–42
Sutherland, Joan, 160
Suzuki, D. T., xi, 6, 23–30, 171; critics of, 42–43; death of, 42; *An Introduction to Zen Buddhism*, 26–36; and Richard Jaffe, 42; and William James, 28; and Kapleau, 36–42; on koan, 25, 30–36, 39, 42, 176, 196n67; legacy of, 43; utopianism of, 35; and Van de Wetering, 43, 45–46, 50–51, 109
Suzuki, Shungo, 86
Suzuki, Shunryu, 6, 46, 55, 82, 86

Tai-san. *See* Shimano Eido
Taisho canon, xx
Tang dynasty, 7, 30, 35
Tanka Tennen (Danxia Tianran), 39
Tantric Buddhism, 18
teacher-student relationships, 61–62, 65–66
Tendai (Tiantai) school, 53–54
tenderness, way of, 93–99, 101

Theravada Buddhism, 14, 27
Thich Nhat Hanh, 144
Tiantai (Tendai) school, 53–54
"time being," 144–46, 159, 160, 165
Tokusan Senkan (Deshan Xuanjian), 59–60, 62–64, 88, 122–23
Tolle, Eckhart, 134–37, 146, 147
Traditional Zen Narrative (TZN), 7
Trump, Donald, 171–72
Trungpa, Chögyam (Rimpoche), 115–16, 127
"Two Buddhisms," 162
two truths doctrine, xii, 79–81; Manuel on, 94–95, 97

utopianism, 5, 51; and orientalism, 15–18; of Suzuki, 35; of Tolle, 134

Vanacker, Sabine, 193n6
Van de Wetering, Janwillem, 21, 24, 44–46, 76–77, 163; *Afterzen*, xii, 105–8, 112–30, 169, 174; on autobiography, 45, 107, 120–21, 128, 186n17; on carnivalesque, 105–8, 124; documentary on, 104, 128; *The Empty Mirror*, xi–xii, 43, 49–54, 77, 105, 108–11, 176–77; on enlightenment, 43, 49–54, 109–11; *A Glimpse of Nothingness*, xii, 107–12, 117, 129; on indifference, 126–27; on koan, 53, 105–7, 112, 117, 120–27, 196n67; on masks, 105, 107, 109, 112–20, 126, 128–29; and Nowick, 195n47; and orientalism, 51–52, 113, 187n42; and Ozeki, 129–30; rewritten koan of, 120; and Suzuki, 6, 43, 45–46, 50–51, 109

Van de Wetering, Thera, 111–12, 195n47
Van Gulik, Robert, 111
Vazimba people, 101
Vimalakirti sutra, 126, 197n82

Walker, Alice, 12
Wang Zhou, 99–100
Warner, Brad, 102–3
Watson, Julia, 19–20
Whalen, Philip, 12
williams, angel Kyodo, 95
Wilson, Jeff, 12
World's Parliament of Religions (Chicago, 1893), 3, 26
writer's block, 138
Wuzhuo Miaozong, 83–84, 101, 163

Xuefeng Yicun (Seppo Gizon), 122–23, 147

Yasutani Hakuun, xi, 16, 39–42, 150

Zen Buddhism, 4–6; essence of, 135–36; golden age of, 121; modernist, 12, 94, 109; and nihilism, 31; postmodernist, 88, 192n57; and psychoanalysis, 24, 188n76; as "rhetoric of immediacy," 98; Rinzai vs. Soto schools, 5; and Theravada, 27; "universal," 94. *See also* American Buddhism
"Zentertainment," 102–3
Zhaozhou Congshen. *See* Joshu Jushin
Zhuangzi, 70, 100

Recent books in the series

STUDIES IN RELIGION AND CULTURE

Desire and the Ascetic Ideal: Buddhism and Hinduism in the Works of T. S. Eliot
EDWARD UPTON

Spirit Deep: Recovering the Sacred in Black Women's Travel
TISHA M. BROOKS

In Search of Justice in Thailand's Deep South: Malay Muslim and Thai Buddhist Women's Narratives
EDITED BY JOHN C. HOLT, COMPILED BY SORAYA JAMJUREE, AND TRANSLATED BY HARA SHINTARO

Precarious Balance: Sinhala Buddhism and the Forces of Pluralism
BARDWELL L. SMITH

Words Made Flesh: Formations of the Postsecular in British Romanticism
SEAN DEMPSEY

A Language of Things: Emanuel Swedenborg and the American Environmental Imagination
DEVIN P. ZUBER

The Pragmatist Turn: Religion, the Enlightenment, and the Formation of American Literature
GILES GUNN

Rethinking Sincerity and Authenticity: The Ethics of Theatricality in Kant, Kierkegaard, and Levinas
HOWARD PICKETT

The Newark Earthworks: Enduring Monuments, Contested Meanings
LINDSAY JONES AND RICHARD D. SHIELS, EDITORS

Ideas to Live For: Toward a Global Ethics
GILES GUNN

The Pagan Writes Back: When World Religion Meets World Literature
ZHANGE NI

Freud and Augustine in Dialogue: Psychoanalysis, Mysticism, and the Culture of Modern Spirituality
WILLIAM B. PARSONS

Vigilant Faith: Passionate Agnosticism in a Secular World
DANIEL BOSCALJON

Postmodernism and the Revolution in Religious Theory: Toward a Semiotics of the Event
CARL RASCHKE

Textual Intimacy: Autobiography and Religious Identities
WESLEY A. KORT

When the Sun Danced: Myth, Miracles, and Modernity in Early Twentieth-Century Portugal
JEFFREY S. BENNETT

Encountering the Secular: Philosophical Endeavors in Religion and Culture
J. HEATH ATCHLEY

Religion after Postmodernism: Retheorizing Myth and Literature
VICTOR E. TAYLOR

Mourning Religion
WILLIAM B. PARSONS, DIANE JONTE-PACE, AND SUSAN E. HENKING, EDITORS

Milton Keynes UK
Ingram Content Group UK Ltd.
UKHW040746261024
450281UK00006B/61